Forecasts

FORECASTS

A Story of Weather and Finance at the Edge of Disaster

Written by Caroline E. Schuster
Illustrated by Enrique Bernardou and David Bueno

UNIVERSITY OF TORONTO PRESS
Toronto Buffalo London

© University of Toronto Press 2023
Toronto Buffalo London
utorontopress.com
Printed in the USA

ISBN 978-1-4875-4220-7 (cloth)   ISBN 978-1-4875-4225-2 (EPUB)
ISBN 978-1-4875-4223-8 (paper)   ISBN 978-1-4875-4224-5 (PDF)

Library and Archives Canada Cataloguing in Publication

Title: Forecasts : a story of weather and finance at the edge of disaster / written by
Caroline E. Schuster ; illustrated by Enrique Bernardou and David Bueno.
Names: Schuster, Caroline E., 1983– author. | Bernardou, Enrique, illustrator. |
Bueno, David (Illustrator), illustrator.
Series: ethnoGRAPHIC (University of Toronto Press)
Description: Series statement: EthnoGRAPHIC | Includes bibliographical references.
Identifiers: Canadiana (print) 20230154751 | Canadiana (ebook) 20230154840 | ISBN 9781487542238
(paper) | ISBN 9781487542207 (cloth) | ISBN 9781487542252 (EPUB) | ISBN 9781487542245 (PDF)
Subjects: LCSH: Sesame industry – Paraguay – Comic books, strips, etc. | LCSH: Sesame industry –
Paraguay – Finance – Comic books, strips, etc. | LCSH: Sesame – Climatic factors –
Paraguay – Comic books, strips, etc. | LCSH: Farmers – Paraguay – Comic books, strips, etc. |
LCSH: Climatic changes – Paraguay – Comic books, strips, etc. | LCSH: Anthropology –
Paraguay – Comic books, strips, etc. | LCGFT: Comics (Graphic works)
Classification: LCC SB299.S4 S38 2023 | DDC 633.8/509892 – dc23

Cover design: Liz Harasymczuk
Cover image: Enrique Bernardou and David Bueno

We welcome comments and suggestions regarding any aspect of our publications – please feel free to contact us at news@utorontopress.com or visit us at utorontopress.com.

Every effort has been made to contact copyright holders; in the event of an error or omission, please notify the publisher.

We wish to acknowledge the land on which the University of Toronto Press operates. This land is the traditional territory of the Wendat, the Anishnaabeg, the Haudenosaunee, the Métis, and the Mississaugas of the Credit First Nation.

University of Toronto Press acknowledges the financial support of the Government of Canada and the Ontario Arts Council, an agency of the Government of Ontario, for its publishing activities.

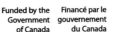

CONTENTS

Foreword

CRITICAL GRAPHICS: FROM ECO-DISASTER SURVIVANCE TO MYTHO-SPECULATIVE THRIVANCE

The planet's heating up, and swiftly. Predatory capitalism is on the rapid rise. People are increasingly forced from homes and lands. Our planet's bountiful biodiversity is dying. In *Forecasts*, Caroline Schuster remarks how Paraguayan sesame seed farmer Don Wilfrido's existence hangs by a "gossamer strand." Severe climate change, along with forced entanglements with global capitalist fintech swindles and Wall Street–traded agriculture insurance derivatives, has him in a financial chokehold. He's not alone. Don Wilfrido, like the great majority of planetary denizens, finds himself grasping at fast-fraying strands of hope to survive another day.

With *Forecasts*, anthropologist and writer Caroline Schuster and comics storytelling virtuosos David Bueno and Enrique Bernardou deliver critical graphic storytelling at its best. That is, *Forecasts* uses visuals and verbal shaping devices to construct a narrative that deeply educates its readers at the micro and macro levels of issues that face life on Earth. In this case, they enrich understanding of the devastating effects of climate change paired with predatory capitalist practices.

Forecasts deeply humanizes those like Don Wilfrido who are forced into debtor schemes that lead to total financial precarity. With heat-trapping greenhouse gases suffocating the Earth and making yesteryear's predictable planting and harvesting seasons totally unpredictable, those like Don Wilfrido find themselves forced to sign with fintech swindlers who seek dollar profits over all forms of life. At one point, his talking dog and horse turn grievously anxious, hoping for a bountiful sesame seed harvest that will ensure that, as the dog states, "we'll be safe for another year." And, at another point the narrator Schuster asks, "Who has the power to alter reality with their narrative – Pomberos? Horses? Farmers? Insurance? Policies? Sesame seeds?" *Forecasts* unravels the deeply disturbing ways those like Don Wilfrido and his creatures big and small – all human and nonhumans in the Americas and across the globe – can no longer forecast what tomorrow will bring, shaking to the core any sense of self-constancy and self-determination.

As critical graphics, *Forecasts* is autoethnographic record. It is also a creative materialization of the counterfactual capacity to imagine alternate futures for Don Wilfrido. If real cannibalistic capitalism and eco devastations predict his tragic end, then, in the hands of Schuster and her creative crew, the speculative becomes the space of the possible. As you'll soon see, *Forecasts* presents a series of other versions and endings to Don Wilfrido's story. Importantly, the creative team construct these imagined alternatives not as rose-colored fairytale endings but as futurities made possible through an eyes-wide-open, critical-optimist worldview.

Schuster and her creative comics storytelling team are not alone. Other creatives of the greater Americas attuned to the wreckage to life with today's global warming and barbarous capitalist practices also turn to the speculative to build their narratives – and always with critical-optimist worldviews. I think readily of those like Angélica Gorodischer, Daína Chaviano, Miguel Collazo, Silvia Moreno-Garcia, Yuri Herrera, and the author known as Yoss. I think, too, of US Latinos like David Bowles, Sabrina Vourvoulias, Julia Rios, Ernest Hogan, Fernando Flores, and the siblings Malka and Daniel José Older, and the many creators that appear in *Latinx Rising* and *Speculative Fiction for Dreamers*. Like *Forecasts*, these creatives are less interested in imagining a high-tech world filled with violence, trauma, and destruction, and more deeply interested in carving out new ways to see how we might create global, bio-harmonious eco-futurities.

Forecasts is not only focused on offering critical optimist futurities in the face of tragic gritty-realisms. It also turns to the deep past: the mythologies of the Tupi-Guaraní peoples. Given that these mythologies weave their way into "daily rhythms of agrarian life in northern Paraguay," as stated in the preface to *Forecasts*, it's not surprising that Tau and Keraná's monstrous offspring Jasy Jateré and the nocturnal trickster the Pombero play a significant role in Don Wilfrido's journey. Their appearances offer strategic pauses in the narrative – ethnohorror pauses that anchor Don Wilfrido's journey within global communities (ethno) that experience the traumas (horror) of eco devastation and predatory capitalism. The appearance of the monstrous elements of Guaraní mythology asks readers to take pause and attend to how Don Wilfrido's experiences function as synecdoche to peoples across the planet experiencing the eco-capitalist horrors of today.

Forecasts is an instantiation of critical graphics that brings a critical-optimistic lens to its construction of Don Wilfrido's ethnohorror-informed present as well as its articulation of a series of speculative futurities. In this regard, *Forecasts* extends the type of critical graphics work seen already in the early 1970s by Ulianov Chalarka. Drawing on interviews with northern Colombian farmers done by sociologist Orlando Fals Borda, Chalarka created a series of comics (*Loma Grande*, *The Tinajones*, *El Boche*, and *Felicita Campos*) that galvanized resistance to social, economic, and political injustices. And more recently, the establishing of the Cartoon Movement as a "global platform for editorial cartoons and comics journalism" shows us that other like-minded creatives exist beyond the geographic borders of South America. They are working hard to create critical graphic narratives that raise awareness of exploitation, oppression, and suffering across the planet. For instance, in the story "Hustling Day in Silicon Savannah" by Gianluca Iazzolino and Michael Kimani (writers) and Maddo (artist) we see how fintech exploitive practices are not just impacting those like Don Wilfrido, but also those in Thika, Kenya.

Since Caroline Schuster began her fieldwork and learned of the plight of those like Don Wilfrido in northern Paraguay, climate change and fintech profiteering continue to bulldoze the everyday lives of all planetary bioforms. Think of the total devastation of El Salvador's economy because of its official adoption of Bitcoin as its legal tender. Think of all those forced to flee homesteads to make deadly crossings across gang-infested lands and militarized borders. The seamless confluence of scholarly research, mytho-based ethnohorror, future-sighted speculation, and story acutely tuned into the human condition make for a critical graphics experience that asks us to *see* ourselves, not as fated to become victims of eco-disasters and fintech profiteering schemes, but rather as agents of progressive, productive, creative change who step up and act. *Forecasts* asks us not to simply survive but to act today so we can thrive tomorrow.

Frederick Luis Aldama
Jacob & Frances Sanger Mossiker Chair in the Humanities
at the University of Texas, Austin
Eisner Award–winning author of *Latinx Superheroes in Mainstream Comics*

Preface

THE PARAGUAYAN PANTHEON

Paraguayan *campesinos* spoke often of the monsters that cohabit the countryside. The pantheon of immortal beings from Guaraní mythology weren't just stories – they intervened powerfully in the daily rhythms of agrarian life in northern Paraguay. Some of those creatures appear in *Forecasts*.

Most folk stories center on the seven monstrous children of **Tau** and **Keraná**. Tau, the spirit of evil, captured Keraná and forced her to become his wife. Their terrible union was cursed by **Angatupyry**, the spirit of good, and Keraná was fated to bear seven monstrous children, seven months apart, each sibling more terrible.

The **Teju Jagua** is the eldest of Tau's descendants. He takes the form of an enormous lizard with seven dog heads. Despite his ferocious appearance, he subsists on fruits and wild honey. As a cave dweller, he is said to protect hidden treasures.

Next comes the **Mbói Tu'i**, a giant snake with a parrot head. He is the protector of waterways, swamps, and estuaries.

The **Moñai** rules the fields, sky, and birds, often stealing crops and harvests and raiding kitchens. He takes human shape with a snake's head topped with massive horns.

The **Jasy Jateré** takes the form of a beautiful blond child. A trickster, his whistling seduces men, women, and children alike. His kiss is deadly for humans.

The **Kurupí** takes hideous human form, short and misshapen. Fiercely loyal to those who aid him, he's a glutton and seducer.

The final two siblings are especially monstrous. The **Ao Ao** is associated with fertility, but takes the monstrous shape of a sheep with a boar's head and vicious teeth. The **Luisón** is the most dangerous of all, a wolf with human traits.

Though not one of Tau and Keraná's children, the **Pombero** figures prominently in more-than-human relations in the countryside. He is conventionally a small, dark, naked figure who comes out primarily at night. A trickster like the Jasy Jateré, he can be charmed with gifts of rum, tobacco, and honey. But should you renege on your gifts, the Pombero will hold a vicious grudge.

ACKNOWLEDGMENTS

It feels inadequate to say that this book is for Don Wilfrido and Ña Neca, whose story takes shape in these pages. We never could have imagined let alone created this graphic novel without the wisdom, guidance, and friendship of the Medina family. I hope that we have lived up to the challenge of bringing Wilfrido's expertly crafted narratives to life. We are deeply indebted to the whole community of *sesameros* for their patience, trust, and hospitality. One of the binds of ethnographic writing is that confidentiality limits the gratitude that we can express to the wider network of participants, including our contacts at InsurTech and their generous spirit of engagement, the members of the Multiactiva who supported and encouraged our research, and various folks in the fintech world in Asunción who immersed us in the design and market for microinsurance.

This book owes an intellectual, creative, and personal debt to Rocío Silvero, whose fieldwork built the foundations of *Forecasts* and all the anthropological thinking that has contributed to this story. The insight and analysis that you brought to the nexus of economic systems and environmental crisis in Paraguay is at the very heart of this book. And your empathy, respect, and friendship with me and with the Medinas held this project together. We hope that it's not too disconcerting to face your comic book doppelgänger. Both your personal warmth and intellectual acuity suffuse this account, start to finish.

While writing is the bread and butter of anthropology, when we began this journey I had no idea that it would prove to be the most challenging project of my career to date. And rewarding! While the whole team shares a deep love of comics, none of us fully grasped the hard work entailed in creating a graphic novel.

I would especially like to thank my colleague at the Australian National University (ANU), Guillaume Molle, for his remarkable vision, boundless encouragement, and deep engagement on a technical level with both the art and writing. From the New Year's Eve pep-talk in 2018 that got the ball rolling, to the writing retreat that resulted in a very early draft of the script, careful editing on countless drafts, and invaluable contributions to my understanding of the archaeology and ethnohistory of Paraguay, this project could not have happened without our sustained collaboration. In the School of Archaeology and Anthropology, Catherine Frieman and Yasmine Musharbash provided generous insights on early drafts. It is a joy to work in a department that takes seriously the idea of anthropological comics.

The support of an Australian Research Council Discovery Early Career Researcher Award (DE170101406, 2017–2020), strategic funds from the ANU School of Archaeology and Anthropology, and support from the Australian National Centre for Latin American Studies made both the fieldwork in Paraguay and the costs of producing the graphic novel possible. In Paraguay I would like to thank Adelina Pulsineri and Raquel Zalazar at the Museo Etnográfico Andres Barbero for their generous insights and archival support in Asunción. Thanks as well to Marilin Rehnfeldt, convenor of the anthropology degree at the Universidad Católica de Asunción, and to Gustavo Setrini at Facultad Latinoamericana de Ciencias Sociales (FLACSO), who organized early conversations, workshops, and roundtables that guided the development of the project.

The ethnoGRAPHIC series at University of Toronto Press has been the perfect home for this project. Anne Brackenbury was the first to see the potential of the book and provided early guidance. Carli Hansen's remarkable editorial stewardship of the manuscript from the proposal stage through to final production has been a sustained and rewarding partnership. We are lucky to have such a generous and dedicated editor. And we have created a much better book thanks to the hands-on guidance, workshopping, walk-throughs, and corrections offered by Marc Parenteau, who gave us an inside view of how comics are really made. We received generous and wonderfully helpful feedback from several anonymous peer reviewers both at the proposal phase as well as on the fully developed manuscript. Christine Folch, Andrew Flachs, and Andrea Ballestero offered lucid and imaginative comments on both the graphic novel and its anthropological argument.

Throughout the project, we had the opportunity to present early versions. Brad Weiss at the College of William and Mary invited us to lead a workshop just after fieldwork wrapped up and went on to provide invaluable feedback on the underlying anthropological analysis in his capacity as a member of the *Cultural Anthropology* editorial collective that oversaw the publication of a related article, "Weedy

Finance: Weather Insurance and Parametric Life on Unstable Grounds" (2021b). We also led a workshop for the American River College Design Hub and got to geek out about art and design – thanks to Randy Schuster for making that conversation happen. We co-convened a "Lab" on anthropology and sequential art at the 2019 Australian Anthropological Society Conference with Guillaume Molle. I also presented aspects of the graphic ethnography at the ANU anthropology seminar series and a Melbourne University seminar. I would like to thank Sian Lazar for her generous invitation to present at the Cambridge Senior Research Seminar for the anthropology department. We would like to thank participants in all those workshops and seminars for contributing to the development of the project.

This book was edited by a whole crew of beta-readers who helped us dial in the narrative, characterization, plot, and illustrations for the comic. Thanks to Megan Kempston, Kristen Schuster, Randy Schuster, Guillaume Molle, Yasmine Musharbash, and the "Bunsen Burners" (Nick Cheeseman, Lia Kent, Rachel Hughes, and Tom Cliff).

Individually, the authors would like to thank the following people:

Caroline: First, a titanic thank you to my co-authors, co-thinkers, peer reviewers, and fellow travelers on this journey – Enrique and David. Hurrah for creating our comics studio in Café Consulado – I can't imagine a better team to work with. I have counted on the unwavering support of my family, including my late grandmother, who encouraged me via weekly Skype calls throughout COVID-19 lockdowns; my dad, whose infectious enthusiasm and sharp eye for accessibility and design made this a much better project; my sister, who did the hard yards as serial beta-reader; and my mum, who has given me more trips to the airport between fieldwork travel and more support for my anthropology career than I can comprehend. And thanks to my partner Dustin – this has not been an easy project to live with over the long haul, and through such tricky and anxious times. Thank you.

Enrique: My deepest thanks to my very own fellowship of the ring, Carly and David, for this amazing journey. My lifelong teacher Kike Olmedo, for his contagious love of comics and many secrets in picture-making. And my better half: Nanu. Love you to the moon and back.

I'd also like to thank Lira Gonzalez, Jimena Zaldivar, Cielo Caballero, Belén Oporto, Karina Jiménez, and Sofía Amarilla for contributing to our initial drafts and explorations for the project even before we began this enterprise. I hope we get to collaborate in a future project soon!

David: I would like to thank my co-authors, who put up with me for months and months; this ever-changing world (for the good and bad); and my beautiful homeland and its people, whose stories we tried to do justice.

THIS STORY STARTS ON A FARM. A SHEEP STATION OUTSIDE OF THE LITTLE TOWN OF GUNDAROO ON THE EAST COAST OF AUSTRALIA, WHERE I LIVE WITH MY HORSES AND DOG.

BUT THIS STORY ISN'T ABOUT MY FARM. I'M *DR. CAROLINE SCHUSTER*, AN ANTHROPOLOGIST TEACHING AT THE AUSTRALIAN NATIONAL UNIVERSITY.

AND I'M GOING TO TELL YOU ABOUT THE TIME I SPENT WITH SESAME FARMERS IN PARAGUAY. MY SHEEP STATION AND THE LITTLE SESAME *CHACRAS** MIGHT SEEM DISCONNECTED...

*LATIN AMERICAN SPANISH, SMALL GARDEN OR FARM, USED FOR A MIX OF SUBSISTENCE AND COMMERCIAL FOOD PRODUCTION

...BUT THEY ARE CONNECTED BY THE IRREVERSIBLE EFFECTS OF CLIMATE CHANGE, EXTREME TEMPERATURES, DEFORESTATION, AND EXTINCTION.

THIS IS A STORY ABOUT HOW ONE FAMILY OF PARAGUAYAN SESAME FARMERS IS COPING WITH THESE CHANGES. I CONNECTED THE DOTS USING ETHNOGRAPHIC FIELDWORK TO TELL A STORY OF MYTHICAL MONSTERS, FINANCIAL SYSTEMS, FAMILY DRAMAS, WEATHER DISASTERS, AND MODERN AGRIBUSINESS.

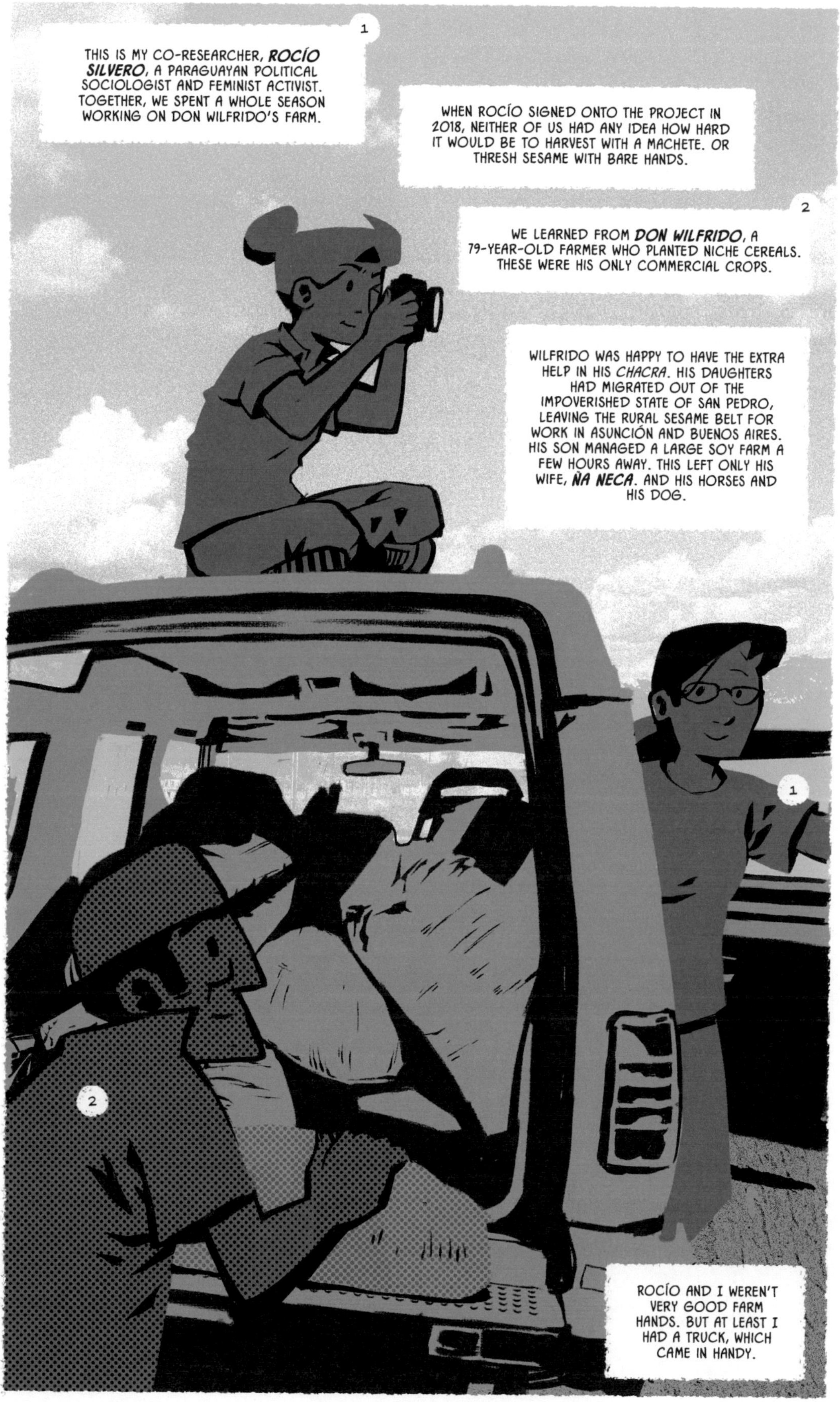
THIS IS MY CO-RESEARCHER, ROCÍO SILVERO, A PARAGUAYAN POLITICAL SOCIOLOGIST AND FEMINIST ACTIVIST. TOGETHER, WE SPENT A WHOLE SEASON WORKING ON DON WILFRIDO'S FARM.
WHEN ROCÍO SIGNED ONTO THE PROJECT IN 2018, NEITHER OF US HAD ANY IDEA HOW HARD IT WOULD BE TO HARVEST WITH A MACHETE. OR THRESH SESAME WITH BARE HANDS.
WE LEARNED FROM DON WILFRIDO, A 79-YEAR-OLD FARMER WHO PLANTED NICHE CEREALS. THESE WERE HIS ONLY COMMERCIAL CROPS.
WILFRIDO WAS HAPPY TO HAVE THE EXTRA HELP IN HIS CHACRA. HIS DAUGHTERS HAD MIGRATED OUT OF THE IMPOVERISHED STATE OF SAN PEDRO, LEAVING THE RURAL SESAME BELT FOR WORK IN ASUNCIÓN AND BUENOS AIRES. HIS SON MANAGED A LARGE SOY FARM A FEW HOURS AWAY. THIS LEFT ONLY HIS WIFE, ÑA NECA. AND HIS HORSES AND HIS DOG.
ROCÍO AND I WEREN'T VERY GOOD FARM HANDS. BUT AT LEAST I HAD A TRUCK, WHICH CAME IN HANDY.

ETHNOGRAPHY INVOLVES LONG-TERM PARTNERSHIPS. FOR THIS PROJECT, TWO OF MY MOST IMPORTANT COLLABORATORS ARE **DAVID BUENO** AND **ENRIQUE BERNARDOU**, PARAGUAYAN ILLUSTRATORS.

WE MET FOR THE FIRST TIME IN A TRENDY CAFE IN THE MICROCENTRO OF ASUNCIÓN IN 2018. SINCE THEN, THEY'VE NOT JUST BEEN FREELANCE ARTISTS - THEY'VE PROVIDED A DEEP PEER REVIEW OF THE PROJECT FROM A PARAGUAYAN PERSPECTIVE.

IT HASN'T BEEN EASY KEEPING THE TEAM TOGETHER THROUGH THE BUSHFIRE CRISIS IN AUSTRALIA, THE COVID-19 PANDEMIC, MORE FIRES IN PARAGUAY, AND THE FINANCIAL COLLAPSE OF AUSTRALIAN UNIVERSITIES.

Caroline: I'm following the news, the second COVID-19 wave in Paraguay sounds bad. Are you ok?

Enrique: We are in lockdown, what else can we do?

David: Take our mind off things with the comic hahaha. Want to see the new pages? Why don't you screenshare…

DON WILFRIDO (CONT'D)
The other ones are in Argentina, working. I'm just an old man, here by myself.

INGENIERO FREDDY
Sure sure Don Wilfrido. It really is just to contact you for updates. The insurance company has the high tech.

Don't you worry.

Mario launches into an explanation -- intercut illustrate what he is talking about (eg satel station, plants/seeds)

LIC. MARIO
This is all for your protection, for your peace of mind, so that you don't have to worry for the next three months.

Because of course you'd be worrying about the weather. Sesame is a crop that likes heat, right? It thrives in the sun.
(panel of small sesame plants)

But with drought -- actually not drought, we in the insurance industry have to be very careful about our words.

Precise contracts, you know. Ha ha! So 'hydrological stress'. Yes, that's where you run into trouble.

THIS IS A BOOK ABOUT CLIMATE-BASED FINANCING AND THE PROMISE OF FINTECH. FROM THE GROUNDED PERSPECTIVE OF PARAGUAYAN FARMERS, INSURANCE AGENTS, AGRONOMISTS, AND POMBEROS – TRICKSTER MONSTERS WHO CAN BE EITHER FRIENDS OR ENEMIES, AND WHO ACCEPT OFFERINGS OF TOBACCO, HONEY, OR RUM.

ALTHOUGH I COMMITTED TO ONGOING COLLABORATIONS WITH MY PARAGUAYAN RESEARCH PARTNERS, AT THE HEART OF THIS BOOK IS A BROKEN PROMISE.

WHEN I SAID GOODBYE IN 2019, I TOLD DON WILFRIDO I WOULD BE BACK THE NEXT YEAR TO CELEBRATE HIS 80TH BIRTHDAY. I EXPECTED TO SHARE A DRAFT OF THIS GRAPHIC ETHNOGRAPHY.

BUT THEN THE BORDERS SLAMMED CLOSED, THE PANDEMIC SPREAD ACROSS THE WORLD. AND I WAS STUCK. I COULDN'T EVEN PHONE, BECAUSE WILFRIDO'S PAY-AS-YOU-GO MOBILE WOULDN'T CONNECT MY INTERNATIONAL CALLS. HIS LIFE WAS TAKING SHAPE IN THESE PAGES, BUT I FELT SO VERY FAR AWAY.

I'VE WRITTEN A STORY THAT INCLUDES MULTIPLE SCENARIOS, MULTIPLE VERSIONS OF EVENTS, MULTIPLE ENDINGS. THIS SPECULATIVE IMAGINATION IS VERY MUCH HOW THE INSURANCE INDUSTRY OPERATES, CLAIMING THE RIGHT TO BUY THE FUTURE.

I AM FILLED WITH SORROW THAT THERE ISN'T A VERSION OF THIS STORY WHERE WE CELEBRATE WILFRIDO'S 80TH BIRTHDAY TOGETHER.

pronóstico

MASCULINE NOUN

(gen) **prediction · forecast**

(in races) **tip**

pronósticos para el año nuevo **predictions for the new year**

pronóstico del tiempo **weather forecast**

I FIRST HEARD ABOUT FINTECH IN 2017 AT AN "AFTER OFFICE" NETWORKING EVENT FOR FINANCIAL SERVICES PROFESSIONALS IN ASUNCIÓN.

SENETÉ, TELEBINGO! TELEBINGO, SENETÉ!

HEY, IF YOU WIN YOU COULD BUY A CATTLE ESTANCIA* IN THE CHACO, JUST LIKE IF YOU HAD A POLITICIAN IN YOUR FAMILY.

OR YOU COULD PAY OFF ALL OF YOUR CREDIT AND START FRESH. MAYBE YOU'LL GET LUCKY THIS TIME.

HEY, DO YOU REALLY THINK SO?

MAYBE.

IT COULD HAPPEN TO ANYBODY.

BUT LUCKIER IF YOU HAD AN UNCLE IN GOVERNMENT.

*A LARGE RANCH. LARGE ESTATES ARE THE DOMINANT LAND-TENURE SYSTEM IN THE NORTHWESTERN CHACO REGION OF PARAGUAY.

HELLO?

A LOAN WITHOUT CHECKING MY CREDIT SCORE YOU SAY?

UP TO $1,000?

WELL, IF I DON'T WIN THE BINGO, AT LEAST I CAN LIVE ON CREDIT.

OR MORE LIKELY A *SUELDO COMPROMETIDO** LIKE THESE FOLKS. DID YOU SEE THIS SIGN – "AFTER OFFICE" NETWORKING EVENT? MAYBE IT'S A SIDE HUSTLE TO PAY THE BILLS.

WELL, THIS IS MY OFFICE! PRETTY STYLISH, RIGHT?

YOU CAN EVEN BUY BINGO WITH A CREDIT CARD THESE DAYS. WE ARE FULL SERVICE.

*INDEBTED WAGE. EACH PAYCHECK IS ALREADY EARMARKED TO PAY DEBTS.

YOU WORK AT THE CENTRAL BANK OF PARAGUAY?
SURE DO, I CAME RIGHT HERE FROM THE OFFICE.
OK, SO TELL ME SOMETHING. WHAT IS FINTECH?
NO IDEA, I'M JUST HERE FOR THE CRAFT BEER.
BZZZZ
RING RING!
TWEET!
loffice
AFTER OFFICE
NETWORKING
Sponsored by Koga

*NATIONAL STRATEGY FOR FINANCIAL INCLUSION, RATIFIED IN DECEMBER 2014

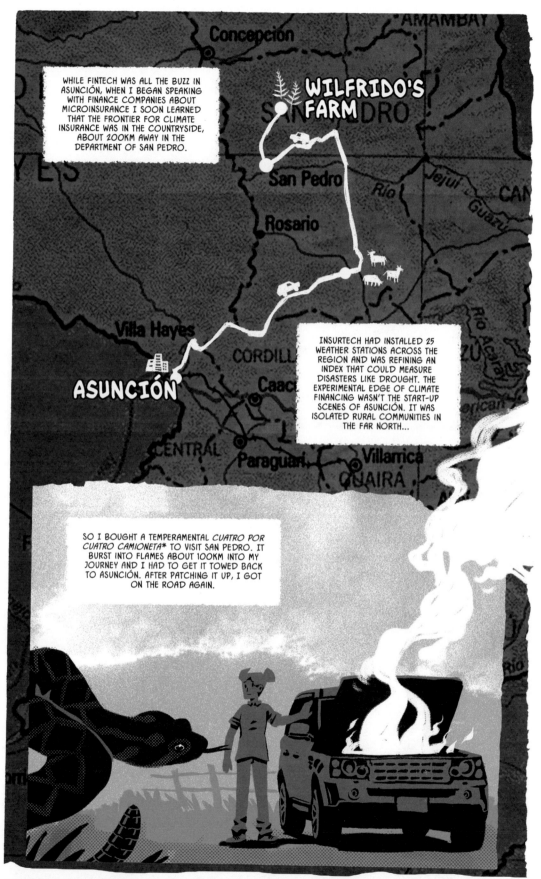

WHILE FINTECH WAS ALL THE BUZZ IN ASUNCIÓN, WHEN I BEGAN SPEAKING WITH FINANCE COMPANIES ABOUT MICROINSURANCE I SOON LEARNED THAT THE FRONTIER FOR CLIMATE INSURANCE WAS IN THE COUNTRYSIDE, ABOUT 200KM AWAY IN THE DEPARTMENT OF SAN PEDRO.

WILFRIDO'S FARM

INSURTECH HAD INSTALLED 25 WEATHER STATIONS ACROSS THE REGION AND WAS REFINING AN INDEX THAT COULD MEASURE DISASTERS LIKE DROUGHT. THE EXPERIMENTAL EDGE OF CLIMATE FINANCING WASN'T THE START-UP SCENES OF ASUNCIÓN. IT WAS ISOLATED RURAL COMMUNITIES IN THE FAR NORTH...

SO I BOUGHT A TEMPERAMENTAL *CUATRO POR CUATRO CAMIONETA** TO VISIT SAN PEDRO. IT BURST INTO FLAMES ABOUT 100KM INTO MY JOURNEY AND I HAD TO GET IT TOWED BACK TO ASUNCIÓN. AFTER PATCHING IT UP, I GOT ON THE ROAD AGAIN.

*AWD VEHICLE. IN THIS CASE A 1994 LAND ROVER AFFECTIONATELY DUBBED *THE LANDIE* (WHEN IT WAS OPERATIONAL). ITS LUMBERING BULK SET US APART FROM THE FLASH TOYOTA HILUX PICKUPS THAT WERE THE NORM FOR NGOS, GOVERNMENT OFFICIALS, AND WEALTHY MENNONITE FARMERS.

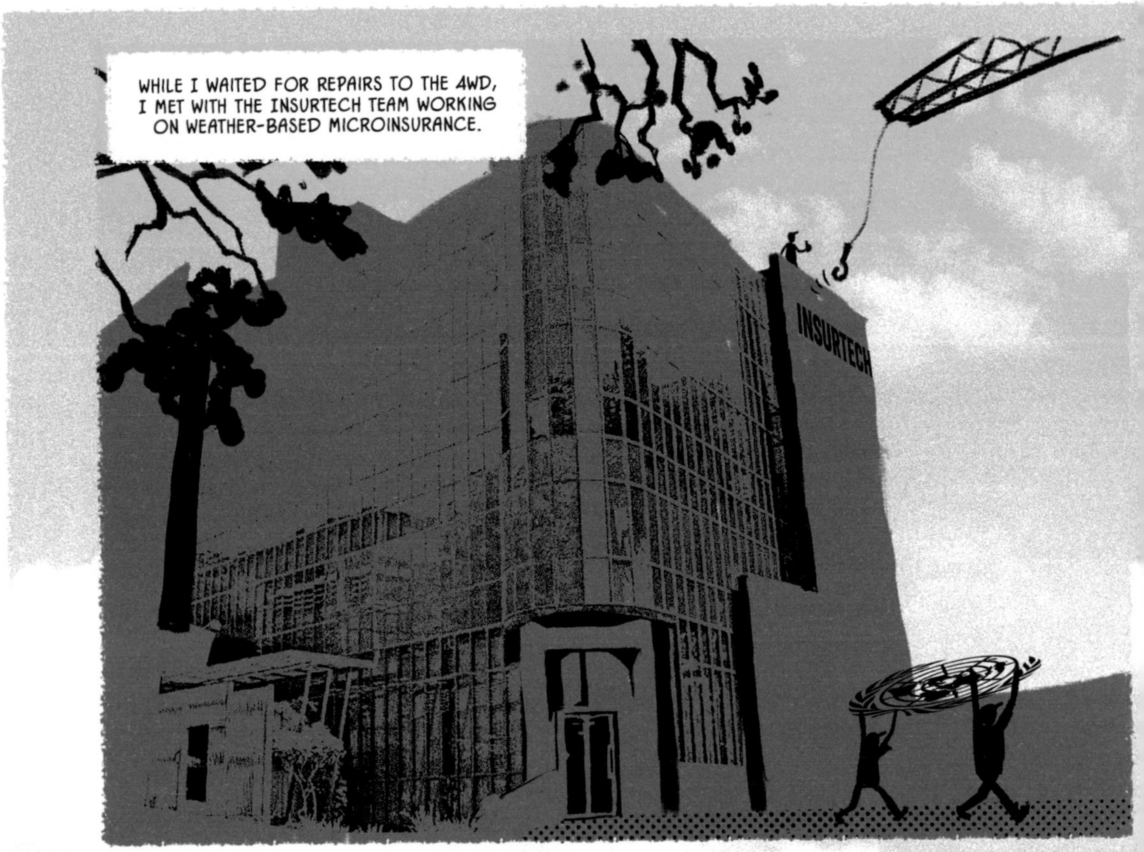
WHILE I WAITED FOR REPAIRS TO THE AWD, I MET WITH THE INSURTECH TEAM WORKING ON WEATHER-BASED MICROINSURANCE.
INSURTECH

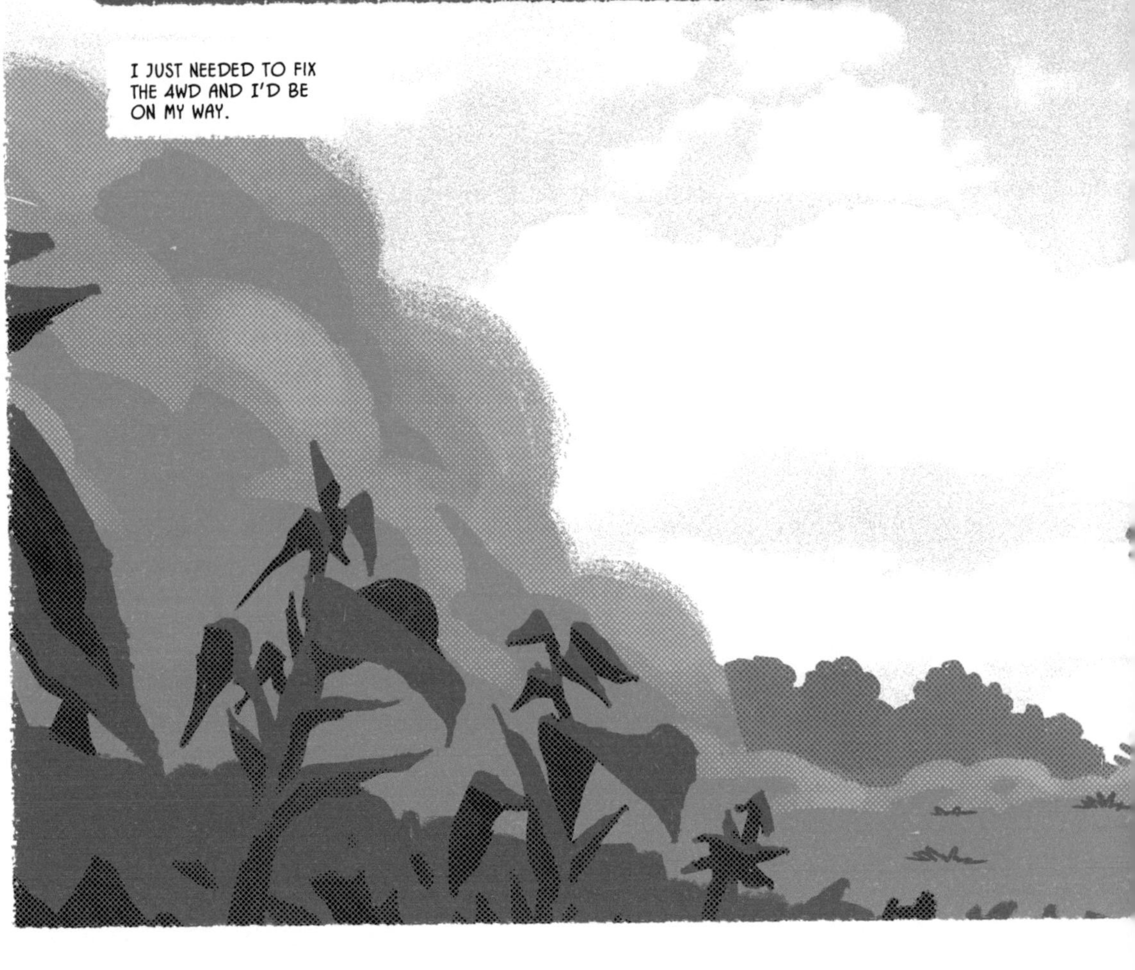
I JUST NEEDED TO FIX THE AWD AND I'D BE ON MY WAY.

THE INSURTECH TEAM HAD ALREADY MET WITH THE LEAD AGRONOMISTS FROM SAN PEDRO AND INTRODUCED THE NEW CROP INSURANCE THEY WERE OFFERING. THE AGRONOMISTS WERE CAUTIOUSLY OPTIMISTIC - BAD WEATHER WAS DISASTROUS FOR THE *CAMPESINOS,** AND OFTEN LEFT THEM DEEPLY IN DEBT TO THE COOPERATIVES THAT LOANED MONEY FOR CHEMICALS, SEEDS, AND OTHER FARM INPUTS. MICROINSURANCE WOULD LEAVE THE COOPERATIVES LESS EXPOSED TO WEATHER RISKS, AND WOULD BE A SAFETY NET FOR FARMERS.

INSURTECH WAS EAGER TO PUT ME IN TOUCH WITH THEIR PARTNERS AT THE COOPERATIVES, AND WERE EXCITED ABOUT THE ON-THE-GROUND PERSPECTIVE THAT AN ANTHROPOLOGIST MIGHT BE ABLE TO GIVE THEM.

AND INSURTECH WAS RIGHT. EXTREME WEATHER WAS COMING...

*PEASANT FARMERS

15

THE EFFECTS OF CLIMATE CHANGE WERE HARD TO IGNORE AS WE WORKED ON THIS BOOK.

DAVID AND ENRIQUE WERE DRAWING *FORECASTS* AS THE AMAZON FIRES BURNED FARTHER AND FARTHER SOUTH FROM BRAZIL DOWN INTO PARAGUAY.

BOY, THE COFFEE STEAM IS KINDA STRONG, ISN'T IT?

COUGH COUGH

YEAH...

JA'UMA HULE. I'M GOING TO HAVE TO TEACH CAROLINE THAT GUARANÍ PHRASE, "EATING THE PLASTIC BAG." WE'VE REALLY STUFFED IT UP.

I BET SHE ALREADY KNOWS IT. SESAME FARMERS DON'T HAVE IT EASY. *HULE* FOR SURE.

MORE THAN 5,000 WILDFIRES BURNED THROUGHOUT DROUGHT-RAVAGED PARAGUAY AMID A RECORD-SETTING HEATWAVE IN 2020.

THIS IS A CATASTROPHE THAT DIDN'T JUST *HAPPEN*. HEAT AND FIRES ARE DIRECTLY LINKED TO PARAGUAY'S ENVIRONMENTAL RECORD. CATTLE RANCHING AND AGRIBUSINESS HAVE LED TO SOME OF THE WORLD'S WORST DEFORESTATION.

BURNING TO CLEAR LAND FOR COWS, SOY, AND MARIJUANA.

EXTREME WEATHER DOESN'T JUST MEAN FIRES AND DROUGHT. IN 2016, FLOODING ACROSS PARAGUAY'S CAPITAL, ASUNCIÓN, DISPLACED THOUSANDS FROM THEIR HOMES NEAR THE RIVER.

THE GOVERNMENT CONSIDERED SUBSIDIZED FLOOD INSURANCE. BUT THE INITIATIVE WAS TOO DIFFICULT TO FINANCE AND WAS NEVER IMPLEMENTED.

FLOOD WATERS RECEDED, PEOPLE MOVED BACK INTO THEIR HOMES TO REBUILD.

2018, AND THE *EL NIÑO* WEATHER PATTERN BROUGHT MORE FLOODING FOLLOWED BY DROUGHT. FARMERS SUCH AS WILFRIDO STRUGGLED TO COPE WITH THE EXTREME WEATHER.

THIS TIME PRIVATE INSURERS WERE ON HAND TO PROVIDE A SAFETY NET. FINTECH ARRIVED IN THE DEPARTMENT OF SAN PEDRO.

18

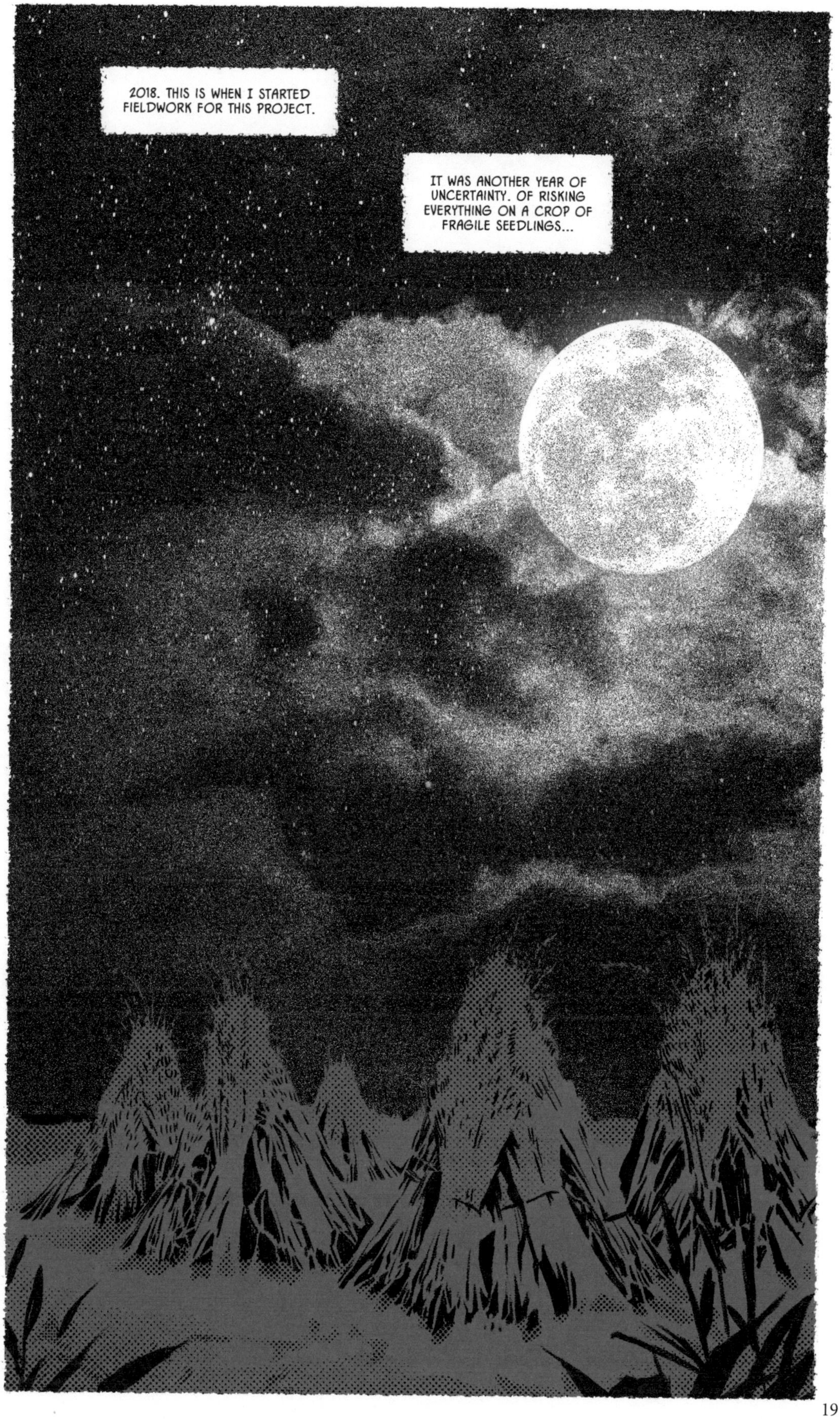
2018. THIS IS WHEN I STARTED FIELDWORK FOR THIS PROJECT.
IT WAS ANOTHER YEAR OF UNCERTAINTY. OF RISKING EVERYTHING ON A CROP OF FRAGILE SEEDLINGS...

DIOS EN EL CIELO, DON WILFRIDO EN EL SUELO. GOD IN HEAVEN, AND ME ON THIS LAND.

THIS LAND THAT GIVES ME NOTHING. THAT WILL *RUIN* ME.

YOU ARE RIGHT, MAYBE IT IS THE JASY JATERE, THE MYTHICAL GOLDEN CHILD FROM OUR STORIES.

THEY SAY HE WHISTLES LIKE A BIRD.

BUT THE HARVEST IS OVER, AND WE HAVE NO CORN FOR HIM. NO WILD HONEY. NO CHILDREN FOR HIM TO ENCHANT AND CARRY AWAY.

IT'S GONE, ALL GONE.

LET ME TELL YOU A STORY...

IT WOULD HAVE BEEN 50 YEARS AGO. I WAS
WORKING IN THE *CHACRA*. I WAS A YOUNG MAN
DATING A GIRL FROM THE NEIGHBORS' FARM.

AND *OPORTUNAMENTE*...

...THERE SHE WAS! STANDING
AT THE EDGE OF MY FIELD.

WILFRIDO!
COME OVER
HERE.

I'LL TAKE YOU
INTO THE FOREST
AND MAKE LOVE
TO YOU.

¡QUE
SUERTE!*

I'M COMING
MY DARLING!

AND I SNUCK OFF FOR
A TRYST IN THE FOREST
WITH MY GIRL.

BUT SHE CHANGED
BEFORE MY EYES.

I FOUND MYSELF
WITH THE TRICKSTER
MONSTER.

A POMBERO HAD
CAPTURED ME.

*WHAT LUCK

BEFORE I KNEW IT...

...SHE WAS JOINED BY HER NASTY TWIN.

HE KICKED, BIT, AND MISTREATED ME.

SHE WAS SWEET AND FED ME HONEY.

EITHER WAY, I COULDN'T ESCAPE.

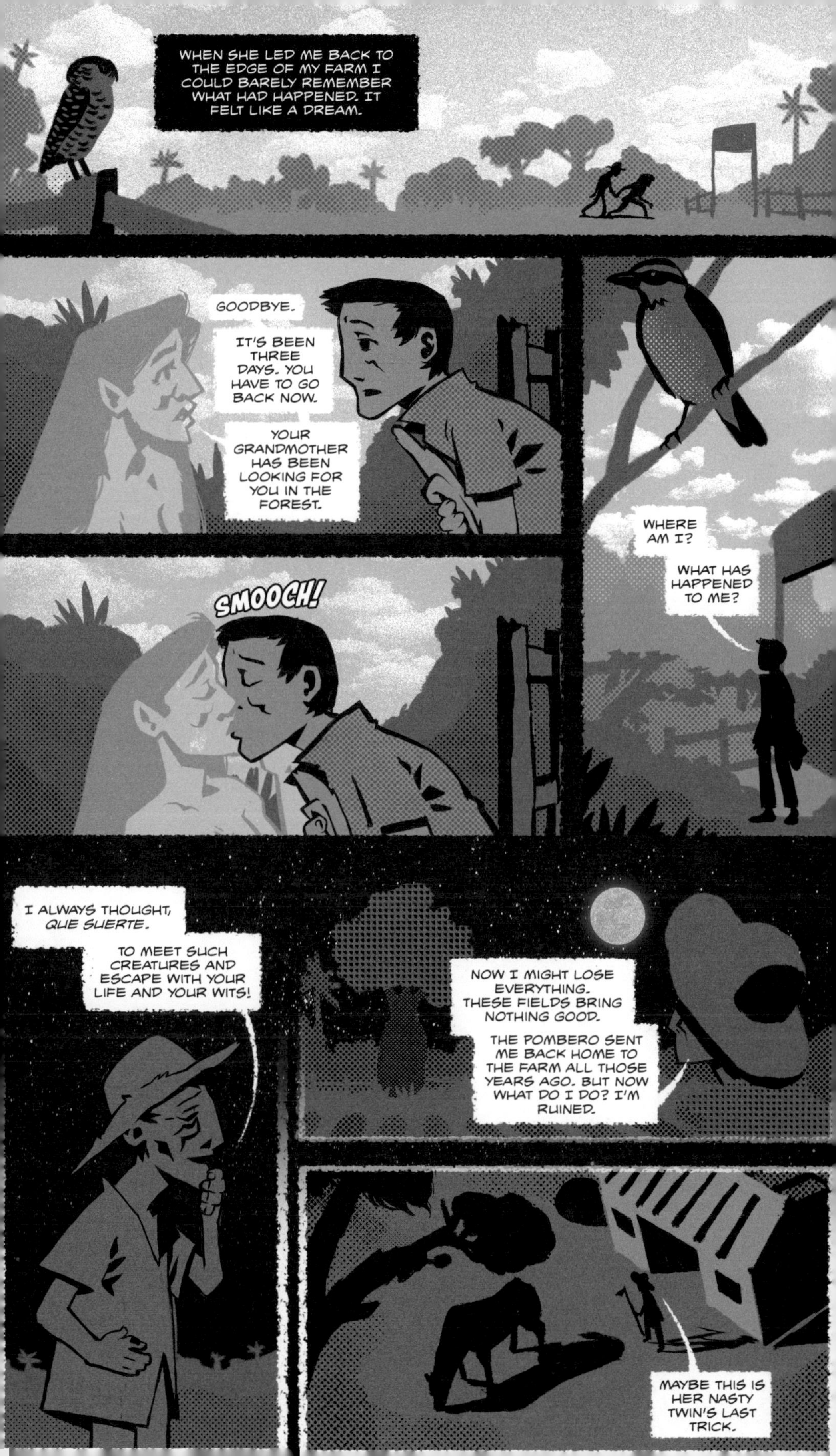
WHEN SHE LED ME BACK TO THE EDGE OF MY FARM I COULD BARELY REMEMBER WHAT HAD HAPPENED. IT FELT LIKE A DREAM.
GOODBYE.
IT'S BEEN THREE DAYS. YOU HAVE TO GO BACK NOW.
YOUR GRANDMOTHER HAS BEEN LOOKING FOR YOU IN THE FOREST.
SMOOCH!
WHERE AM I?
WHAT HAS HAPPENED TO ME?
I ALWAYS THOUGHT, *QUE SUERTE*.
TO MEET SUCH CREATURES AND ESCAPE WITH YOUR LIFE AND YOUR WITS!
NOW I MIGHT LOSE EVERYTHING. THESE FIELDS BRING NOTHING GOOD.
THE POMBERO SENT ME BACK HOME TO THE FARM ALL THOSE YEARS AGO. BUT NOW WHAT DO I DO? I'M RUINED.
MAYBE THIS IS HER NASTY TWIN'S LAST TRICK.

WILFRIDO TOLD ME THIS STORY AT THE END OF THE HARVEST, WHEN HE THOUGHT THAT HE WOULD ONLY MAKE A PITTANCE FROM HIS SESAME CROP.

WE SPOKE OFTEN OF LUCK AND FORTUNE. NOT JUST MONSTERS THAT HAUNTED HIS PAST OR FEARS FOR THIS SEASON'S HARVEST.

HIS FIELDS AND FARM HANG BY A GOSSAMER STRAND - A THREAD OF HOPE AND MONEY.

WILL HIS GAMBLE ON FINTECH PAY OFF? WILL HIS MARE TRIUMPH IN THE HORSE RACE AT THE END OF THE SEASON?

WHO HAS THE POWER TO ALTER REALITY WITH THEIR NARRATIVE - POMBEROS? HORSES? FARMERS? INSURANCE? POLICIES? SESAME SEEDS?

TO ANSWER THESE QUESTIONS, WE SHOULD START AT THE BEGINNING OF THE CYCLES OF PLANTS AND POLICIES...

WILFRIDO'S FARM, 2018. FARMERS AROUND THE REGION BURN OFF THE LAST OF THE WEEDS AND CORN STALKS TO CLEAR THE FIELDS FOR SESAME.

WILFRIDO TOLD ME ABOUT THE TIME *INGENIERO FREDDY,** THE AGRONOMIST FROM THE MULTIACTIVA COOPERATIVE, CAME OUT TO HIS FARM TO EXPLAIN A NEW TYPE OF CROP INSURANCE.

FREDDY WAS GUIDING MARIO, AN INSURANCE AGENT FROM ASUNCIÓN, AROUND TO ALL THE FARMS IN THE AREA, INTRODUCING HIM TO MEMBERS OF MULTIACTIVA THAT GREW SESAME.

SO THIS MEANS THAT MY SESAME CROP IS INSURED? AND THROUGH THIS?

YOU GOT IT. IT'S *FINTECH* – THIS IS THE FUTURE!

AH, DON WILFRIDO IS AN OLD MAN. HE JUST WANTS TO REST.

MAYBE HE'LL JUST TAKE A SIESTA AND CUDDLE UP WITH DOÑA NECA.

MAYBE HE'LL JUST WATCH SOME TELENOVELAS.

BUT THIS IS THE FUTURE YOU SAY? THE FUTURE SOUNDS LIKE A LOT OF WORK TO ME IF I HAVE TO CARRY MY PHONE ALL THE TIME.

NOT ALL THE TIME, YOU'LL JUST GET WEEKLY UPDATES.

*INGENIERO MEANS ENGINEER, AND IS THE COMMON TITLE FOR AGRONOMISTS. FREDDY STUDIED AGRONOMY IN ASUNCIÓN BEFORE MOVING BACK HOME TO SAN PEDRO, WHERE HE PURCHASED A PROPERTY THAT HE SLOWLY BUILT INTO A CATTLE RANCH. HE HAD BEEN THE LEAD AGRONOMIST FOR MULTIACTIVA FOR TEN YEARS.

IT'S NOT EVEN REALLY MINE, YOU SEE. IT'S MY WIFE'S PHONE. ÑA NECA'S, SO SHE CAN COO AT OUR GRANDKIDS.

WE CAN ONLY AFFORD TO BUY PAY-AS-YOU-GO MINUTES, MINICARGA, GS. 3,000 AT A TIME.

ARE YOU SURE IT WILL WORK?

I JUST HAVE THIS OLD THING, MY DAUGHTER HAS A NEW ONE BUT SHE IS IN ASUNCIÓN.

ALL OF THEM ARE AWAY.

THE OTHER ONES ARE IN ARGENTINA, WORKING. I'M JUST AN OLD MAN, HERE BY MYSELF.

SURE, SURE DON WILFRIDO. IT REALLY IS JUST TO CONTACT YOU FOR UPDATES.

DOESN'T LOOK SOPHISTICATED ENOUGH TO ME...

THE INSURANCE COMPANY HAS THE HIGH TECH.

DON'T YOU WORRY.

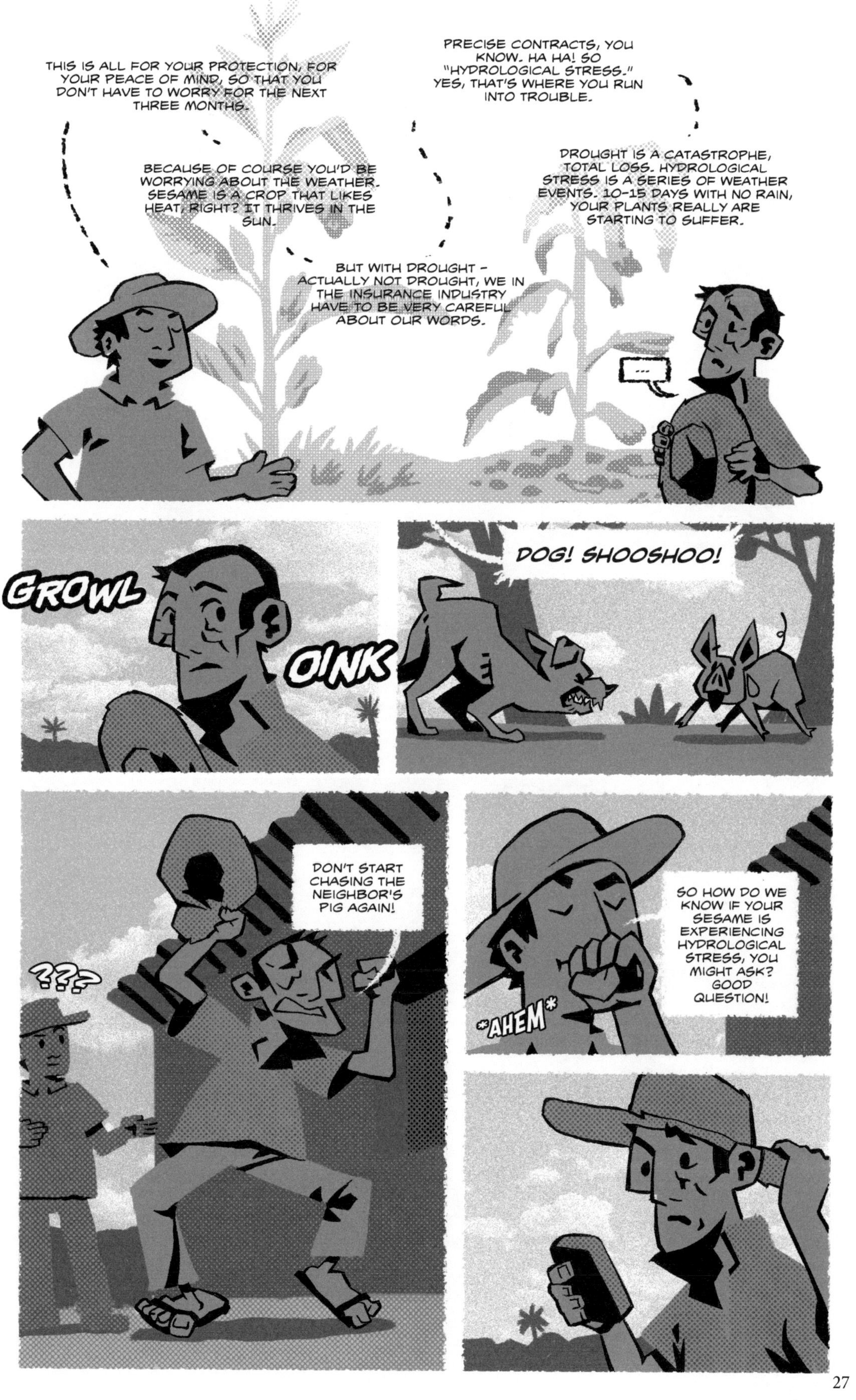
THIS IS ALL FOR YOUR PROTECTION, FOR YOUR PEACE OF MIND, SO THAT YOU DON'T HAVE TO WORRY FOR THE NEXT THREE MONTHS.
BECAUSE OF COURSE YOU'D BE WORRYING ABOUT THE WEATHER. SESAME IS A CROP THAT LIKES HEAT, RIGHT? IT THRIVES IN THE SUN.
BUT WITH DROUGHT - ACTUALLY NOT DROUGHT, WE IN THE INSURANCE INDUSTRY HAVE TO BE VERY CAREFUL ABOUT OUR WORDS.
PRECISE CONTRACTS, YOU KNOW. HA HA! SO "HYDROLOGICAL STRESS." YES, THAT'S WHERE YOU RUN INTO TROUBLE.
DROUGHT IS A CATASTROPHE, TOTAL LOSS. HYDROLOGICAL STRESS IS A SERIES OF WEATHER EVENTS. 10-15 DAYS WITH NO RAIN, YOUR PLANTS REALLY ARE STARTING TO SUFFER.
...
GROWL
OINK
DOG! SHOOSHOO!
DON'T START CHASING THE NEIGHBOR'S PIG AGAIN!
???
AHEM
SO HOW DO WE KNOW IF YOUR SESAME IS EXPERIENCING HYDROLOGICAL STRESS, YOU MIGHT ASK? GOOD QUESTION!

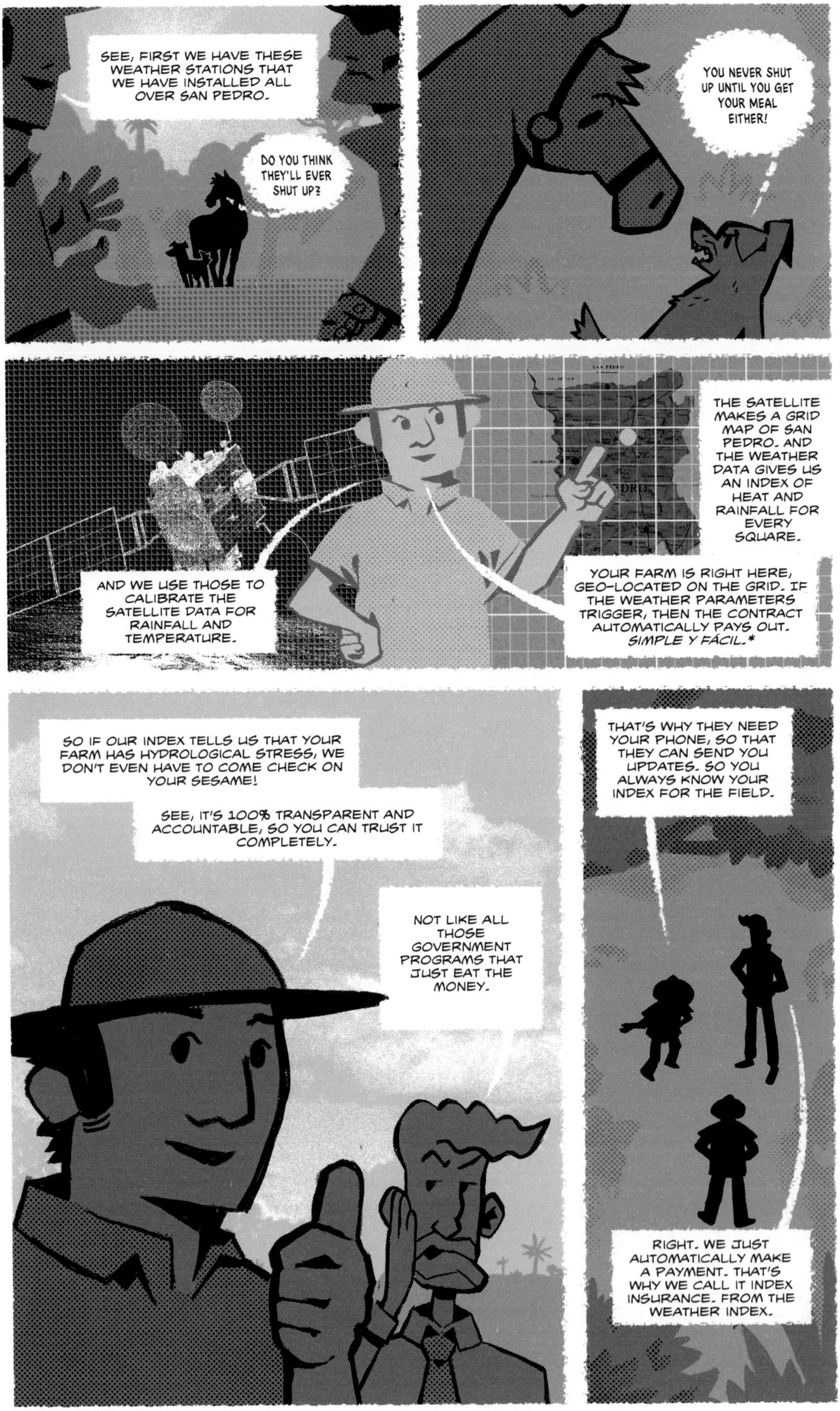
SEE, FIRST WE HAVE THESE WEATHER STATIONS THAT WE HAVE INSTALLED ALL OVER SAN PEDRO.
DO YOU THINK THEY'LL EVER SHUT UP?
YOU NEVER SHUT UP UNTIL YOU GET YOUR MEAL EITHER!
AND WE USE THOSE TO CALIBRATE THE SATELLITE DATA FOR RAINFALL AND TEMPERATURE.
THE SATELLITE MAKES A GRID MAP OF SAN PEDRO. AND THE WEATHER DATA GIVES US AN INDEX OF HEAT AND RAINFALL FOR EVERY SQUARE.
YOUR FARM IS RIGHT HERE, GEO-LOCATED ON THE GRID. IF THE WEATHER PARAMETERS TRIGGER, THEN THE CONTRACT AUTOMATICALLY PAYS OUT. *SIMPLE Y FÁCIL.**
SO IF OUR INDEX TELLS US THAT YOUR FARM HAS HYDROLOGICAL STRESS, WE DON'T EVEN HAVE TO COME CHECK ON YOUR SESAME!
SEE, IT'S 100% TRANSPARENT AND ACCOUNTABLE, SO YOU CAN TRUST IT COMPLETELY.
NOT LIKE ALL THOSE GOVERNMENT PROGRAMS THAT JUST EAT THE MONEY.
THAT'S WHY THEY NEED YOUR PHONE, SO THAT THEY CAN SEND YOU UPDATES. SO YOU ALWAYS KNOW YOUR INDEX FOR THE FIELD.
RIGHT. WE JUST AUTOMATICALLY MAKE A PAYMENT. THAT'S WHY WE CALL IT INDEX INSURANCE. FROM THE WEATHER INDEX.

*SIMPLE AND EASY

WILFRIDO'S INSURANCE POLICY IS KNOWN AS INDEX-BASED AGRICULTURAL INSURANCE (IBAI).

ACTUALLY, IT'S A FINANCIAL PRODUCT CLOSER IN KIND TO A WEATHER DERIVATIVE, NOT INSURANCE IN THE CONVENTIONAL SENSE.

IT'S A CONTRACT TRIGGERED BY FUTURE WEATHER CONDITIONS, NOT INDEMNITY FOR ACTUAL LOST CROPS.

THE VALUE IS DERIVED FROM AN UNDERLYING ENTITY, WHETHER MORTGAGES OR INTEREST RATES OR THE PRICE OF CORN. DERIVATIVES ARE STRANGE, SHAPESHIFTING BEASTS - WITH BOTH AN INVESTMENT AND INSURANCE SIDE...

FORECLOSURE

SOCIAL SCIENTISTS HAVE TAKEN AN INTEREST IN DERIVATIVES BECAUSE THEY PARTICIPATE IN A SPECULATIVE LOGIC THAT HAS PROFOUNDLY REORDERED THE ECONOMY, POLITICS, AND CULTURE. SOME CALL IT "CAPITAL'S SECURITY FORM" - THAT IS, "IT AIMS TO PROVIDE OFFSETTING COMPENSATION (INSURANCE) FOR AN UNDESIRED EVENT OR, CONVERSELY, TO TAKE A BET ON SUCH AN UNDESIRED EVENT BY SPECULATING THAT THE PARTY SEEKING INSURANCE IS WRONG ABOUT THE FUTURE VALUE OF THE UNDERLYING ASSET."*

IBAI IS A WEATHER HEDGE - A DERIVATIVE FOR CROP INSURANCE. BUT RECALL, THESE MUTATING MONSTERS HAVE TWO FACES. MANY ARE USED TO INCREASE RATHER THAN LIMIT EXPOSURE TO VOLATILITY, HOPING TO PROFIT BY BETTING ON THE CORRECT SIDE OF PRICE FLUCTUATIONS. WHEN THE BETS GO BADLY WRONG, IT'S NOT JUST TRADERS WHO LOSE - WHEN HOUSE PRICES FLUCTUATE, FAMILIES CAN'T AFFORD THEIR MORTGAGES. THE INVENTION OF COLLATERALIZED DEBT OBLIGATIONS (CDOS) AND CREDIT DEFAULT SWAPS IN THE 1990S AND 2000S CATALYZED THE GLOBAL FINANCIAL CRISIS IN 2007-8.

HOMEOWNERS IN THE UNITED STATES AND SESAME FARMERS IN PARAGUAY BOTH FIND THEMSELVES CAUGHT UP IN SPECULATIVE FINANCE.

*(KOMPOROZOS-ATHANASIOU 2022, 18)

29

THANK YOU FRIEND. YOUR *TERERÉ** IS DELICIOUS. THIS SUN IS BRUTAL.

SO DID YOU UNDERSTAND? ABOUT OUR INDEX? AND YOUR SESAME?

SURE, SURE. WELL, *INGENIERO FREDDY* HERE TELLS ME THAT I DON'T HAVE A CHOICE. IT'S INCLUDED WITH MY CREDIT WITH MULTIACTIVA. I NEED THAT CREDIT TO PLANT MY SESAME.

THE POLICY, IT COSTS GS. 140,000,** RIGHT?

ACTUALLY, WE NEGOTIATED THE PREMIUMS DOWN TO GS. 136,000. BASED ON THE QUALITY OF OUR PRODUCT.

SURE, SURE.

BUT I DO NEED THAT CREDIT, HOW ELSE AM I GOING TO BUY THE HERBICIDE? THE FERTILIZER? IT ALL HAS COSTS.

AND I'M JUST AN OLD MAN, HERE ALONE ON MY FARM.

I'LL PLANT ALRIGHT, *VA A SALIR ALGO.****

TERERÉ IS COLD YERBA MATE TEA.
**THE EXCHANGE RATE BETWEEN THE US DOLLAR AND PARAGUAYAN GUARANI IS ABOUT GS. 6,500. THE POLICY COSTS ABOUT $21.50. IF THE POLICY TRIGGERS, THE PAYMENT IS $230.
***SOMETHING WILL COME OF IT.

DESPITE THE POURING RAIN, THE NEXT DAY WILFRIDO WENT TO MULTIACTIVA TO BORROW THE COOPERATIVE'S SEEDER MACHINE.

THE STORM GREW EVEN MORE INTENSE. DARK CLOUDS THREATENED...

VROOM

FREDDY! MBA'EICHAPA.*

IPORÁ.** HOW DID YOU EVEN GET HERE DON WILFRIDO?

IT'S 20KM TO YOUR FARM AND THE ROADS ARE A *DISASTER.* AND ALL YOU HAVE IS THAT OLD *CACHAPÉ.****

*GREETING IN GUARANÍ **ALL IS WELL ***HORSE-DRAWN WAGON

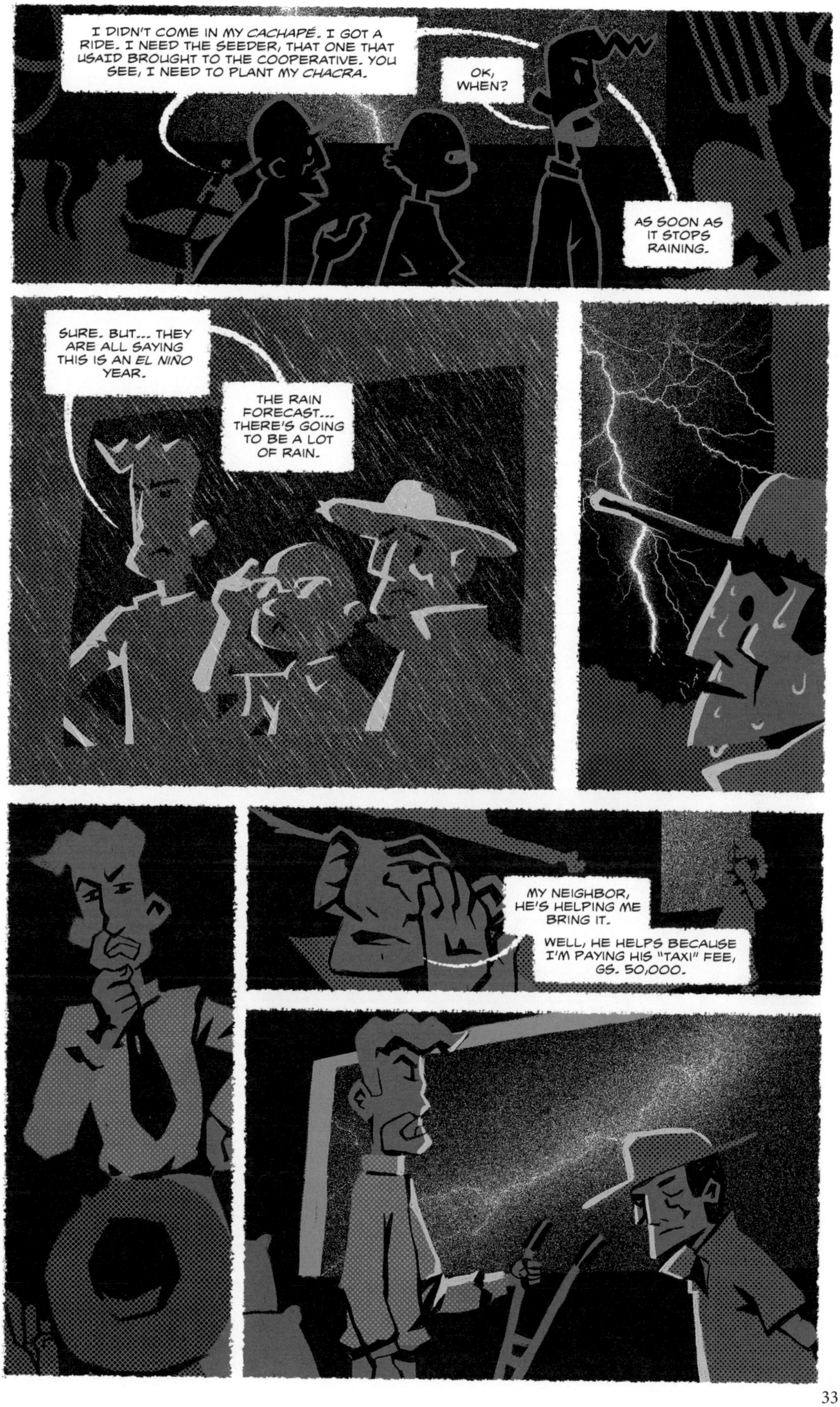
I DIDN'T COME IN MY *CACHAPÉ*. I GOT A RIDE. I NEED THE SEEDER, THAT ONE THAT USAID BROUGHT TO THE COOPERATIVE. YOU SEE, I NEED TO PLANT MY *CHACRA*.
OK, WHEN?
AS SOON AS IT STOPS RAINING.
SURE. BUT... THEY ARE ALL SAYING THIS IS AN *EL NIÑO* YEAR.
THE RAIN FORECAST... THERE'S GOING TO BE A LOT OF RAIN.
MY NEIGHBOR, HE'S HELPING ME BRING IT.
WELL, HE HELPS BECAUSE I'M PAYING HIS "TAXI" FEE, GS. 50,000.

OPORTUNAMENTE, A BREAK IN THE RAIN!

TRY TURNING IT THE OTHER WAY. IT HAS TO FIT.

THIS IS HOW I MET WILFRIDO FOR THE FIRST TIME.

SQUELCH SQUELCH

HEY, WHAT'S ALL THIS?

OH, THAT'S ONE OF OUR SESAME PRODUCERS. HE WANTS TO PLANT HIS FIELD AS SOON AS IT STOPS RAINING.

THEY'LL NEVER GET THE SEEDER IN THAT CAR!

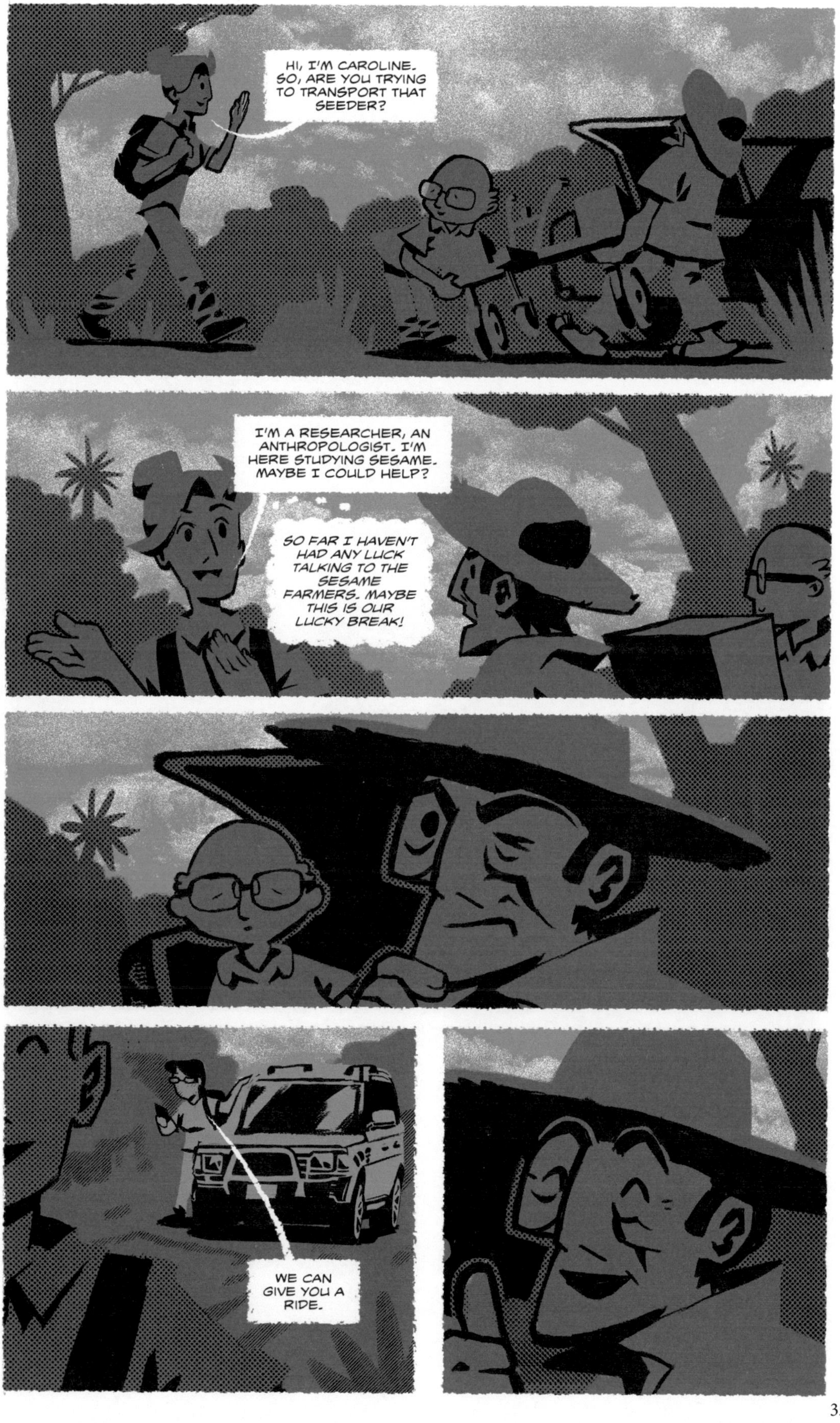
HI, I'M CAROLINE. SO, ARE YOU TRYING TO TRANSPORT THAT SEEDER?
I'M A RESEARCHER, AN ANTHROPOLOGIST. I'M HERE STUDYING SESAME. MAYBE I COULD HELP?
SO FAR I HAVEN'T HAD ANY LUCK TALKING TO THE SESAME FARMERS. MAYBE THIS IS OUR LUCKY BREAK!
WE CAN GIVE YOU A RIDE.

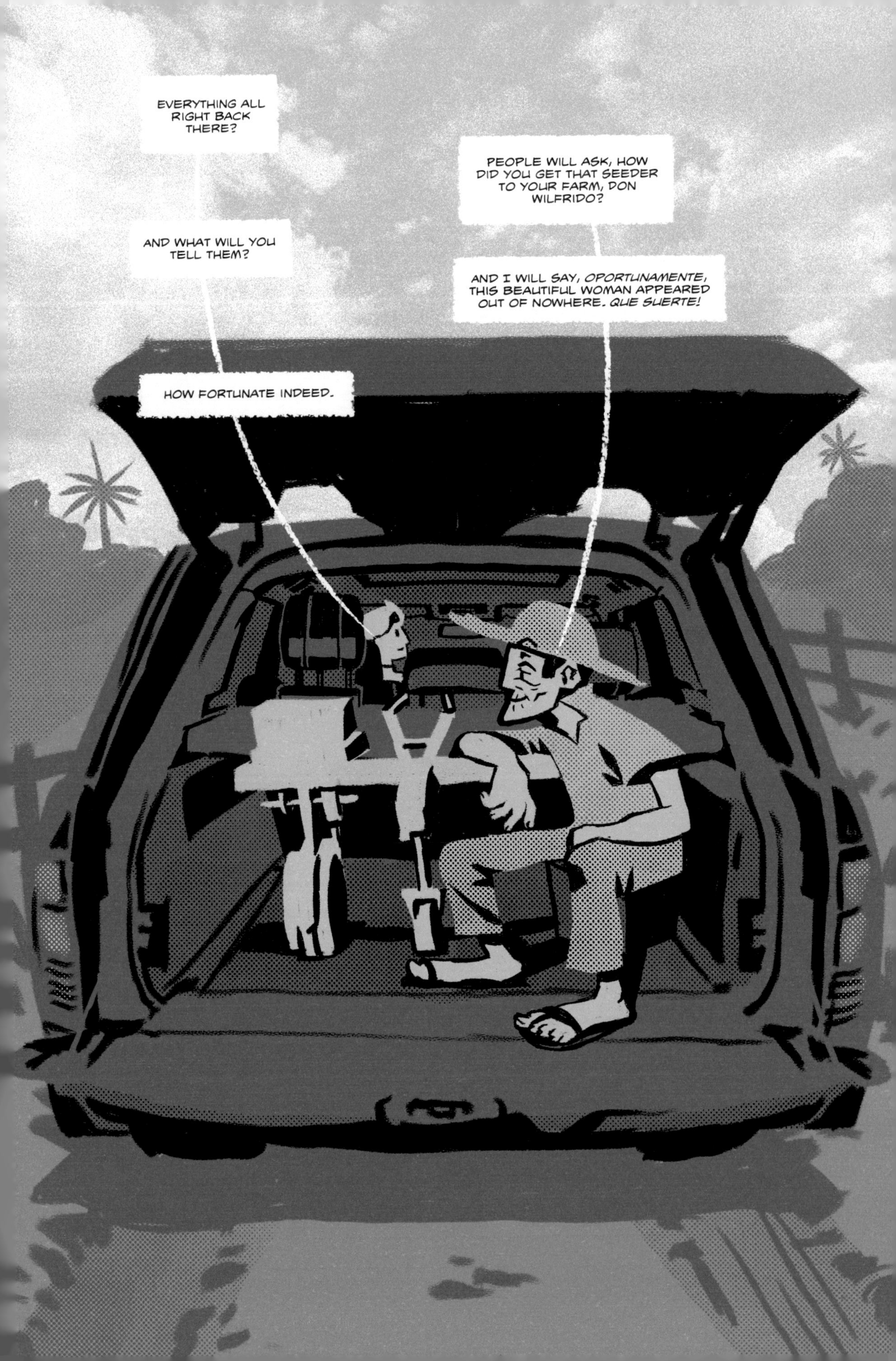
EVERYTHING ALL RIGHT BACK THERE?
PEOPLE WILL ASK, HOW DID YOU GET THAT SEEDER TO YOUR FARM, DON WILFRIDO?
AND WHAT WILL YOU TELL THEM?
AND I WILL SAY, *OPORTUNAMENTE*, THIS BEAUTIFUL WOMAN APPEARED OUT OF NOWHERE. *QUE SUERTE!*
HOW FORTUNATE INDEED.

BY THE FOLLOWING WEEK THE WEATHER CLEARED AND WE STARTED WORKING ON WILFRIDO'S FARM EVERY DAY.

USUALLY BLANCA AND SARITA, HIS DAUGHTERS, HELPED HIM PLANT THE SESAME. BUT BLANCA LIVES IN BUENOS AIRES AND COULD ONLY COME FOR THE HARVEST. AND SARITA MOVED TO ASUNCIÓN LAST YEAR...

JALE JALE JALE!

COME ON, YOU CAN WALK FASTER. I KNOW YOU ARE AN OLD BEAST, BUT PUT SOME ENERGY INTO IT.

DOES HE HAVE A NAME? LIKE SHOOSHOO THE DOG, BECAUSE HE'S ALWAYS UNDERFOOT?

WHAT, THIS HORSE? HMMM, HE'S JUST OLD HORSE, KAVAJÚ TUJA.

IS KAVAJÚ TUJA REALLY THAT OLD?

FIFTEEN YEARS OLD. THAT'S WHY HE'S SO TAME, AND I CAN TRUST HIM WITH THE SEEDER.

YEGUA, MY MARE, SHE'S TOO SPIRITED TO PULL THE SEEDER.

I USED TO BE QUITE THE JINETE IN MY YOUTH. DO YOU KNOW WHAT THAT MEANS? I WAS THE BEST JOCKEY IN THE REGION.

AN OLD MAN AND AN OLD HORSE. I, OF COURSE, AM STILL BLESSED WITH YOUTH. DON WILFRIDO. HE IS LIKE A CHILD, FULL OF ENERGY.

MAYBE THAT RIDICULOUS STORY HE TELLS ABOUT THE LADY POMBERO HAS SOMETHING TO IT. HE DOES SEEM TO HAVE AN UNNATURAL ENERGY.

OLD HORSE, EH? *KAVAJÚ TUJA.* DIDN'T KNOW THAT WAS MY NAME. I ALWAYS THOUGHT IT WAS *JALE.*

TO HIM, I'M JUST A TRACTOR, ONE THAT DOESN'T EVEN NEED DIESEL. THAT'S OK, WE EACH PLAY OUR PART. AND AT LEAST THE GRASS IS GOOD ON THIS FARM.

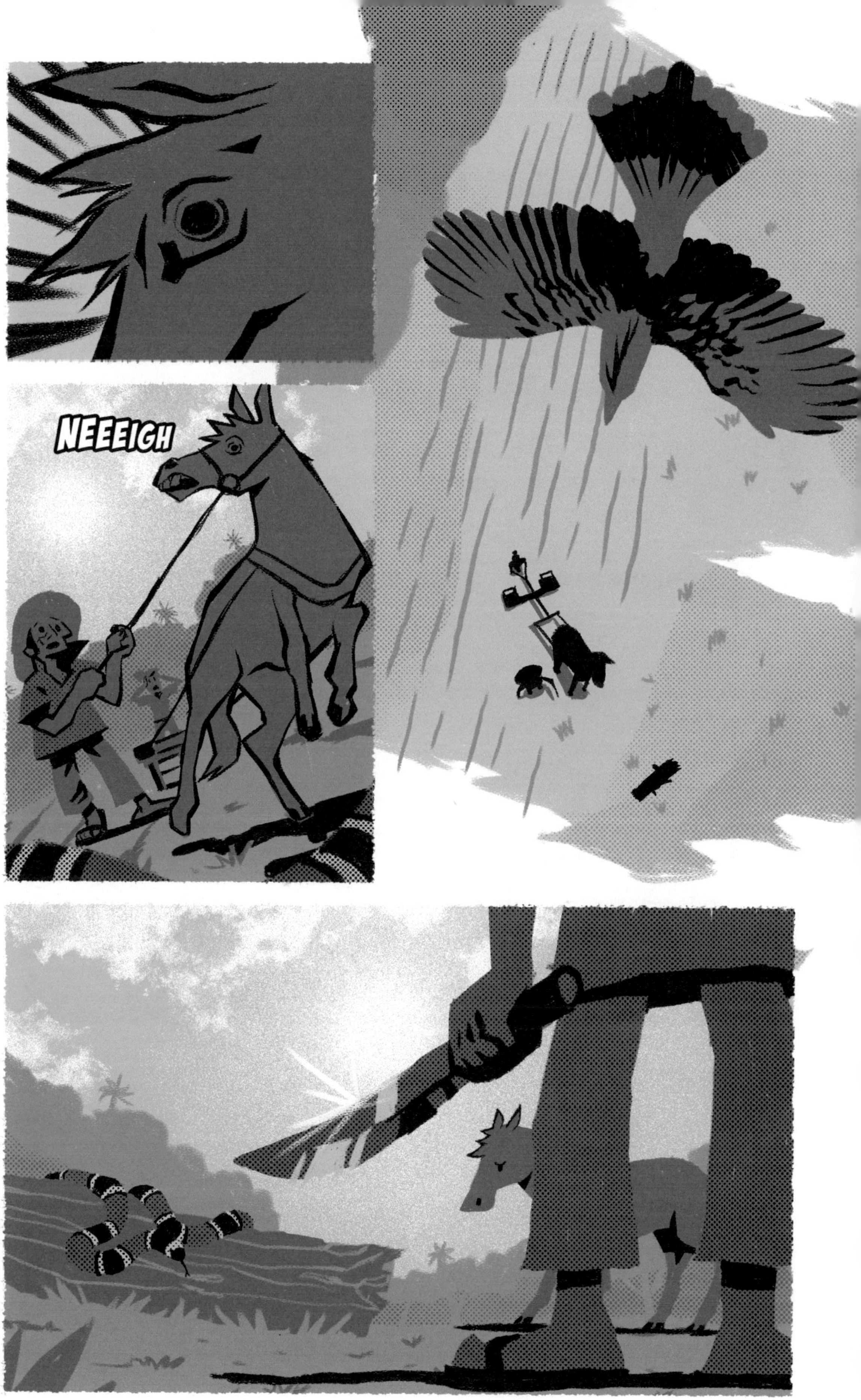
NEEEIGH

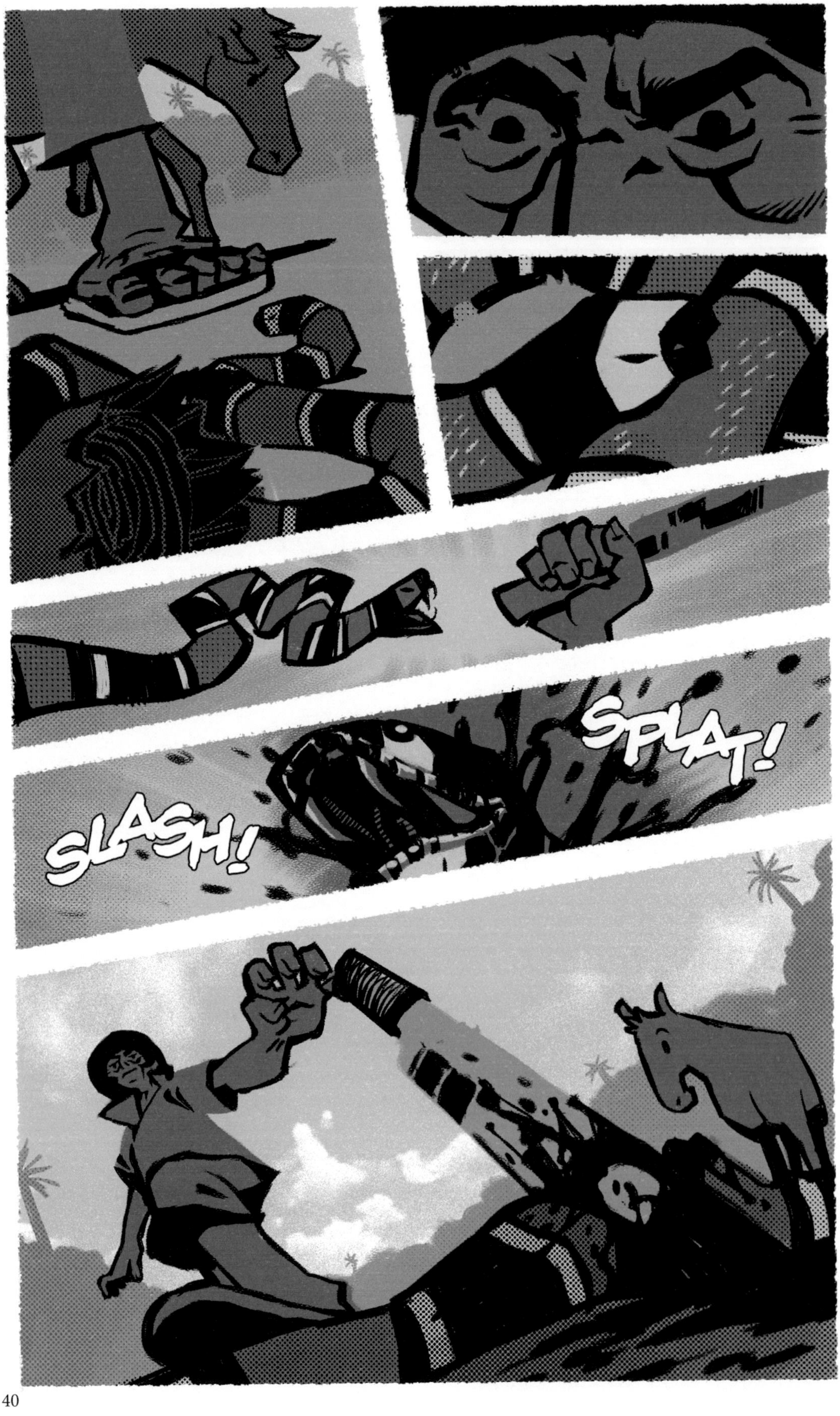
SPLAT!
SLASH!

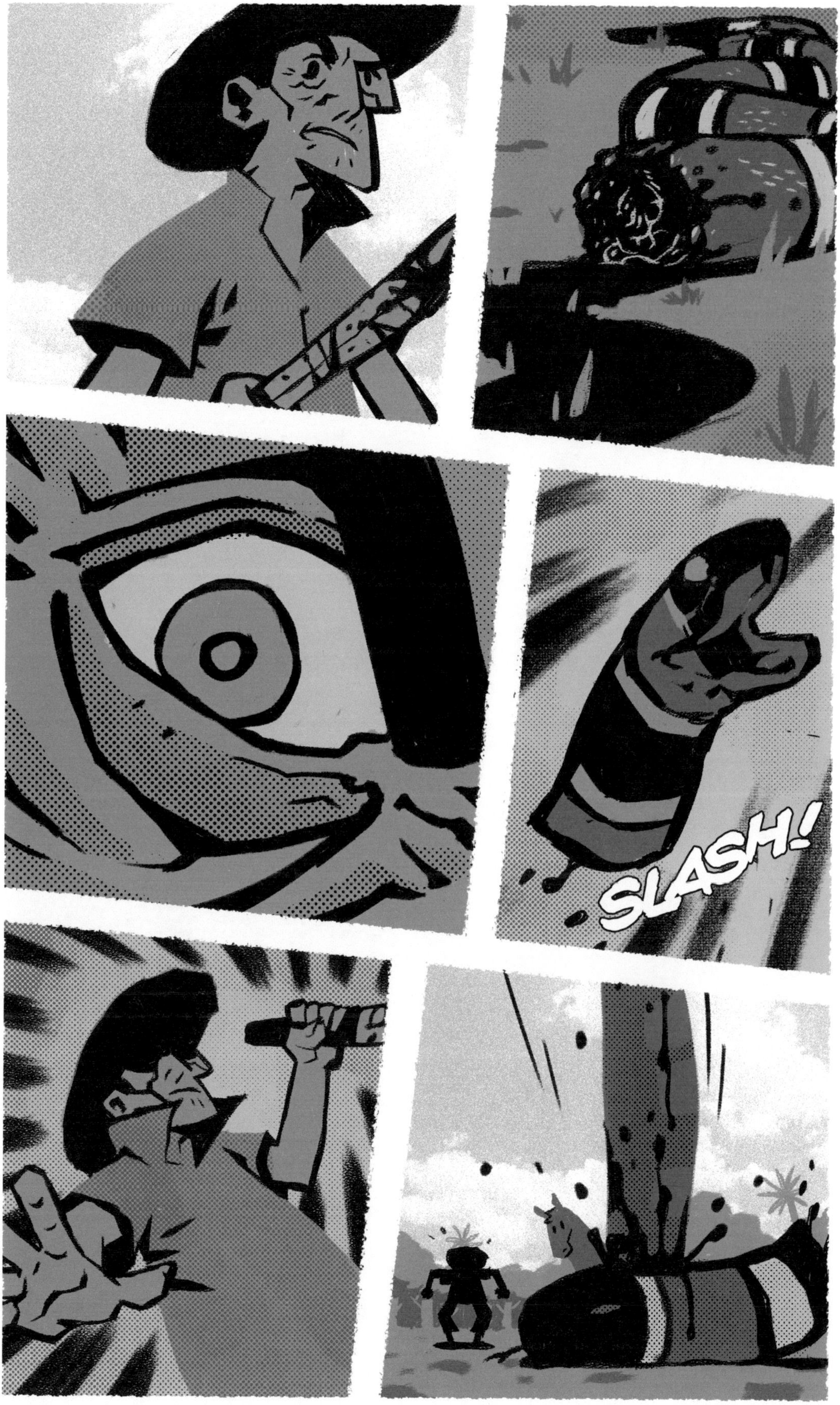
SLASH!

A LA GRAN SIETE, THAT WAS CLOSE!

LA GRAN SIETE IS RIGHT, LUCKY SEVEN FOR CARDS AND DICE... AND SNAKES TOO.

IT'S A GOOD THING I'VE SEEN MY FAIR SHARE. BY ALL'S RIGHT I SHOULD BE GALLOPING BACK HOME, DRAGGING THIS MACHINE BEHIND ME.

YIKES! IT'S A GOOD THING KAVAJÚ TUJA IS SENSIBLE. WE COULD HAVE BEEN IN REAL TROUBLE.

EH!

REALLY?

HE'S NOT SENSIBLE AT ALL. PUERCO, PIG! HE'S IMPOSSIBLE TO CATCH, STUBBORN BEAST.

BUT HE'S MY SOCIO DE TRABAJO.* I HAVE TO PUT UP WITH HIM.

HE WAS STEADY THIS TIME, I'LL GIVE HIM THAT. BUT USUALLY HE'S A PIG.

*WORK COLLEAGUE

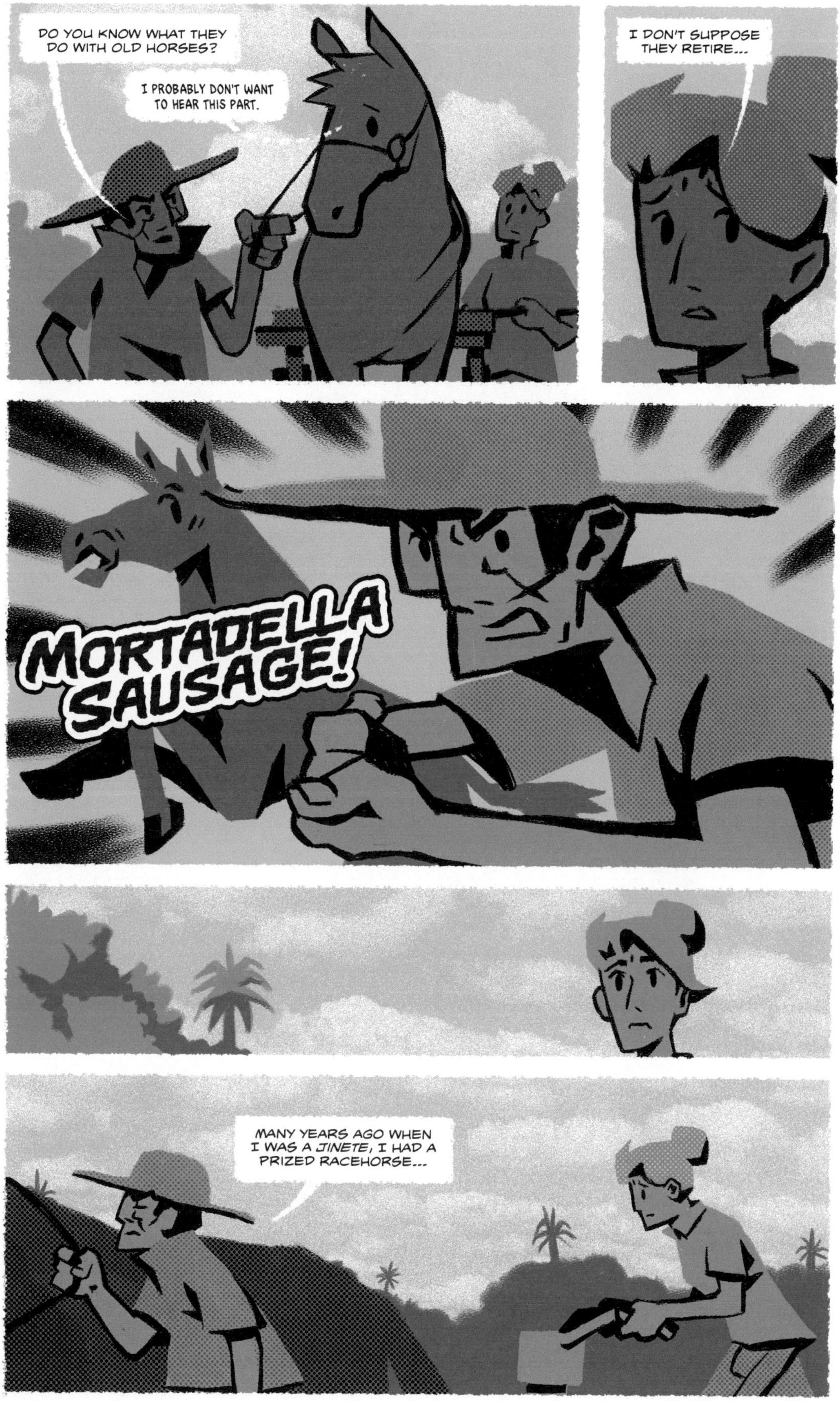
DO YOU KNOW WHAT THEY DO WITH OLD HORSES?
I PROBABLY DON'T WANT TO HEAR THIS PART.
I DON'T SUPPOSE THEY RETIRE...
MORTADELLA SAUSAGE!
MANY YEARS AGO WHEN I WAS A *JINETE*, I HAD A PRIZED RACEHORSE...

I RAISED HIM FROM A COLT.

WELL EVENTUALLY MY OLD HORSE WAS USED UP. USELESS.

BUT WHEN THE MAN CAME TO TAKE AWAY THE OLD HORSES I COULDN'T DO IT.

WELL, THAT'S A RELIEF.

SO I SAID, NECA, QUICK, DO IT WHILE I'M AWAY AND DON'T TELL ME.

HUH??

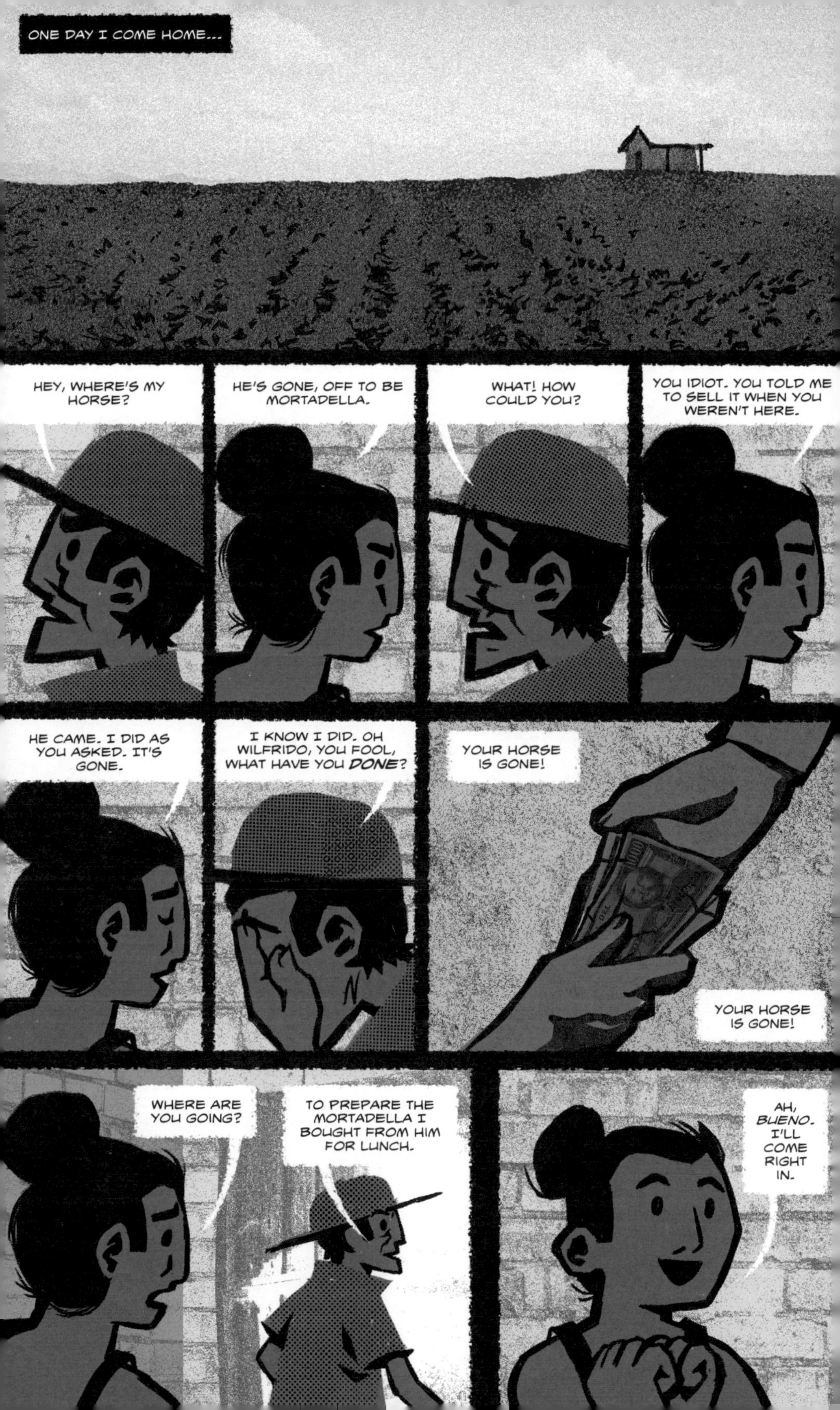
ONE DAY I COME HOME...
HEY, WHERE'S MY HORSE?
HE'S GONE, OFF TO BE MORTADELLA.
WHAT! HOW COULD YOU?
YOU IDIOT. YOU TOLD ME TO SELL IT WHEN YOU WEREN'T HERE.
HE CAME. I DID AS YOU ASKED. IT'S GONE.
I KNOW I DID. OH WILFRIDO, YOU FOOL, WHAT HAVE YOU *DONE*?
YOUR HORSE IS GONE!
YOUR HORSE IS GONE!
WHERE ARE YOU GOING?
TO PREPARE THE MORTADELLA I BOUGHT FROM HIM FOR LUNCH.
AH, *BUENO*. I'LL COME RIGHT IN.

WELL, *KAVAJÚ TUJA*, YOU DID ALRIGHT TODAY WITH THE SNAKE. GOOD WORK *SOCIO*.

CLOP CLOP

PAT PAT

46

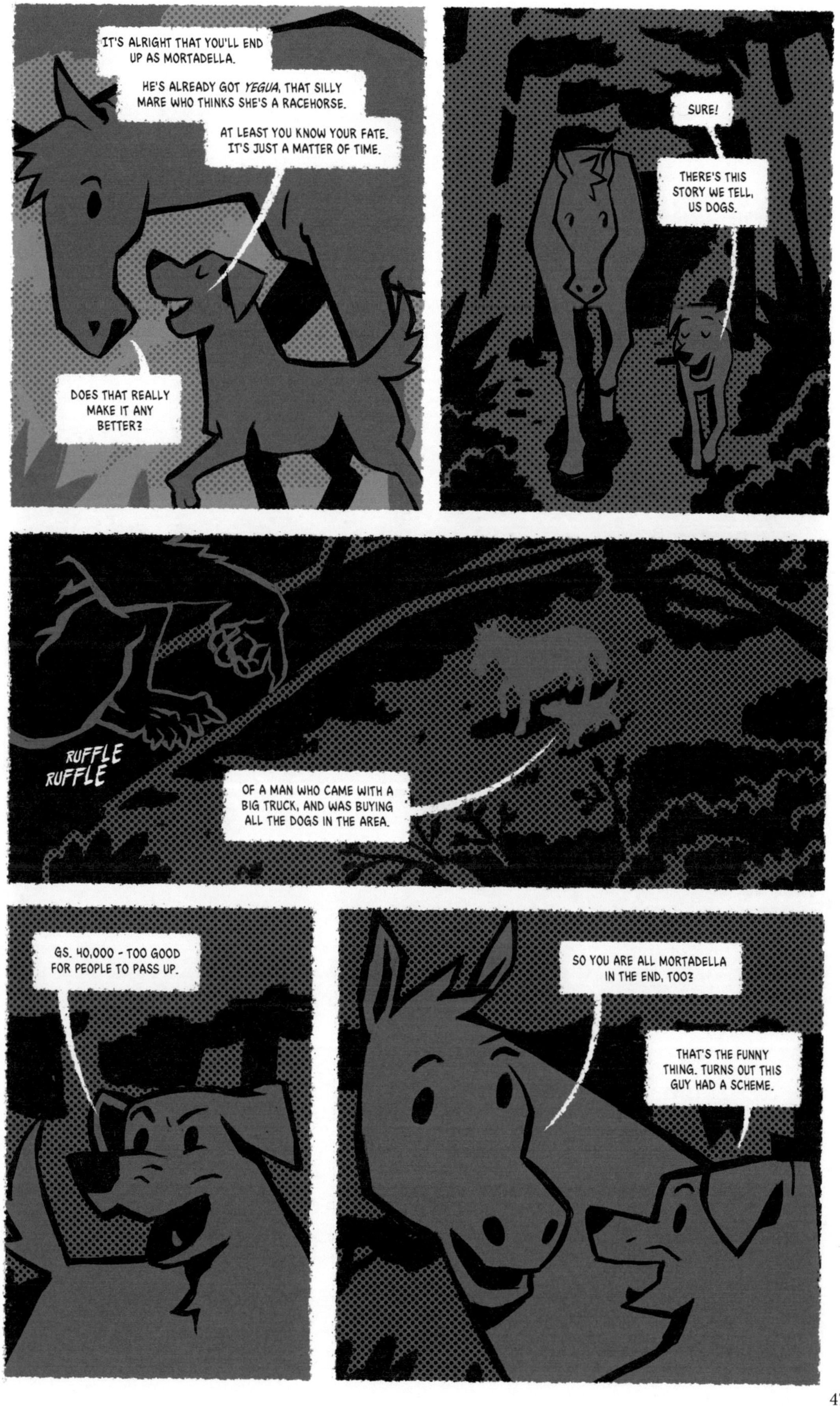
IT'S ALRIGHT THAT YOU'LL END UP AS MORTADELLA.
HE'S ALREADY GOT *YEGUA*, THAT SILLY MARE WHO THINKS SHE'S A RACEHORSE.
AT LEAST YOU KNOW YOUR FATE. IT'S JUST A MATTER OF TIME.
DOES THAT REALLY MAKE IT ANY BETTER?
SURE!
THERE'S THIS STORY WE TELL, US DOGS.
RUFFLE RUFFLE
OF A MAN WHO CAME WITH A BIG TRUCK, AND WAS BUYING ALL THE DOGS IN THE AREA.
GS. 40,000 - TOO GOOD FOR PEOPLE TO PASS UP.
SO YOU ARE ALL MORTADELLA IN THE END, TOO?
THAT'S THE FUNNY THING. TURNS OUT THIS GUY HAD A SCHEME.

HE HAD A WHOLE RUN OF THOSE GS. 50,000 BILLS, FROM THAT TIME THE CENTRAL BANK OF PARAGUAY LOST A SHIPMENT OF MONEY WHEN IT WAS SENT FROM THE OVERSEAS COMPANY THAT MINTED IT. IN FRANCE I THINK.

THEY SAID IT WAS ATTACKED BY PIRATES, BUT I SUSPECT AN INSIDE JOB. SOMEBODY ATE THE MONEY. ANYWAY. THE WHOLE SERIES WAS DECLARED INVALID, COUNTERFEIT.

SO HE PAID FOR THE DOGS WITH THOSE WORTHLESS *MAU** GS. 50,000 BILLS.

AND GOT GS. 10,000 BACK IN CHANGE FROM EVERY HOUSE. MONEY THAT ACTUALLY HAD VALUE.

A TIDY CON.

WHAT DID HE DO WITH THE DOGS?

IT'S SAID THAT THEY ALL CAME RUNNING DOWN THE SIDE OF THE HIGHWAY - HE GOT AS FAR AS SANTANÍ AND DUMPED THEM.

DON'T YOU THINK THAT'S WORSE? YOU KNOW YOU'RE DONE FOR, OFF TO BE SAUSAGE FOR SURE. NEXT THING YOU KNOW YOU'VE GOT A 40KM HIKE HOME!

*COUNTERFEIT, FAKE, ILLEGAL

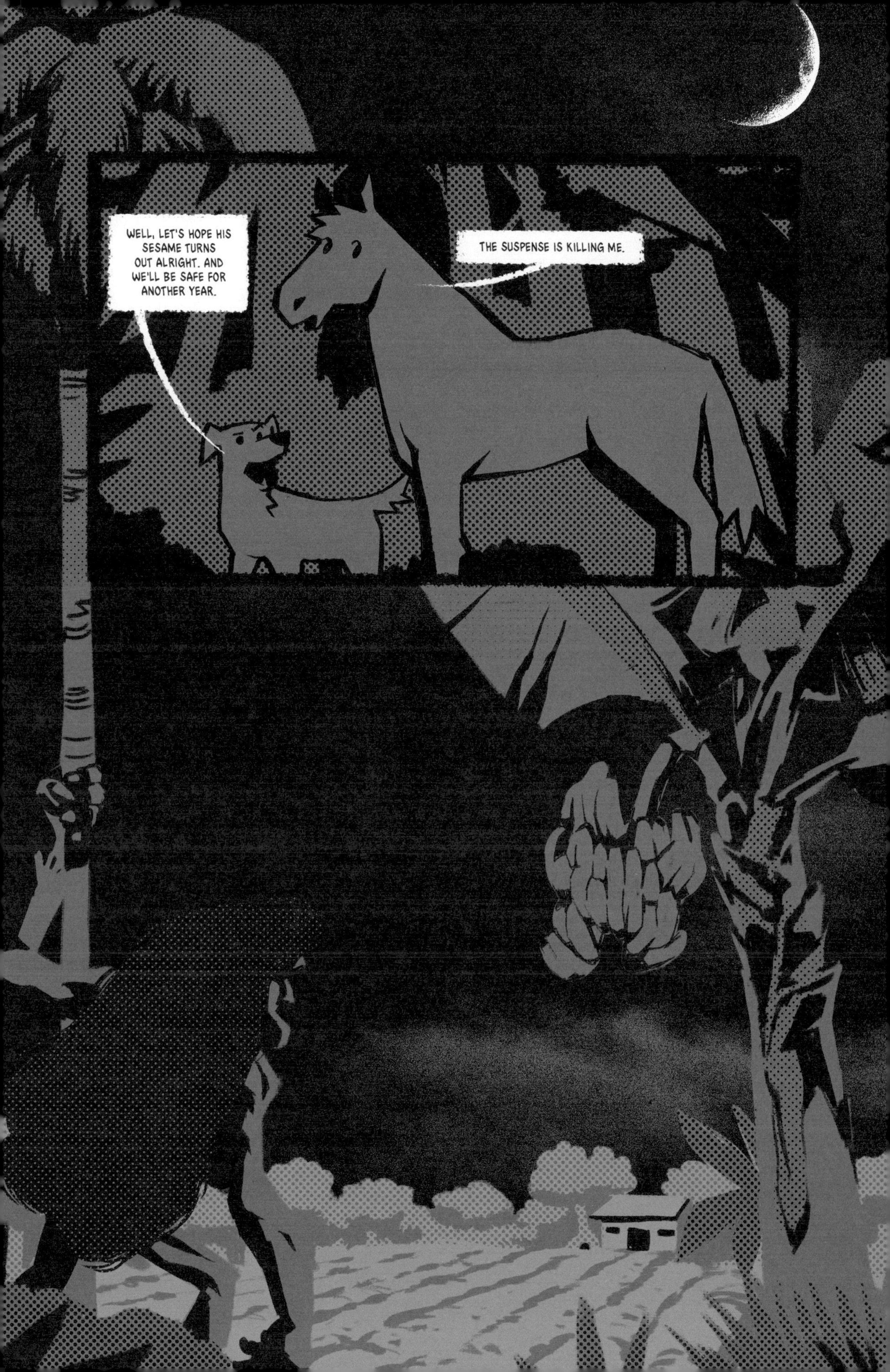
WELL, LET'S HOPE HIS SESAME TURNS OUT ALRIGHT. AND WE'LL BE SAFE FOR ANOTHER YEAR.
THE SUSPENSE IS KILLING ME.

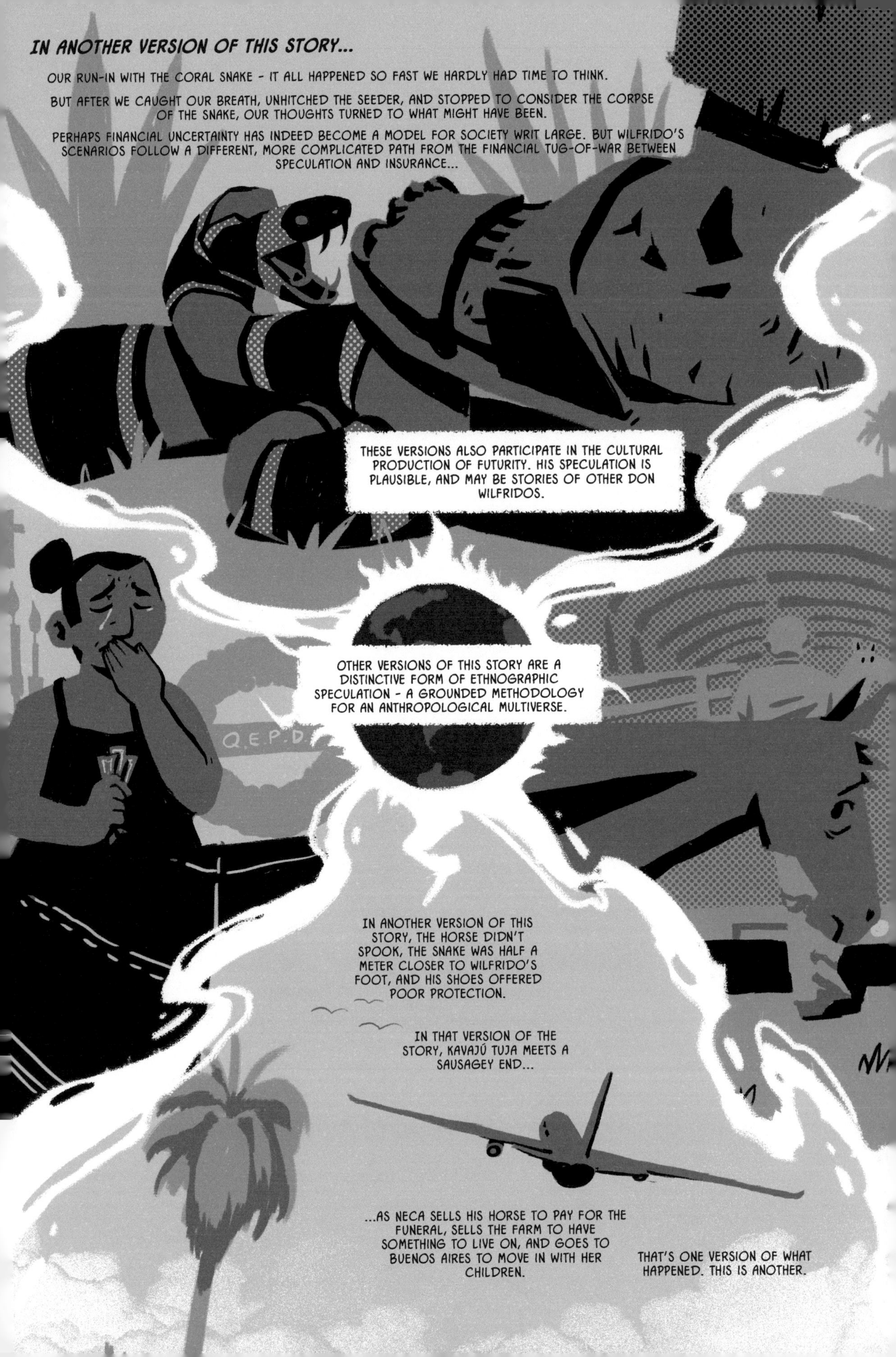

IN ANOTHER VERSION OF THIS STORY...
OUR RUN-IN WITH THE CORAL SNAKE - IT ALL HAPPENED SO FAST WE HARDLY HAD TIME TO THINK.
BUT AFTER WE CAUGHT OUR BREATH, UNHITCHED THE SEEDER, AND STOPPED TO CONSIDER THE CORPSE OF THE SNAKE, OUR THOUGHTS TURNED TO WHAT MIGHT HAVE BEEN.
PERHAPS FINANCIAL UNCERTAINTY HAS INDEED BECOME A MODEL FOR SOCIETY WRIT LARGE. BUT WILFRIDO'S SCENARIOS FOLLOW A DIFFERENT, MORE COMPLICATED PATH FROM THE FINANCIAL TUG-OF-WAR BETWEEN SPECULATION AND INSURANCE...
THESE VERSIONS ALSO PARTICIPATE IN THE CULTURAL PRODUCTION OF FUTURITY. HIS SPECULATION IS PLAUSIBLE, AND MAY BE STORIES OF OTHER DON WILFRIDOS.
OTHER VERSIONS OF THIS STORY ARE A DISTINCTIVE FORM OF ETHNOGRAPHIC SPECULATION - A GROUNDED METHODOLOGY FOR AN ANTHROPOLOGICAL MULTIVERSE.
Q.E.P.D.
IN ANOTHER VERSION OF THIS STORY, THE HORSE DIDN'T SPOOK, THE SNAKE WAS HALF A METER CLOSER TO WILFRIDO'S FOOT, AND HIS SHOES OFFERED POOR PROTECTION.
IN THAT VERSION OF THE STORY, KAVAJÚ TUJA MEETS A SAUSAGEY END...
...AS NECA SELLS HIS HORSE TO PAY FOR THE FUNERAL, SELLS THE FARM TO HAVE SOMETHING TO LIVE ON, AND GOES TO BUENOS AIRES TO MOVE IN WITH HER CHILDREN.
THAT'S ONE VERSION OF WHAT HAPPENED. THIS IS ANOTHER.

STORMS CAME AND WENT.
AND WE WAITED FOR THE
SESAME TO GERMINATE.

I NEED TO SHOW YOU SOMETHING.

OK, DON WILFRIDO, WE'LL COME RIGHT OUT TO THE FARM.

SINCE WE'VE SPENT THE LAST FEW WEEKS WORKING WITH FREDDY AND PLANTING SESAME ON OTHER FARMS, WE HAVEN'T SEEN DON WILFRIDO. I HOPE HE'S NOT CROSS WITH US.

HE SOUNDED EXCITED ON THE PHONE. LET'S PICK UP SOME *CERVEZA** TO SHARE IN CASE IT'S SOME GOOD NEWS.

THE RAIN IS EXPECTED TO CONTINUE AS PARAGUAY EXPERIENCES THE EFFECTS OF EL NIÑO...

EL NIÑO, EL NIÑO, LIKE A CAPRICIOUS CHILD. THIS WEATHER FEELS LIKE NATURE'S TEMPER TANTRUM.

I THINK IT'S NAMED AFTER THE BABY JESUS, SINCE THE WEATHER PATTERN USUALLY TAKES SHAPE AROUND CHRISTMAS.

OH.

WELL, IT'S STILL CAPRICIOUS.

*BEER

ROCÍO! CAROLINA! COME QUICKLY.

HERE, THIS IS WHAT I WANTED TO SHOW YOU.

YOUR SESAME! *IT'S SPROUTED!*

I WAS AFRAID THAT YESTERDAY'S RAIN WOULD WASH AWAY THE SEEDS. SEE, COME LOOK. HERE, THESE TINY SEEDS ARE TOO WEAK TO PUSH UP THROUGH THE SOIL. IF THEY GET BURIED TOO DEEP.

I'VE BEEN EXPERIMENTING. IF I SCRAPE THE SOIL LIKE THIS...

IT FREES UP THE SEEDLINGS.

THERE.

NOW THEY CAN GROW.

I'M SURE THAT'S NOT SOMETHING THAT FREDDY, THE UPTIGHT AGRONOMIST FROM THE COOPERATIVE, TAUGHT YOU.

NO NO.

THEY HAVE A CHEMICAL FOR EVERYTHING, BUT WHO CAN AFFORD THAT?

I ALWAYS SAY, WE *CAMPESINOS* ARE AGRONOMIST ENGINEERS IN OUR OWN FIELDS.

WE SHOULD PROBABLY GET GOING. IT LOOKS LIKE IT MIGHT RAIN AGAIN.

IT'S TOO BAD YOU BOUGHT DROUGHT INSURANCE, DON WILFRIDO! BAD LUCK THIS YEAR, WITH ALL THE RAIN.

HAIKUEPÉTE!* DROUGHT. BAH! THOSE ENGINEERS DON'T KNOW ANYTHING.

BEEP BEEP

HERE, CAN YOU READ THIS FOR ME?

SURE. IT'S AN SMS FROM YOUR INSURTECH COMPANY. THE INDEX THIS WEEK IS AT 3.2/16.8. SO IT HAS TO BE MUCH HIGHER TO GET A PAYOUT! NO DANGER OF IT TRIGGERING NOW.

LET'S HOPE THE WEATHER COLLABORATES.

BUT IT LOOKS LIKE A STORM IS BREWING.

EH.

WELL, I'M GOING TO CLEAR MY LAST PARCEL OF LAND TO PLANT. THE SEEDER IS STILL HERE — NOBODY ELSE IS PLANTING. WAITING FOR CLEAR SKIES...

I SAY YOU HAVE TO TAKE A CHANCE, UN MOMENTO OPORTUNO.

*GUARANÍ EXCLAMATION OF SURPRISE OR DISBELIEF

THAT NIGHT...

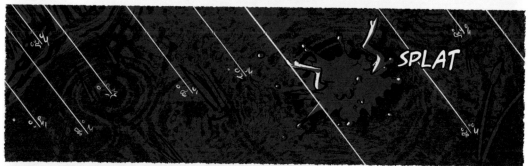

SPLAT

FWOOOO

NEEEIGH!

KRAKOOM

AWOO!

AFTER THE STORM CLEARED, WILFRIDO STARTED WORKING ON FIXING HIS ROOF.

DRIP

DRIP

I HAD A DREAM ON THE NIGHT OF THE STORM. LAST NIGHT. THAT I LOST IT ALL.

SLURP

I LOST ALL THE SESAME. I WENT UP TO THE *CHACRA* AND IT WAS EMPTY. THERE WAS NOTHING LEFT AFTER ALL THAT RAIN.

IT WAS JUST GONE...

WASHED AWAY.

AND IN THE DREAM, I THINK IT'S OVER NOW. *SE SUICIDA*, DARK DREAMS OF SUICIDE.

IT'S THE END.

AND THEN IN THE DREAM, YOU SAY...

NO, NO!

WILFRIDO, YOU ARE MISTAKEN.

LOOK, YOUR CROPS ARE FINE. NO HAY *PÉRDIDAS.*

AND THEN I WAKE UP...

AND I HEAR THE STORM OUTSIDE.

THAT WAS MY DREAM LAST NIGHT.

I WENT TO THE PARCEL OF SESAME THIS MORNING. AND THE SEEDLINGS WERE THERE.

THEY WERE ALL THERE. THEY SURVIVED THE STORM.

IT'S A MIRACLE.

WHAT ARE WE?

WE ARE 'MEDIUM,' NOT RICH OR POOR. SOME PEOPLE DON'T EVEN HAVE A HORSE. THEY DON'T HAVE ANYTHING. EH. WE ARE IN THE MIDDLE.

BUT IF THAT STORM HAD DROWNED MY CROP...

IN ANOTHER VERSION OF THIS STORY...

THERE IS A COMMON SAYING IN GUARANÍ, *TOIKO LA OIKÓTA, QUE PASE LO QUE TENGA QUE PASAR.* WHAT MUST HAPPEN WILL HAPPEN.

SOMETIMES WHAT HAPPENS IS A MIRACLE.

IN ONE VERSION OF THIS STORY, THE SESAME WAS GONE. ACTUALLY, IT WAS THE MOST COMMON VERSION OF THE STORY.

ALL OF THE SESAME FARMERS IN THE NEARBY VILLAGES OF ESCALERA AND REDONDO WENT BACK WITH THEIR TRACTORS AND DISKED THE SOIL AGAIN, TURNING THE WASTED, UNGERMINATED SEEDS BACK INTO THE MUD. AND THEN THEY WAITED FOR BETTER WEATHER.

THERE'S NO MUNICIPAL TRACTOR, NO HELP FROM THE MULTIACTIVA, NO POLITICAL FAVORS FROM THE DIRECTORATE OF AGRICULTURAL EXTENSION TO HELP WILFRIDO PLOUGH HIS FIELDS AGAIN.

BUT IN THIS VERSION OF THE STORY, THE FRAGILE SESAME SEEDS SENT DELICATE SHOOTS UP THROUGH THE MUDDY SOIL.

AND WILFRIDO'S DREAM WAS JUST THAT.

WATER SCARCITY AND LOW CROP YIELDS. EXTREME RAINFALL AND FLOODING. THE MANY VERSIONS OF DON WILFRIDO RESPOND AS BEST THEY CAN TO WEATHER CONDITIONS ON THE FARM.

AT A GLOBAL SCALE, OCEANIC AND ATMOSPHERIC VARIATIONS ARE KNOWN AS THE EL NIÑO SOUTHERN OSCILLATION (ENSO) AND CAN IMPACT WEATHER PATTERNS WORLDWIDE. WARM CONDITIONS IN THE TROPICAL PACIFIC CAN SLOW DOWN OR EVEN REVERSE THE TRADE WINDS THAT USUALLY BLOW TOWARDS INDONESIA AND AUSTRALIA. LA NIÑA HAPPENS WHEN THE PACIFIC HAS COLD OCEANIC AND ATMOSPHERIC CONDITIONS.

EL NIÑO AND LA NIÑA EVENTS HAPPEN ROUGHLY EVERY TWO TO SEVEN YEARS, THOUGH THIS IS CHANGING WITH GLOBAL WARMING.

DISASTER SCIENCE HAS AMBITIONS TO TAME EL NIÑO. ENSO PREDICTIONS HAVE IMPROVED, WITH LEAD TIMES UP TO 14 MONTHS. EXPERTS HOPE THAT RELIABLE FORECASTS CAN ALLOW FOR EARLY WARNING AND ACTION BY LOCAL GOVERNMENTS AND HUMANITARIAN AID ORGANIZATIONS. THIS IS PART OF A BROADER SHIFT TO PREVENTATIVE RISK MANAGEMENT.*

EL NIÑO SCENARIOS OFTEN MEAN A SECOND OR THIRD PLANTING FOR *SESAMEROS*.** SOME VERSIONS OF THIS STORY END IN TOTAL CROP FAILURE. OTHERS, METEOROLOGICAL MIRACLES.

MEANWHILE, FINANCIAL INTERMEDIARIES BENEFIT FROM BETTER EL NINO FORECASTS. MICROFINANCE COMPANIES CAN TAKE OUT PORTFOLIO-LEVEL INSURANCE AGAINST NATURAL DISASTERS, ANTICIPATING THAT THEIR BORROWERS WILL EXPERIENCE FINANCIAL STRESS AND MAY EVEN DEFAULT ON THEIR LOANS.***

AND INSURANCE COMPANIES THEMSELVES HOLD MASSIVE INVESTMENT PORTFOLIOS. THESE ASSETS ARE ALSO VULNERABLE TO EL NINO WEATHER RISKS - BETTER FORECASTS CAN PROTECT THEIR CAPITAL.

WILFRIDO HAD A NIGHTMARE. HIS BANKERS HAD A RISK ASSESSMENT PROCESS.

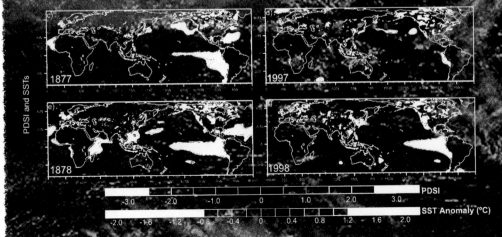

PDSI and SSTs

1877

1997

1878

1998

PDSI

-3.0 -2.0 -1.0 0 1.0 2.0 3.0

SST Anomaly (°C)

-2.0 -1.6 -1.2 -0.8 -0.4 0 0.4 0.8 1.2 1.6 2.0

*(NOBRE ET AL. 2019)   **SESAME FARMERS   ***(COLLIER AND SKEES 2012)

WHILE WE WAITED FOR WILFRIDO'S SESAME TO GROW, WE SPENT TIME AT MULTIACTIVA. FREDDY AND THE AGRICULTURAL TECHNICIANS HAD PLANTED 0.6 HECTARES OF SESAME AT THE CENTRO DE INVESTIGACIÓN REGIONAL (CIR)* TO TEST HERBICIDES, PESTICIDES, AND FERTILIZERS.

WE ALSO LEARNED THAT THE CIR HAD PURCHASED AN IBAI WEATHER INSURANCE POLICY FROM INSURTECH.

YOU ARE LUCKY THAT THE EXPERIMENTAL STATION DIDN'T LOSE THE FIRST PLANTING.

I'VE HEARD THERE HAVE BEEN PLENTY OF PROBLEMS IN THE REGION.

FROM THE RAIN?

IT JUST HASN'T LET UP.

I WONDER HOW MUCH FELL IN THAT HUGE STORM LAST WEEK.

FREDDY, YOU'VE GOT A WEATHER STATION FROM INSURTECH ON YOUR OWN FARM IN PEGUAJÓ!

HMM... WELL, THEY ARE SUPPOSED TO COME DO MAINTENANCE ON THEM.

THE WEBSITE IS DOWN, SO WE CAN'T ACCESS REAL-TIME UPDATES.

I'LL REQUEST THE DATA WHEN THEY COME OUT FOR REPAIRS.

*REGIONAL EXPERIMENTAL STATION

61

HI! MARIO, HOW ARE YOU?

GOOD GOOD. LOOK, I WAS WONDERING WHEN YOU WERE SENDING YOUR MAINTENANCE TEAM OUT TO FIX THE WEATHER STATIONS IN OUR AREA.

NEXT WEEK? I'M LOOKING AT ACCUWEATHER NOW...

WELL IT LOOKS LIKE IT MIGHT RAIN AGAIN.

OK, WE'LL KEEP IN TOUCH.

TAP

THE CROP INSURANCE SPECIALISTS AT INSURTECH REALLY PERSUADED ME. THE COOPERATIVE FACES HUGE RISKS IN THE YEARS WITH *PÉRDIDAS*, WHEN ALL OUR MEMBERS LOSE THEIR CROPS.

SLURP

PECK PECK

THIS YEAR WE ARE EXPERIMENTING WITH FERTILIZER – WE'LL SET UP THE GRID LINES TOMORROW AND APPLY THE CHEMICALS ONCE THE SEEDS SPOUT.

THESE WEED KILLERS WE WERE JUST SPRAYING, THEY AREN'T THE SAME CHEMICALS THAT THE BIG SOY GROWERS USE, RIGHT?

HMMMM.

THIS IS ALL ORGANIC SESAME. WE CAN USE GLYPHOSATE NOW BECAUSE THE PLANTS HAVEN'T GERMINATED YET.

BUT THEN THERE ARE ORGANIC PRODUCTS THAT WE CAN APPLY LATER. THEY HELP CONTROL PESTS AND BOOST YIELDS.

WE USED TO CALL OUR PRODUCTS AGROCHEMICALS. NOW, THE PREFERRED TERM IS *DEFENSORES AGRÍCOLAS*, AGRICULTURAL DEFENCES.

BUT ALL THE PRODUCTS IN THE WORLD WON'T HELP IF THE WEATHER DOESN'T COOPERATE.

THE FOLLOWING WEEK, I WAS AT THE MULTIACTIVA WITH FREDDY AGAIN, ENDURING ANOTHER STORM.

INSURTECH CANCELLED AGAIN?

HEẼ.*
AGAIN.

THEY HAVE SUSPICIOUSLY BAD TIMING FOR A COMPANY THAT'S ALL ABOUT RISK MANAGEMENT.

HOW DO THEY ALWAYS PICK THE ONE DAY OF THE WEEK IT'S CERTAIN IT'S GOING TO RAIN?

MAYBE BECAUSE THEY NEED TO FIX THEIR MALFUNCTIONING WEATHER STATIONS.

OR MAYBE THEY JUST WANT TO STAY WARM AND DRY IN THEIR CUSHY OFFICE IN ASUNCIÓN!

*YES

OH, AND THAT SPRAYING WE DID LAST WEEK? USELESS! IT RAINED THE NEXT NIGHT. I'M SURE IT WASHED AWAY ALL OF THE HERBICIDE.

OH WELL. THE COOPERATIVE HAS GIVEN US A GENEROUS BUDGET FOR THE EXPERIMENTAL PARCEL. WE CAN BUY OTHER PRODUCTS.

NO REAL LOSS.

THE NEXT WEEK, INSURTECH SENT MARIO AND AN IT SPECIALIST TO CHECK ALL 25 WEATHER STATIONS IN SAN PEDRO.

OK, WATCH OUT!

BZZZ

BZZZ

WHIFF

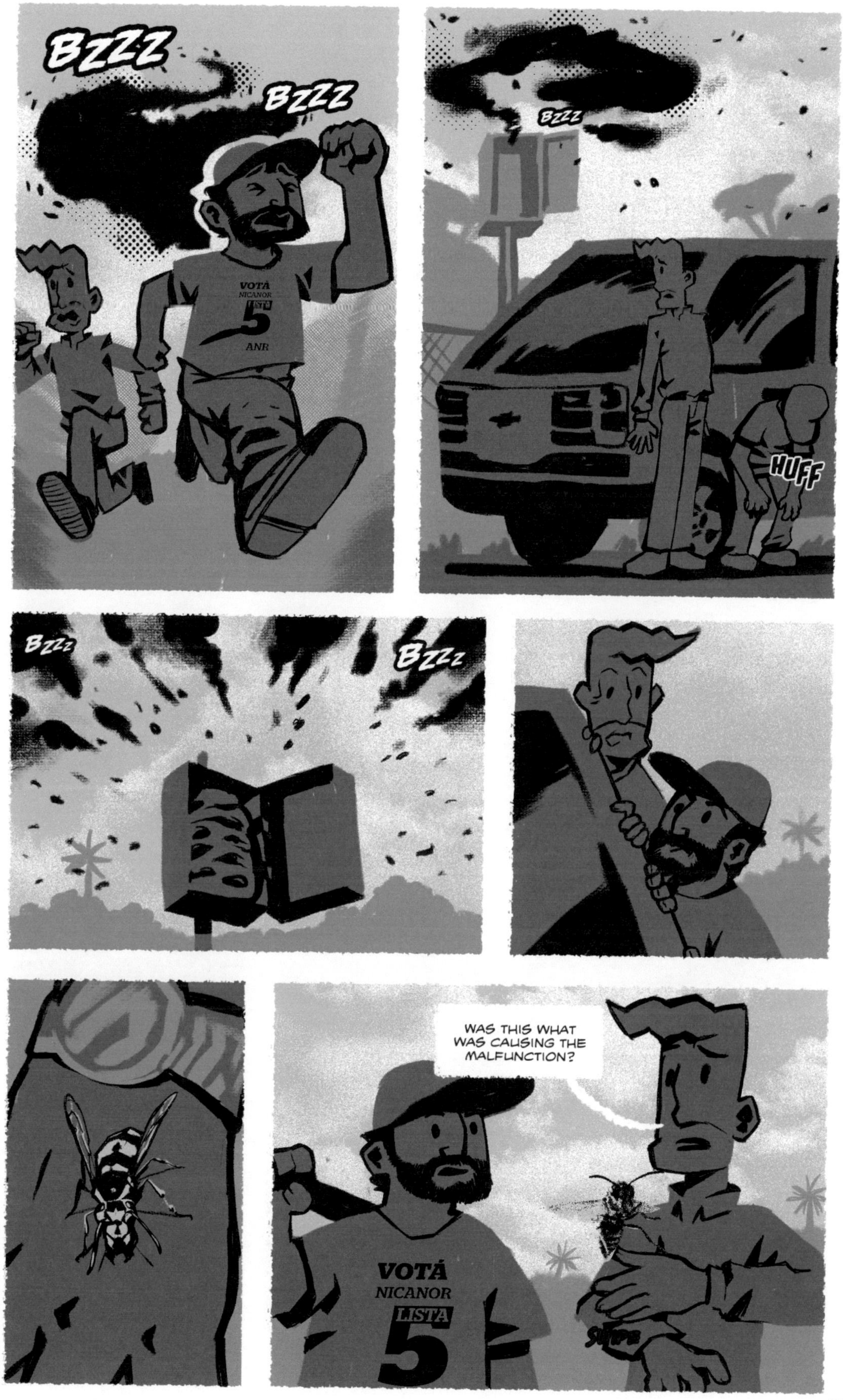
BZZZ
BZZZ
VOTÁ NICANOR LISTA 5 ANR
BZZZ
HUFF
BZZZ
BZZZ
WAS THIS WHAT WAS CAUSING THE MALFUNCTION?
VOTÁ NICANOR LISTA 5

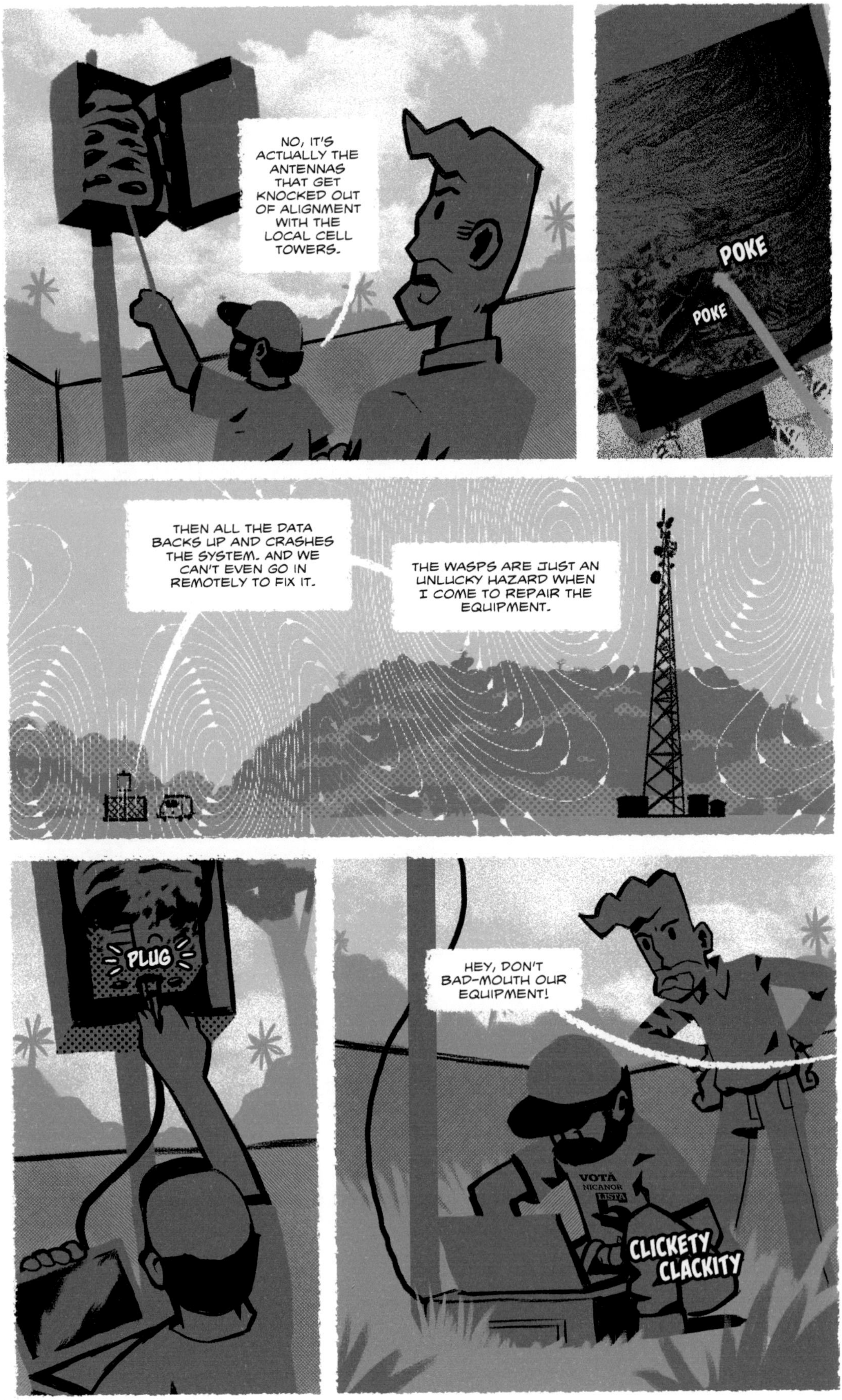
NO, IT'S ACTUALLY THE ANTENNAS THAT GET KNOCKED OUT OF ALIGNMENT WITH THE LOCAL CELL TOWERS.
POKE
POKE
THEN ALL THE DATA BACKS UP AND CRASHES THE SYSTEM. AND WE CAN'T EVEN GO IN REMOTELY TO FIX IT.
THE WASPS ARE JUST AN UNLUCKY HAZARD WHEN I COME TO REPAIR THE EQUIPMENT.
PLUG
HEY, DON'T BAD-MOUTH OUR EQUIPMENT!
VOTÁ NICANOR LISTA
CLICKETY CLACKITY

OUR STATIONS ARE THE BEST MODELS THERE ARE — DESIGNED BY A COMPANY IN AUSTRIA. FUNDING FROM AUSTRALIAN AID AND THE INTER-AMERICAN DEVELOPMENT BANK.

IT'S THE LOCAL TELECOM. THAT'S THE PROBLEM. A *PORQUERÍA.** FINTECH ONLY WORKS IF THEIR TECH WORKS!

SEE? WE ARE GETTING THE FIRMWARE UPDATES FROM AUSTRIA RIGHT NOW! NOW THAT WE'VE FIXED THE SIGNAL....

WASPS AND LOCAL TELECOMS ARE VERY SPECIFIC RISKS. INSURANCE DEALS WITH LARGER, SYSTEMIC RISKS...

DON'T WORRY, ALL THE DATA IS BACKED UP. I'M DOWNLOADING IT NOW.

*WHAT CRAP

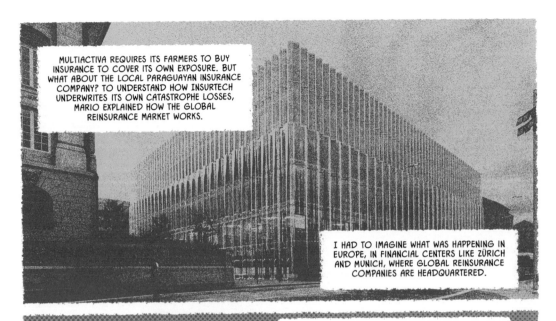

MULTIACTIVA REQUIRES ITS FARMERS TO BUY INSURANCE TO COVER ITS OWN EXPOSURE. BUT WHAT ABOUT THE LOCAL PARAGUAYAN INSURANCE COMPANY? TO UNDERSTAND HOW INSURTECH UNDERWRITES ITS OWN CATASTROPHE LOSSES, MARIO EXPLAINED HOW THE GLOBAL REINSURANCE MARKET WORKS.

I HAD TO IMAGINE WHAT WAS HAPPENING IN EUROPE, IN FINANCIAL CENTERS LIKE ZÜRICH AND MUNICH, WHERE GLOBAL REINSURANCE COMPANIES ARE HEADQUARTERED.

THIS IS WHAT MARIO EXPLAINED TO ME.

THEIR AGROCLIMATOLOGIST IS PRETTY GOOD. CALIBRATING THE SATELLITE DATA USING LOCAL WEATHER STATIONS HAS MADE A VERY ACCURATE DROUGHT MODEL.

SEE, HERE'S THE HISTORICAL DATA. THIS HELPS US ESTABLISH THE LIKELIHOOD OF CERTAIN WEATHER CONDITIONS.

WELL, AS ACCURATE AS WE MIGHT HOPE FOR, GIVEN THE CLIMATE UNCERTAINTIES AND EXTREME WEATHER EVENTS.

FOR INSTANCE, IT'S PROBABLE THAT A DROUGHT WILL REACH THIS LEVEL ONCE A DECADE, OR EVERY 20 YEARS, OR EVERY 100 YEARS.

THAT'S NOT TO SAY IT HAPPENS ON SCHEDULE, LIKE CLOCKWORK.

WE DEAL IN PROBABILITIES, STATISTICAL DISTRIBUTIONS, RISK.

AND PRICE IT ACCORDINGLY. THE PREMIUM FOR THIS INSURANCE SHOULD CORRESPOND TO THE LIKELIHOOD OF THE EVENT.

AND THE LOCAL INSURANCE COMPANY ACCESSES LARGER POOLS OF CAPITAL THROUGH GLOBAL FINANCIAL MARKETS.

AND WE DEAL WITH THE LATEST CLIMATE SCIENCE AND SCENARIO PLANNING.

RISK TRANSFER.

WE REINSURE CATASTROPHES THAT ARE LIKELY TO HAPPEN ONCE IN TEN YEARS.

THAT WAY THEY DON'T HAVE TO MAINTAIN RIDICULOUSLY HIGH RESERVES TO PAY OUT CLAIMS.

THE INSURANCE COMPANY BUYS INSURANCE.

SO WE CAN REINSURE INSURTECH AT A LOWER RATE THAN LAST YEAR? SINCE THEIR WEATHER INDEX IS PRETTY GOOD AND WE CAN PRICE THE RISK ACCURATELY?

SO YOU ARE WILLING TO REINSURE OUR IBAI SESAME POLICY? SO THAT IN THE EVENT OF CATASTROPHIC CLAIMS, OUR LOSSES WILL BE COVERED?

YES SIR. WE ARE VERY INTERESTED IN CLIMATE INSURANCE. IT'S A GROWING MARKET.

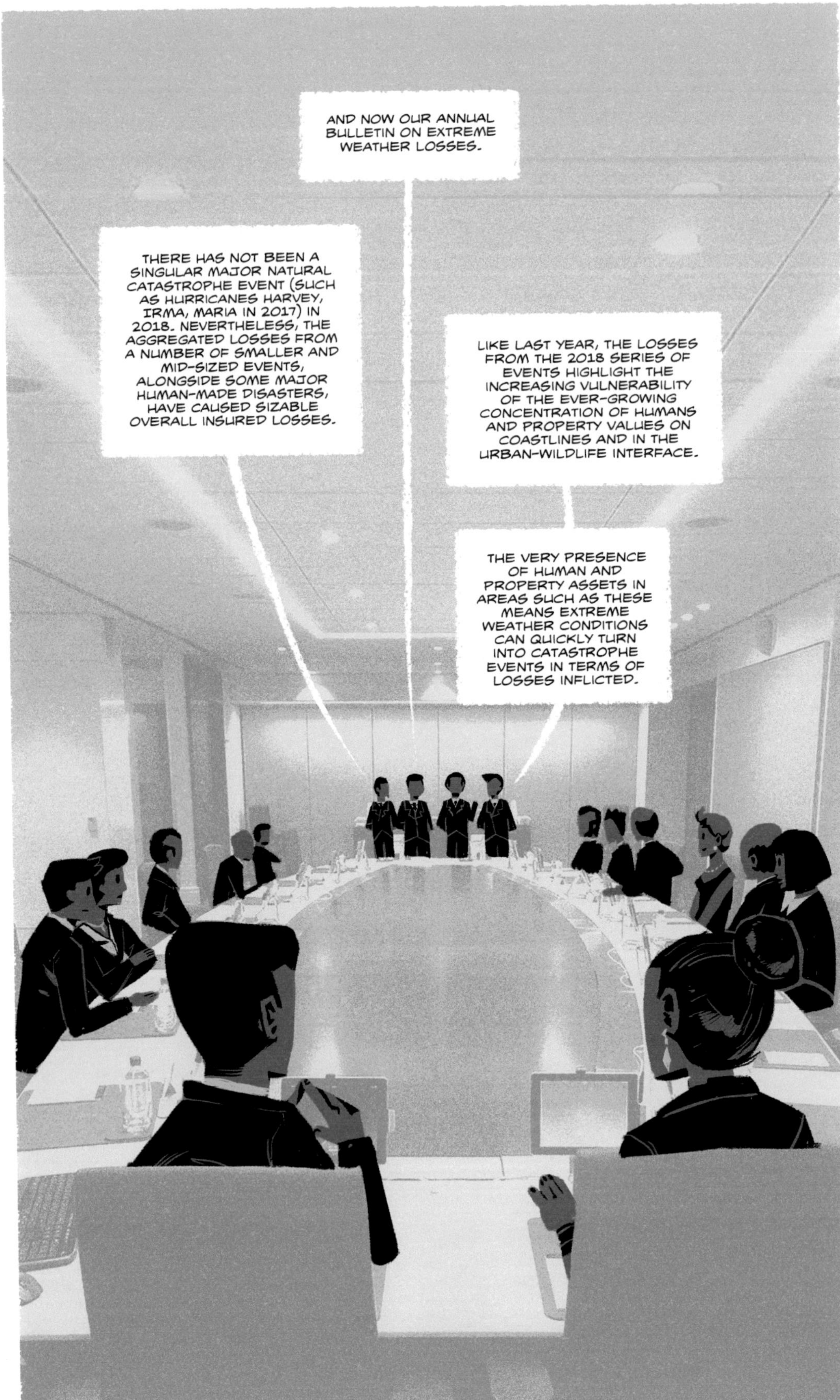
AND NOW OUR ANNUAL BULLETIN ON EXTREME WEATHER LOSSES.
THERE HAS NOT BEEN A SINGULAR MAJOR NATURAL CATASTROPHE EVENT (SUCH AS HURRICANES HARVEY, IRMA, MARIA IN 2017) IN 2018. NEVERTHELESS, THE AGGREGATED LOSSES FROM A NUMBER OF SMALLER AND MID-SIZED EVENTS, ALONGSIDE SOME MAJOR HUMAN-MADE DISASTERS, HAVE CAUSED SIZABLE OVERALL INSURED LOSSES.
LIKE LAST YEAR, THE LOSSES FROM THE 2018 SERIES OF EVENTS HIGHLIGHT THE INCREASING VULNERABILITY OF THE EVER-GROWING CONCENTRATION OF HUMANS AND PROPERTY VALUES ON COASTLINES AND IN THE URBAN-WILDLIFE INTERFACE.
THE VERY PRESENCE OF HUMAN AND PROPERTY ASSETS IN AREAS SUCH AS THESE MEANS EXTREME WEATHER CONDITIONS CAN QUICKLY TURN INTO CATASTROPHE EVENTS IN TERMS OF LOSSES INFLICTED.

EXAMPLES OF THIS YEAR'S DEVASTATING NATURAL CATASTROPHE EVENTS INCLUDE HURRICANES MICHAEL AND FLORENCE; TYPHOONS JEBI, TRAMI, AND MANGKHUT; HEAT WAVES, DROUGHTS, AND WILDFIRES IN EUROPE AND CALIFORNIA; WINTER AND THUNDERSTORMS AROUND THE WORLD; FLOODS IN JAPAN AND INDIA; EARTHQUAKES IN JAPAN, INDONESIA, AND PAPUA NEW GUINEA; AND VOLCANO ERUPTIONS IN HAWAII.

INSURANCE CONTRIBUTED USD 79 BILLION IN PAID CLAIMS TO LESSEN THE HARDSHIP FOR PEOPLE AND BUSINESSES AFFECTED BY THIS YEAR'S DISASTER EVENTS.

IN OTHER WORDS, MORE THAN 50% OF ALL ECONOMIC LOSSES WERE INSURED, DEMONSTRATING AGAIN THE SIGNIFICANT CONTRIBUTION OF THE INSURANCE SECTOR TO MITIGATING CATASTROPHE RISK.*

*AFTER DISCUSSING GLOBAL REINSURANCE WITH MARIO, I READ SEVERAL REPORTS ON DISASTER RISK MANAGEMENT PUBLISHED BY SIGMA, SWISS RE'S RESEARCH THINK TANK.

AFTER DOWNLOADING THE DATA, THE TEAM WAS PACKING UP...

ANÓ

ANÓ

I'VE BEEN IN TOUCH WITH OUR AGROCLIMATOLOGIST IN THE UNITED STATES. THE PROFESSOR. HE'S EAGER TO GET THE WEATHER DATA FROM THIS YEAR.

RUMBLE

RUMBLE

WITH *EL NIÑO*, THE CATASTROPHIC RAIN WILL HELP US MODEL EXTREME WEATHER. A BETTER IDEA OF THE WORST CASE SCENARIO.

HE'S REALLY EXCITED ABOUT THE DATA. THIS IS A GREAT OPPORTUNITY.

YOU KNOW WHAT? I'LL BE REALLY EXCITED IF WE CAN FINISH UP BEFORE THE STORM COMES AND STARTS DROPPING LIGHTNING BOLTS ON US.

KRRRAK

LET'S GET PACKED UP, I'M ALMOST DONE HERE.

AFTER FIXING THE WEATHER STATIONS, WE GATHERED AT A *CANTINA** FOR LUNCH NEAR THE MULTIACTIVA.

WHOOSH!

TUMBLE

SPLASH!

YOU KNOW, IT WOULD BE GOOD TO EXPAND THE PROGRAM – THE CURRENT POLICY ONLY COVERS DROUGHT. WIND IS A MAJOR FACTOR TOO.

YOU COULD LOSE THE WHOLE CROP, NOT JUST LOW YIELDS LIKE WITH DROUGHT. SESAME IS A TALL PLANT AND ESPECIALLY SUSCEPTIBLE.

WE ARE LEARNING FROM THE WHOLE PROCESS, *ENSAYANDO TAMBIÉN*. IT'S A CONSTANT PROCESS OF FEEDBACK. WE WOULD LIKE TO ADD MORE RISKS. AND WE HOPE THE WEATHER DATA WILL HELP WITH THAT.

IT TOOK THREE YEARS WORKING WITH THE AGROMETEOROLOGIST TO BUILD THE DROUGHT INDEX. YOU HAVE TO UNDERSTAND THE CLIMATE MODEL. AND ALSO THE PLANT SCIENCE – WHAT ARE THE CONDITIONS THAT AFFECT SESAME YIELDS?

EVEN WITH THE LIMITATIONS THE BOARD OF THE MULTIACTIVA IS CONSIDERING MAKING THE INSURANCE MANDATORY FOR SESAME GROWERS. A BAD HARVEST COULD TRIGGER A WAVE OF DEFAULTS, AND THREATEN THE FINANCES OF THE COOPERATIVE.

*OUTDOOR PATIO

WE HAD BETTER GET BACK ON THE ROAD – WE HAD TO LEAVE ASUNCIÓN AT 4AM AND I'LL GET HOME LONG AFTER MY KIDS HAVE GONE TO BED. MANAGING INSURANCE ISN'T JUST A DESK JOB. NOT WHEN OUR CLIENTS AND THE WEATHER STATIONS ARE ALL THE WAY OUT HERE.

THAT'S FOR SURE. THE SESAMEROS ARE INTERESTED IN THE COVERAGE BUT YOU EXPLAIN IT TO THEM 10 TIMES AND STILL NEED THE 11TH...

WHAT YOU SAID BACK THERE ABOUT THE FINANCIAL EXPOSURE OF THE COOPERATIVE – AT INSURTECH WE HAVE TO DEAL WITH THAT TOO. IT'S WHY WE BID FOR FUNDING TO BUILD ALL THESE WEATHER STATIONS. PART OF IT IS TO CALIBRATE THE INDEX AND LIMIT BASIS RISK.*

BUT IT'S ALSO FOR OUR BROKER TO NEGOTIATE WITH OUR EUROPEAN UNDERWRITER. ON THE GLOBAL REINSURANCE MARKET, LITTLE COMPANIES LIKE OURS TRANSFER RISK TO BIG COMPANIES LIKE MUNICH RE AND SWISS RE. REINSURANCE COMPANIES THAT COVER CATASTROPHE LOSSES.

IF WE HAD A TERRIBLE YEAR AND ALL THE DROUGHT POLICIES TRIGGERED AT ONCE, *JA'UMA HULE.* JUST LIKE MULTIACTIVA. SO WE BUY INSURANCE FOR INSURTECH TOO *¡JAJAJA!*

*BASIS RISK GENERALLY REFERS TO A HEDGE THAT DOES NOT PERFECTLY OFFSET AN UNDERLYING POSITION. IN INDEX INSURANCE, BASIS RISK APPEARS WHEN THE INDEX'S MEASUREMENT DOES NOT ACCURATELY REFLECT THE INSURED INDIVIDUAL'S ACTUAL LOSSES.

RUMBLE

CIR

CIR

IT WON'T BE SAFE TO DRIVE ALL THE WAY BACK TO ASUNCIÓN IN THIS STORM!

DEFINITELY NOT. I'LL CALL AHEAD TO TANNENHOF, THAT NICE HOTEL AT THE MENNONITE COLONY JUST UP THE ROAD. IT FEELS LIKE A GERMAN LODGE, EXCEPT THEY ALSO HAVE TOUCANS!

CAROLINA, WOULD YOU LIKE TO JOIN US FOR DINNER? THE SCHNITZEL IS VERY GOOD!

BOOM

KRAKOOM

SURE WHY NOT? WE CAN STOP BY THE "MOTHER" STATION FOR THE WEATHER NETWORK – IT'S ON THE MENNONITE COLONY TOO, RIGHT?

IT SURE IS, BUT WE AREN'T GETTING OUT IN THIS WEATHER. COME ON, LET'S GET TO SOMEWHERE CIVILIZED, OUT OF THIS MUD AND RAIN.

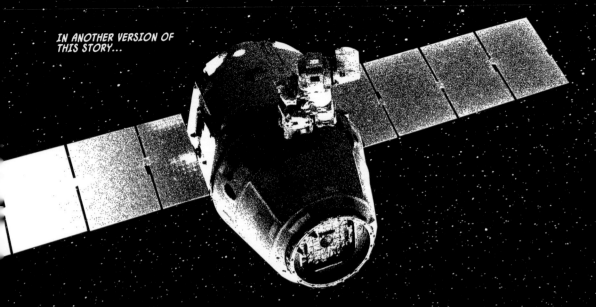

IN ANOTHER VERSION OF THIS STORY...

IN ONE VERSION OF THIS STORY, NO WEATHER STATIONS WERE BUILT IN SAN PEDRO. THE FUNDS FOR THE PROJECT WERE NOT APPROVED BY THE INTERNATIONAL DEVELOPMENT AGENCIES THAT INVEST IN TECHNOLOGY AND INNOVATION IN LATIN AMERICA.

WITHOUT OUTSIDE INVESTMENT, CROP INSURANCE FOR SMALL FARMERS IS SIMPLY TOO RISKY (AND HENCE TOO EXPENSIVE). CAPITAL INTENSIVE PROJECTS LIKE WEATHER STATIONS DON'T GET OFF THE GROUND.

THE INTER-AMERICAN DEVELOPMENT BANK, THE FOMIN INNOVATION AND ENTREPRENEURSHIP FUND, AND AUSTRALIAN AID TOGETHER INVESTED HUNDREDS OF THOUSANDS OF DOLLARS IN INSURTECH'S PILOT PROJECT.

THE WEATHER-INDEXED SESAME INSURANCE WAS NOT DESIGNED TO BE PROFITABLE, AT LEAST NOT IN THE SHORT TERM. IT WAS DESIGNED WITH A LONGER VIEW, WITH THE HOPE OF ENGINEERING MARKETS THAT CAN ABSORB THE FINANCIAL COSTS OF CLIMATE CHANGE.

*WEEDS AND PESTS
**THERE IS A PRODUCT FOR EVERYTHING

SESAME WAS ACTUALLY A BIT LIKE FINTECH, IN
ITS DAY. IT WAS A PROMISING DEVELOPMENT
PROJECT NEGOTIATED THROUGH A BILATERAL
AID PROGRAM BETWEEN PARAGUAY AND USAID,
THE UNITED STATES DEVELOPMENT AGENCY.

DEVELOPMENT EXPERTS SAW SESAME AND OTHER
NICHE CEREALS AS AN INNOVATIVE COMMERCIAL
CASH CROP THAT COULD BOOST FARM INCOME IN
POOR RURAL COMMUNITIES. PARAGUAYAN FARMERS
HAD BEEN SEVERELY IMPACTED IN THE 1990S WITH
THE GLOBAL COLLAPSE OF COTTON PRICES.

ALTHOUGH SESAME REQUIRES MINIMAL OR ZERO LEVELS OF AGROCHEMICALS, THE NEW CROP PROMISED A FRONTIER OF EXPANSION FOR A NEW GENERATION OF AGRICULTURAL ENTERPRISES. COMPANIES LIKE SHIROSAWA CO. EXPORTED TO JAPAN. A NEW FINANCING MODEL THAT ENHANCED THE ROLE OF INTERMEDIARIES, AS BOTH SUPPLIERS OF FARM INPUTS AS WELL AS BUYERS AND EXPORTERS, MEANT SHIROSAWA COULD DISTRIBUTE RISK ACROSS MANY SMALL FARMS.

AT ITS PEAK IN 2004-5 THE MINISTRY OF AGRICULTURE CENSUS RECORDED 37,540 HECTARES PLANTED WITH SESAME IN SAN PEDRO, UP FROM 6,800 IN 2000-1.

CAMPESINOS RELY ON AGRONOMISTS LIKE FREDDY AND DEVELOPMENT TECHNICIANS FROM USAID FOR KNOWLEDGE ABOUT THESE UNFAMILIAR CROPS. AND TECHNICIANS FROM USAID DEPENDED ON FREDDY AND MULTIACTIVA FOR ON-THE-GROUND KNOWLEDGE AND RELATIONSHIPS WITH LOCAL FARMERS. SO, THE NEW INSURTECH WEATHER INSURANCE WAS ONLY ONE SMALL PIECE OF THE PUZZLE. SESAME HAD BEEN A CRUCIBLE OF EXPERIMENTATION FOR AT LEAST 20 YEARS.

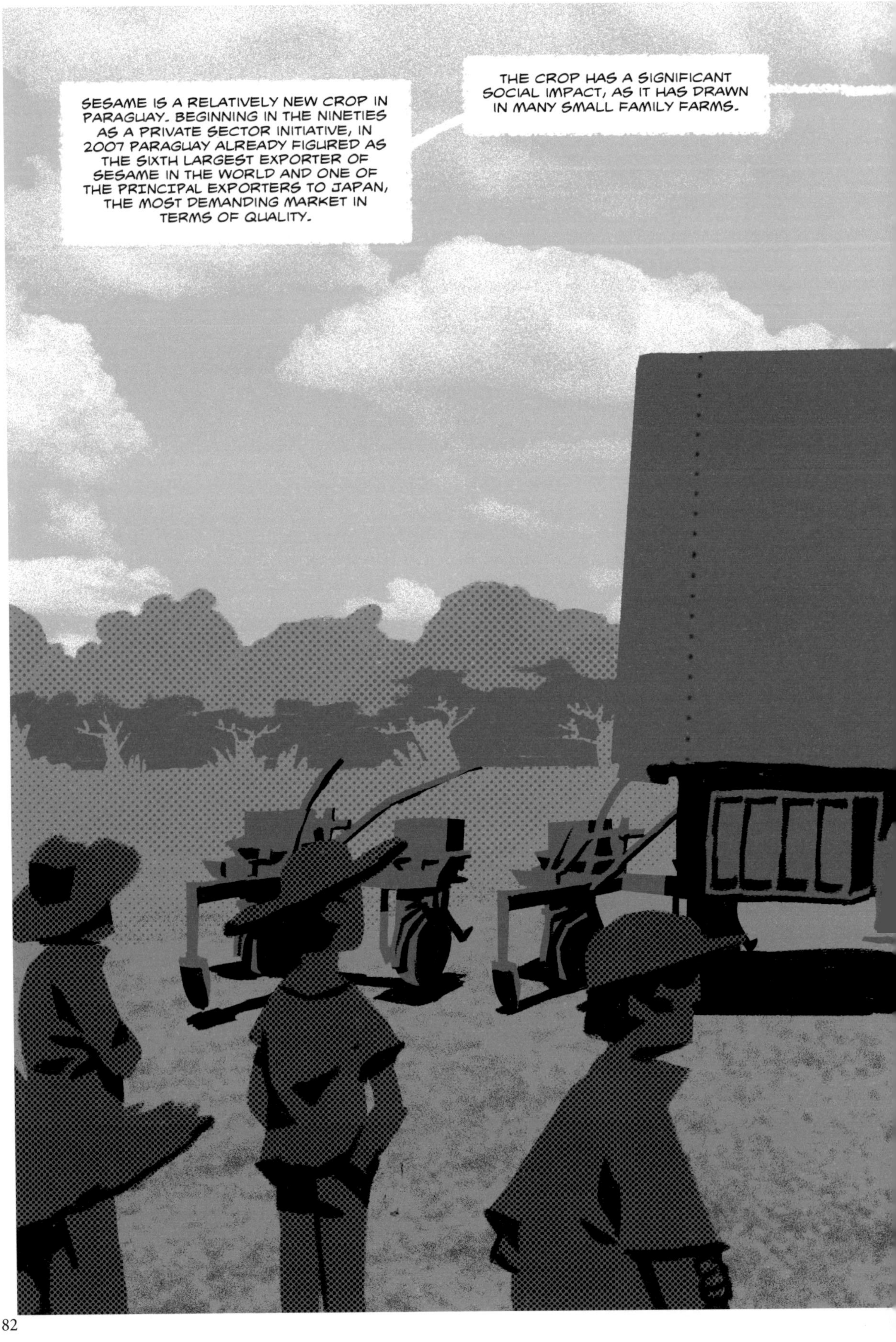
SESAME IS A RELATIVELY NEW CROP IN PARAGUAY. BEGINNING IN THE NINETIES AS A PRIVATE SECTOR INITIATIVE, IN 2007 PARAGUAY ALREADY FIGURED AS THE SIXTH LARGEST EXPORTER OF SESAME IN THE WORLD AND ONE OF THE PRINCIPAL EXPORTERS TO JAPAN, THE MOST DEMANDING MARKET IN TERMS OF QUALITY.
THE CROP HAS A SIGNIFICANT SOCIAL IMPACT, AS IT HAS DRAWN IN MANY SMALL FAMILY FARMS.

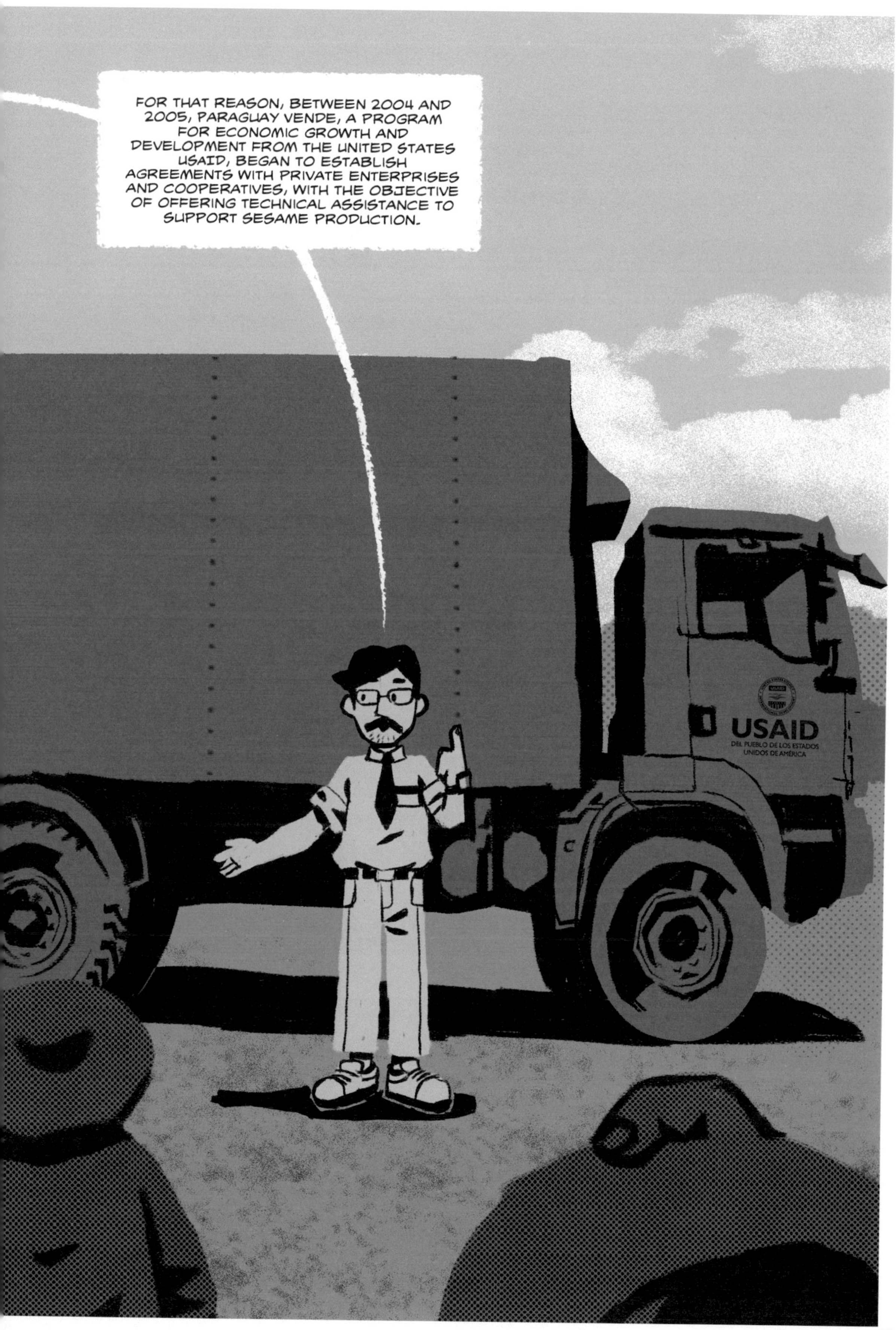
FOR THAT REASON, BETWEEN 2004 AND 2005, PARAGUAY VENDE, A PROGRAM FOR ECONOMIC GROWTH AND DEVELOPMENT FROM THE UNITED STATES USAID, BEGAN TO ESTABLISH AGREEMENTS WITH PRIVATE ENTERPRISES AND COOPERATIVES, WITH THE OBJECTIVE OF OFFERING TECHNICAL ASSISTANCE TO SUPPORT SESAME PRODUCTION.
USAID
DEL PUEBLO DE LOS ESTADOS UNIDOS DE AMÉRICA

SESAME SHOULD BE ECONOMICALLY, ENVIRONMENTALLY, AND SOCIALLY SUSTAINABLE. IN THIS SENSE, IT'S ABSOLUTELY CLEAR THAT NO CROP CAN BE COMPETITIVE, OR FUNCTION HARMONIOUSLY, IF SOME PARTS OF ITS VALUE CHAIN FAIL. THEREFORE, THE SUSTAINABILITY OF SESAME, LIKE ANY CROP, DEPENDS ON A HARMONIOUS SUPPLY CHAIN.

FOR THE CROP TO BE SUSTAINABLE AS A BUSINESS AND TO ACHIEVE RESULTS, IT HAS BEEN CRUCIAL TO WORK EFFICIENTLY AND WITHOUT DEPENDENCY ON THE GOVERNMENT ASISTENCIALISMO.*

TO KEEP GROWING IN BOTH VOLUME AND QUALITY, TECHNICAL ASSISTANCE REMAINS KEY, ESPECIALLY THE DIFFUSION OF BEST PRACTICES.

PARTICIPATION OF THE GOVERNMENT, IN HARMONY WITH EXPORTERS AND PRODUCERS, WILL YIELD THE SYNERGIES NEEDED TO FOSTER THE MEANS TO GUARANTEE THE SUCCESS OF THIS CROP IN OUR COUNTRY.

USAID AGRONOMISTS WILL BE IN YOUR AREA SOON...

REINALDO PENNER (ECONOMIST), DIRECTOR EJECUTIVO USAID / PARAGUAY VENDE. REPORT, *SESAMO INNOVACIÓN EN AGRONEGOCIOS* (2009)

*NEGATIVE EUPHEMISM FOR WELFARE DEPENDENCY AND CLIENTELISM

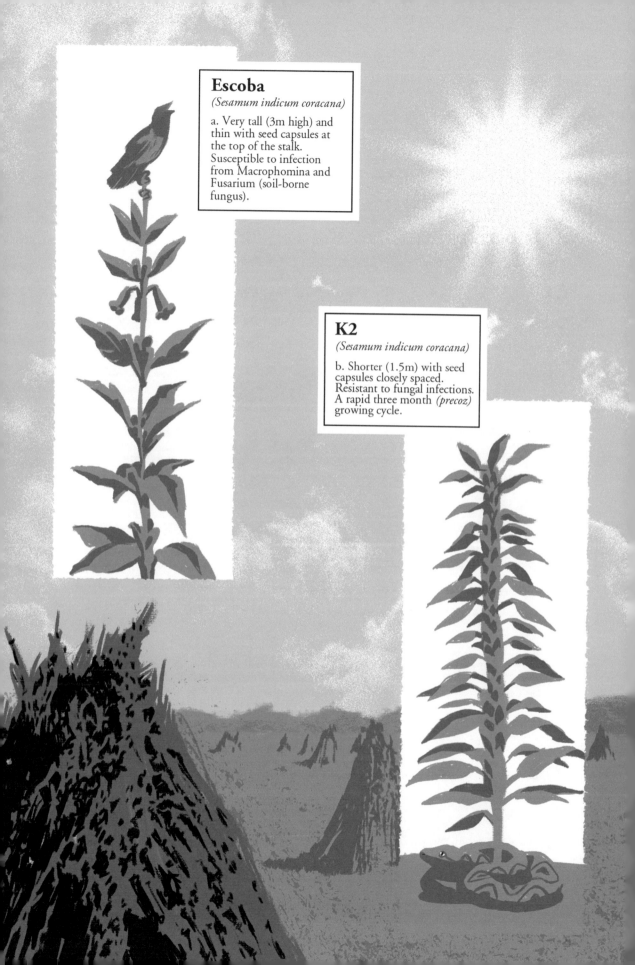

Escoba

(Sesamum indicum coracana)

a. Very tall (3m high) and thin with seed capsules at the top of the stalk. Susceptible to infection from Macrophomina and Fusarium (soil-borne fungus).

K2

(Sesamum indicum coracana)

b. Shorter (1.5m) with seed capsules closely spaced. Resistant to fungal infections. A rapid three month *(precoz)* growing cycle.

AN AGRONOMIST AT THE DIRECTORATE OF AGRICULTURAL EXTENSION CALLED MY BOOM YEARS "THE SESAME CRAZE."

YOU COULDN'T FIND AN EMPTY CORNER IN THE WHOLE COUNTRY THAT WASN'T PLANTED WITH SESAME. PEOPLE WERE NUTS, *LOCOS!*

BUT THEN YOU HAD TO GO GET A FUNGAL INFECTION. DO YOU KNOW HOW MANY FARMERS TOOK ON DEBT TO PLANT EVERY SPARE HECTARE WITH ESCOBA? AND THEN IT ALL WENT TO SHIT.

FROM ONE YEAR TO THE NEXT, SESAME DISAPPOINTED AND DISAPPEARED.

THE FUNGAL INFECTION STARTS AT THE ROOT AND MOVES UP THE STEM, TURNING THE SESAME STALKS BLACK AND WITHERING THE WHOLE PLANT.

AND LOOK HOW THAT ENDED...

HEY! I WAS SUPPOSED TO BE THE ENGINE OF DEVELOPMENT. A PURELY CASH CROP. MODERNIZATION OF THE COUNTRYSIDE.

I WAS THE FUTURE.

THEY SAY YOU ARE THE NEXT BOONDOGGLE. ORGANIC SESAME.

MORE RESILIENT TO PESTS AND ADVERSE WEATHER. A MORE PRODUCTIVE HYBRID WITH BETTER YIELDS.

BUT PEOPLE REMEMBER. THEY ARE STILL CRUSHED UNDER THE DEBTS FROM CROP FAILURES DURING THE FIRST BOOM. DO YOU THINK THEY'LL BE SO KEEN THE SECOND GO-ROUND?

WELL, **USAID** IS INVESTING AGAIN. IT'S A DEVELOPMENT PROJECT, SOME PEOPLE WILL GET HOOKED.

*FEVER OF WHITE GOLD
**INTERMEDIARIES

THE HEAT OF PARAGUAYAN SUMMER WAS INTENSE. AFTER MONTHS OF RAIN, THE REGION WAS NOW DEEP IN DROUGHT.

IN OUR LAST FREE TIME BEFORE THE HARVEST, WILFRIDO INVITED US OUT TO THE SOY FARM WHERE HIS SON LIVED AND WORKED AS MANAGER.

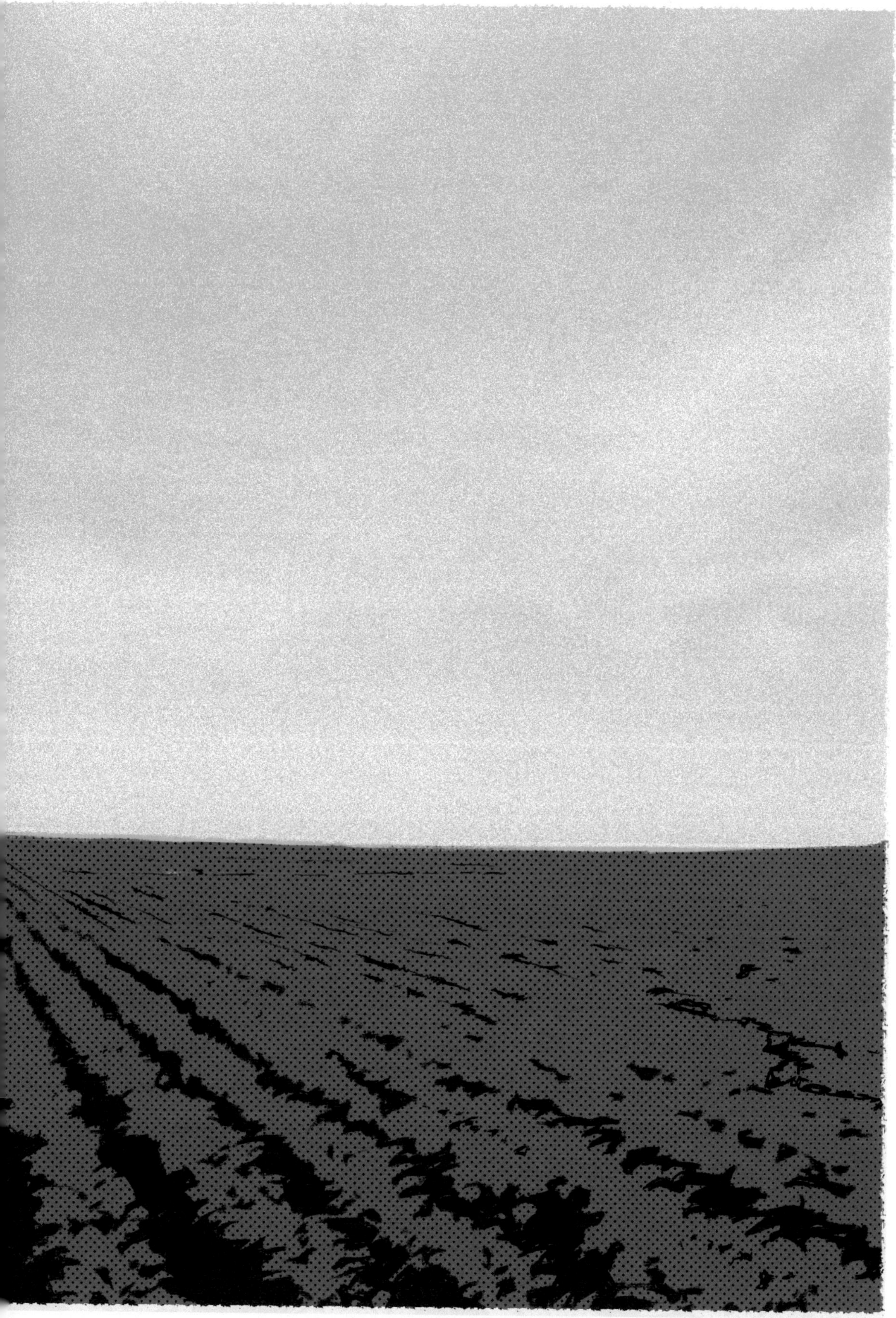

I'M IMPRESSED BY YOUR WORK HERE, MY BOY. MANAGING 500 HECTARES IS VERY SERIOUS.

SURE, FATHER. BUT THAT'S BECAUSE YOU GOT YOUR FIRST 8 HECTARE FARM WHEN YOU WERE 25 YEARS OLD, DURING STROESSNER'S PRESIDENCY. BACK THEN FOR GS. 25,000 YOU COULD ENTER A LOTTERY AND GET A LAND TITLE.

DID I EVER TELL YOU ABOUT HOW I TRICKED THEM? YOU HAD TO BE MARRIED TO ENTER THE LOTTERY.

YEAH, YEAH. AND YOU TOLD THEM YOU WERE ABOUT TO PROPOSE TO YOUR GIRLFRIEND. WHICHEVER ONE THAT WAS AT THE TIME.

WELL, THEY NEVER CHECKED TO SEE IF WE ACTUALLY MARRIED. IT DIDN'T LAST LONG, AFTER ALL. BUT I GOT THE LAND TITLE! THAT LASTS FOREVER.

YOU WERE QUITE THE ROOSTER WAY BACK WHEN.

WAY BACK WHEN!? I'M OFFENDED.

DO YOU KNOW WHY THEY CALLED ME THE ROOSTER?

BECAUSE YOU HAD LOTS OF CHICKENS.

QUE PUCHA. I CAN'T BELIEVE THIS. FIRST WE GET DROWNED WITH RAIN. AND NOW WEEKS WITHOUT A CLOUD IN THE SKY. THIS DROUGHT IS GOING TO KILL THE SOY YIELDS THIS YEAR.

MY SESAME CROPS ARE FEELING THE EFFECTS. *SECO SECO SECO,* IT'S BONE DAY IN THE *CHACRA.*

THIS IS FOR MY *PATRÓN** TO WORRY ABOUT, DON'T WORRY PAPÁ. I JUST LOOK AFTER THE FIELDS.

WELL, NOT EVEN REALLY THE *PATRÓN.* DO YOU KNOW, THE ONLY PEOPLE WHO HAVE EVER SHOWED UP HERE ARE REPRESENTATIVES FROM THE BANK?

THE BANK? A BIG BANK, NOT LIKE MY COOPERATIVE?

THE ACCOUNT THAT PAYS OUR SALARY. NOBODY EVEN KNOWS WHO OWNS THIS FARM. THEY SAY IT'S A SYNDICATE OF INVESTORS. MAYBE FROM BRAZIL, MAYBE FROM ARGENTINA, MAYBE FROM THE USA. WHO KNOWS.

THERE'S NO FOREST LEFT HERE – IF I'D LIVED HERE AS A YOUNG MAN, PERHAPS I WOULDN'T HAVE MET THE POMBEROS.

THOSE CREATURES CAN'T HIDE IN *SOJALES.***

*LANDLORD AND EMPLOYER   **SOY FIELDS

THE OLD MAN IS *PILA'I** THESE DAYS. I HOPE SOME OF OUR TRANSGENIC SEED CORN WILL CHEER HIM UP!

IT'S EXTRA RESILIENT AND SHOULD THRIVE NO MATTER WHAT THIS CRAZY WEATHER THROWS AT IT.

LET'S LOAD UP SOME MANGOES FOR HIM.

HERE, BE SURE TO TREAT THE SOIL WITH THIS BEFORE PLANTING. IT'S *MATA TODO*, KILLS EVERYTHING.

SINCE MY SIBLINGS ARE IN BUENOS AIRES AND ASUNCIÓN AND CAN'T HELP YOU WITH THE WEEDING AND HOEING.

*MELANCHOLY, LOW ENERGY. GUARANÍ DERIVED FROM THE SPANISH WORD FOR BATTERY.

WE DROVE THROUGH *COLONIA FRIESLAND*, A LARGE AND PROSPEROUS MENNONITE COLONY. THEY PIONEERED IMPROVED GMO CROPS IN THE REGION.

SEE THERE, AT THE MENNONITE COLONY? *LOS MENONITAS*, THEY PLANT ALL THE NEW VARIETIES, ALL IMPROVED SEEDS. LIKE YOU *CHE RA'A.**

COLONIA FRIESLAND SUPPORTS THE MULTIACTIVA, I'M THANKFUL FOR THAT. BUT OUR SEEDS, BAH, A *PORQUERIA.*

I'M NEVER PLANTING THIS ORGANIC SESAME AGAIN, WHAT A NIGHTMARE.

THE AGRONOMISTS COME AND SAY, YOU NEED TO HOE BETWEEN THE ROWS DON WILFRIDO, GS. 500,000. YOU NEED THIS SPECIAL INSECTICIDE DON WILFRIDO, GS. 100,000. YOU NEED THIS CROP INSURANCE DON WILFRIDO, GS. 140,000. CLEAN UP YOUR PARCEL AGAIN, DON WILFRIDO, GS. 500,000.

IF IT HAD BEEN CONVENTIONAL AND NOT ORGANIC I COULD HAVE PASSED WEED KILLER OVER THE WHOLE PARCEL, *MATA TODO* AND CLEANED THE FIELDS. IT WOULD HAVE TURNED OUT *LINDO, LINDO, LINDO,* VERY PRETTY.

TOO BAD, BUT... AT LEAST I HAVE YOU.

*MY FRIEND

"THE DAMAGE FROM THE DROUGHT WAS HUGE," AS REPORTED BY MAJOR SOY PRODUCERS IN PARAGUAY. THE FARMS THAT PLANTED EARLY WERE ALL HIT HARD. LOSSES WERE ESTIMATED AT 37% BELOW NORMAL YIELDS.

IN ANOTHER VERSION OF THIS STORY, WILFRIDO DOESN'T HAVE A FAMILY CONNECTION TO THE BIG PRODUCERS, AND PLANTS THE LOCAL VARIETY OF MAIZE INSTEAD. MOST OF HIS CHILDREN SEND MONEY HOME TO THE FARM, OF COURSE.

BUT THE CONNECTION BETWEEN A *SOJAL* OWNED BY AN INVESTMENT FUND AND WILFRIDO'S FARM IS CLOSER THAN WE MIGHT EXPECT. CONNECTIONS TRACED BY KINSHIP AND CORN AND AGROCHEMICALS.

IN THIS VERSION OF HIS STORY, THE FAMILY FARM DEPENDS ON A SUBSIDY FROM THE BIG GROWERS, BUT ONE ORCHESTRATED BY A DUTIFUL SON.

AND IN THIS VERSION OF THE STORY, THE SPECIAL SEEDS USUALLY RESERVED FOR COLONIA FRIESLAND, AND FOR THE BIG PRODUCERS, FOUND THEIR WAY TO WILFRIDO'S *CHACRA* AS A SAFEGUARD INSURANCE IF HIS SESAME WERE TO FAIL.

WILFRIDO WAS EXPECTING BLANCA, HIS DAUGHTER, TO ARRIVE ANY DAY FROM BUENOS AIRES.

BUT IF WE DIDN'T COME OUT TO THE FARM TO HELP, HE WORKED BY HIMSELF.

NEEEIGH

WITH THE REINS OF KAVAJÚ TUJA LOOPED AROUND HIS NECK...

...THERE WERE RISKS TO WORKING THE *CHACRA* ON HIS OWN.

WHICH IS WHY, IN EARLY JANUARY, WE CAME TO HELP WITH THE HARVEST.

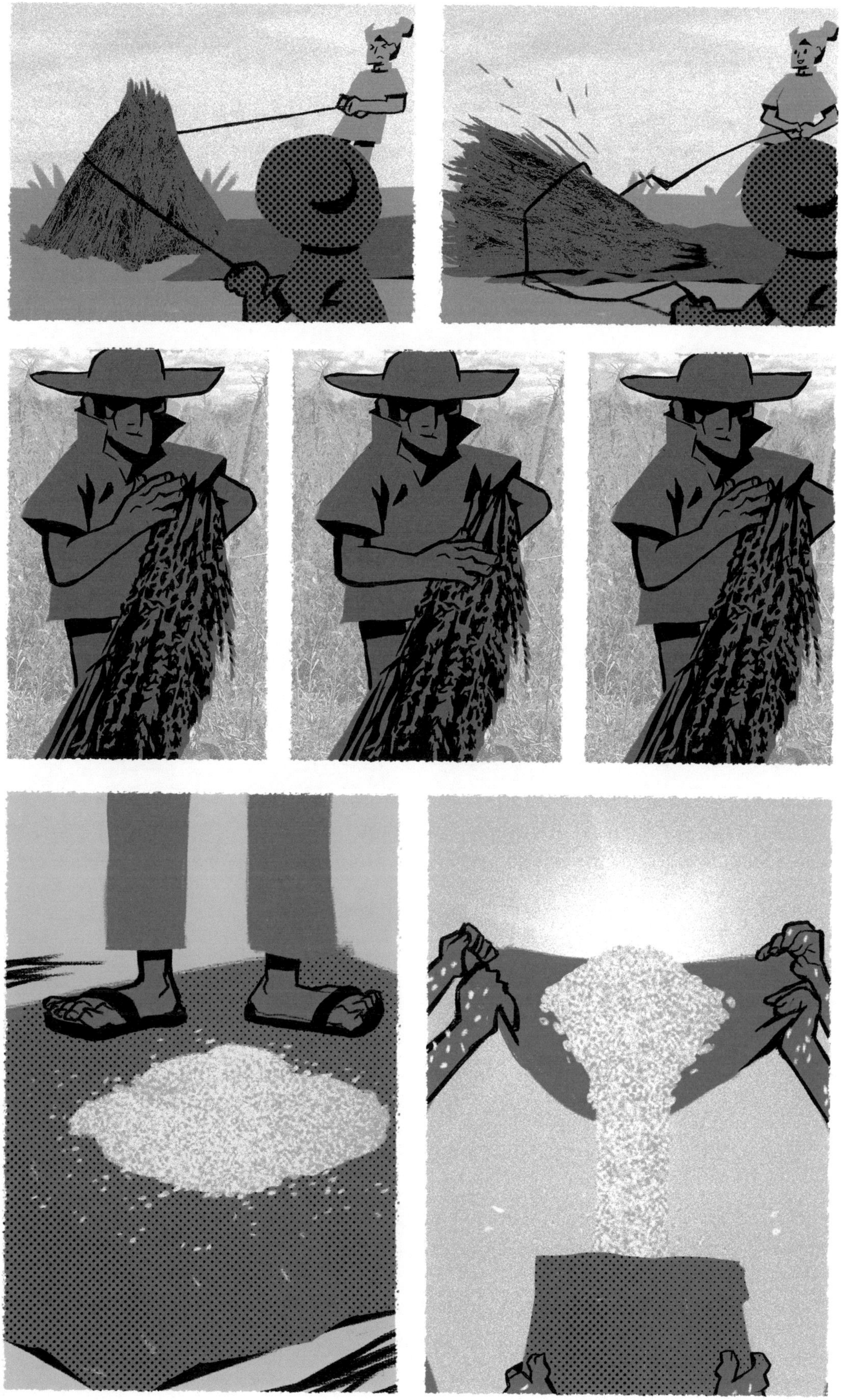

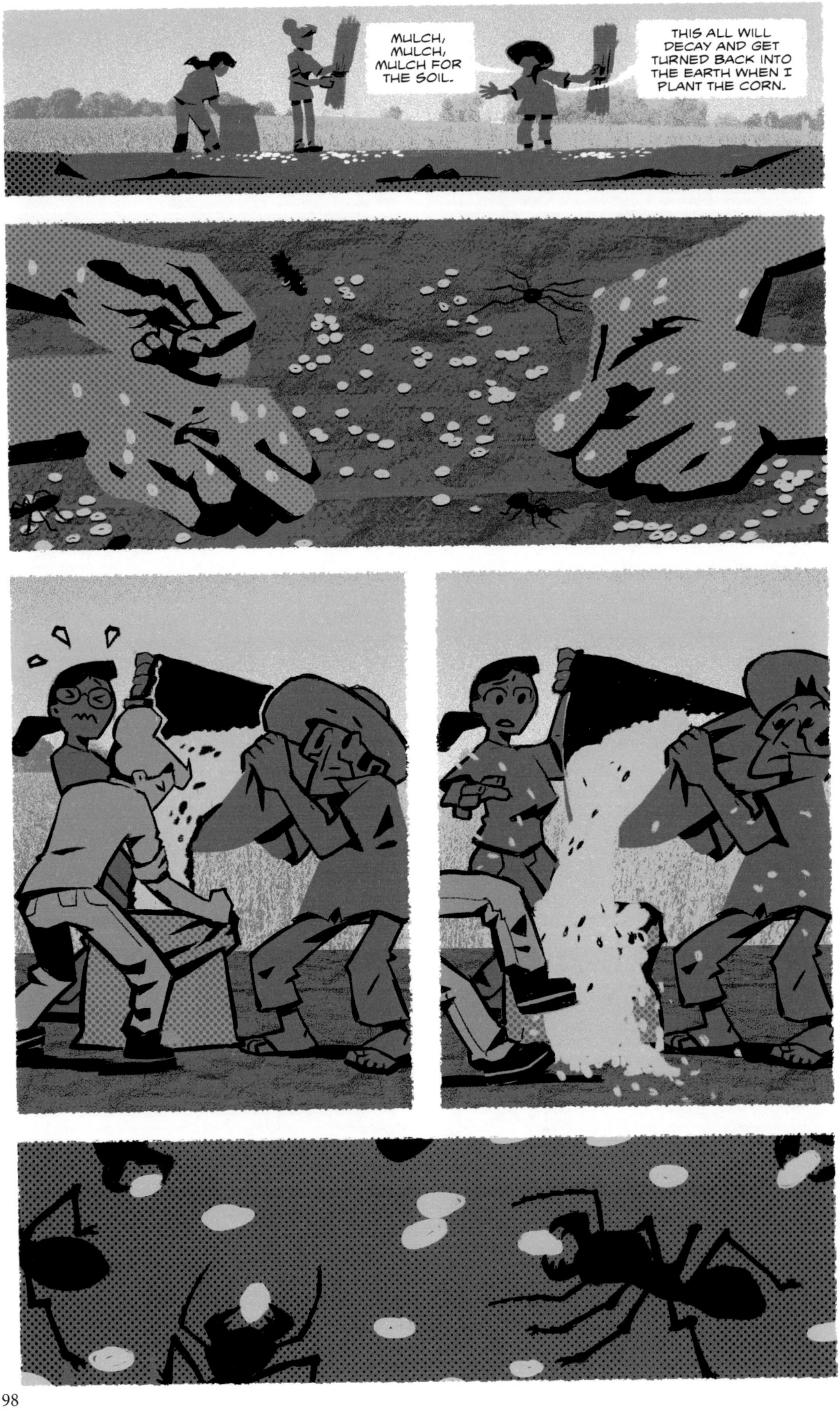
MULCH, MULCH, MULCH FOR THE SOIL.
THIS ALL WILL DECAY AND GET TURNED BACK INTO THE EARTH WHEN I PLANT THE CORN.

THEY WANT TO HELP, AND ÑA NECA LOVES FEEDING THEM. SHE IS LONELY AT HOME, WORKING ALL DAY WITH THE COWS, AND MILKING, AND POULTRY, AND CHEESE, AND CLEANING, AND COOKING, AND MENDING.

MY DAUGHTERS HAVE ALWAYS HELPED WITH THE HARVEST. BLANCA WILL BE HERE SOON. BUT THIS YEAR THEY'RE GONE, JUST CAROL AND ROCÍO.

MULCH, IT'S COMPOST FOR THE SOIL.

I'M SO SORRY DON WILFRIDO. THAT MULCH IS WORTH GS. 6,500 PER KILO.

DRY, DRY, DRY.

NOBODY THINKS ABOUT THE LOSSES.

THEY SET AN AMOUNT TO PAY, AND WHAT ABOUT ALL THE COSTS?

"IT HAS TO BE THIS AMOUNT," THEY SAY. FOR YOUR MONTHLY DEBT QUOTA.

FOR THE INSURANCE. TO BUY CHEMICALS AND PERSONNEL. *ESO, ESO, ESO.*

BUT WHAT ABOUT THE YEARS IT DOESN'T TURN OUT?

WHAT IF THE WEATHER DOESN'T COLLABORATE? IF THE PLANTS DON'T GROW?

STILL THE SAME AMOUNT, AND THEY WILL DO ANYTHING TO COLLECT.

THEY NEVER HAVE TO ADJUST. THOSE WHO COLLECT ALWAYS GET PAID. NOTHING AFFECTS THEM.

SOMEDAY THERE WILL BE A RECKONING.

MUCHA GENTE QUE TUVO Y QUE YA NO TENDRÍA. LOTS OF WEALTHY PEOPLE WHO WON'T HAVE WEALTH ANY MORE.

RECOMPENSA. ACKNOWLEDGMENT. RETRIBUTION.

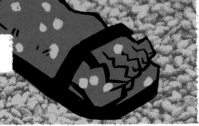

I THINK WE ARE DONE HERE. LET'S LOAD THE BAG.

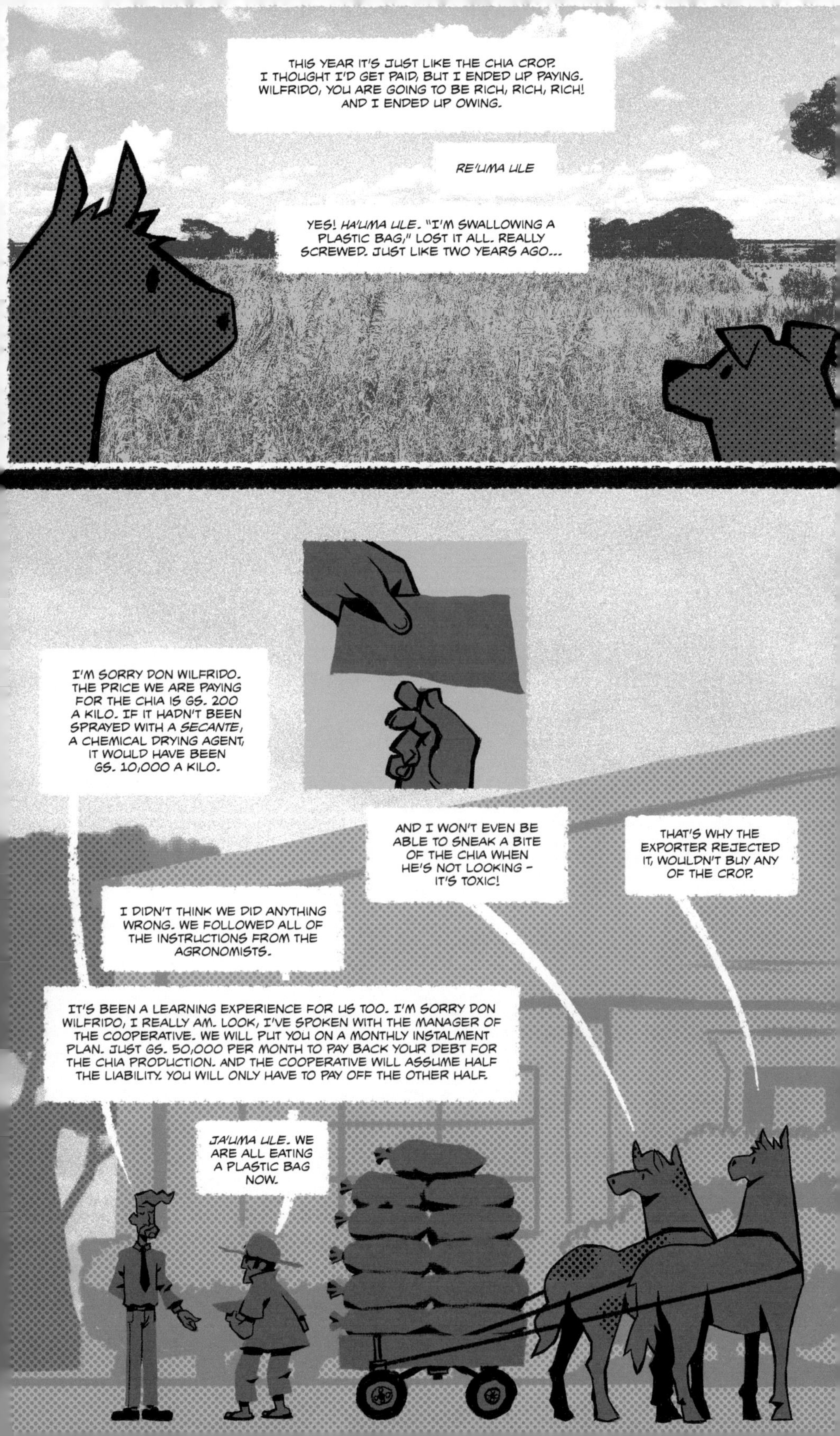
THIS YEAR IT'S JUST LIKE THE CHIA CROP. I THOUGHT I'D GET PAID, BUT I ENDED UP PAYING. WILFRIDO, YOU ARE GOING TO BE RICH, RICH, RICH! AND I ENDED UP OWING.
RE'UMA ULE
YES! *HA'UMA ULE*. "I'M SWALLOWING A PLASTIC BAG," LOST IT ALL. REALLY SCREWED. JUST LIKE TWO YEARS AGO...
I'M SORRY DON WILFRIDO. THE PRICE WE ARE PAYING FOR THE CHIA IS GS. 200 A KILO. IF IT HADN'T BEEN SPRAYED WITH A *SECANTE*, A CHEMICAL DRYING AGENT, IT WOULD HAVE BEEN GS. 10,000 A KILO.
AND I WON'T EVEN BE ABLE TO SNEAK A BITE OF THE CHIA WHEN HE'S NOT LOOKING – IT'S TOXIC!
THAT'S WHY THE EXPORTER REJECTED IT, WOULDN'T BUY ANY OF THE CROP.
I DIDN'T THINK WE DID ANYTHING WRONG. WE FOLLOWED ALL OF THE INSTRUCTIONS FROM THE AGRONOMISTS.
IT'S BEEN A LEARNING EXPERIENCE FOR US TOO. I'M SORRY DON WILFRIDO, I REALLY AM. LOOK, I'VE SPOKEN WITH THE MANAGER OF THE COOPERATIVE. WE WILL PUT YOU ON A MONTHLY INSTALMENT PLAN. JUST GS. 50,000 PER MONTH TO PAY BACK YOUR DEBT FOR THE CHIA PRODUCTION. AND THE COOPERATIVE WILL ASSUME HALF THE LIABILITY. YOU WILL ONLY HAVE TO PAY OFF THE OTHER HALF.
JA'UMA ULE. WE ARE ALL EATING A PLASTIC BAG NOW.

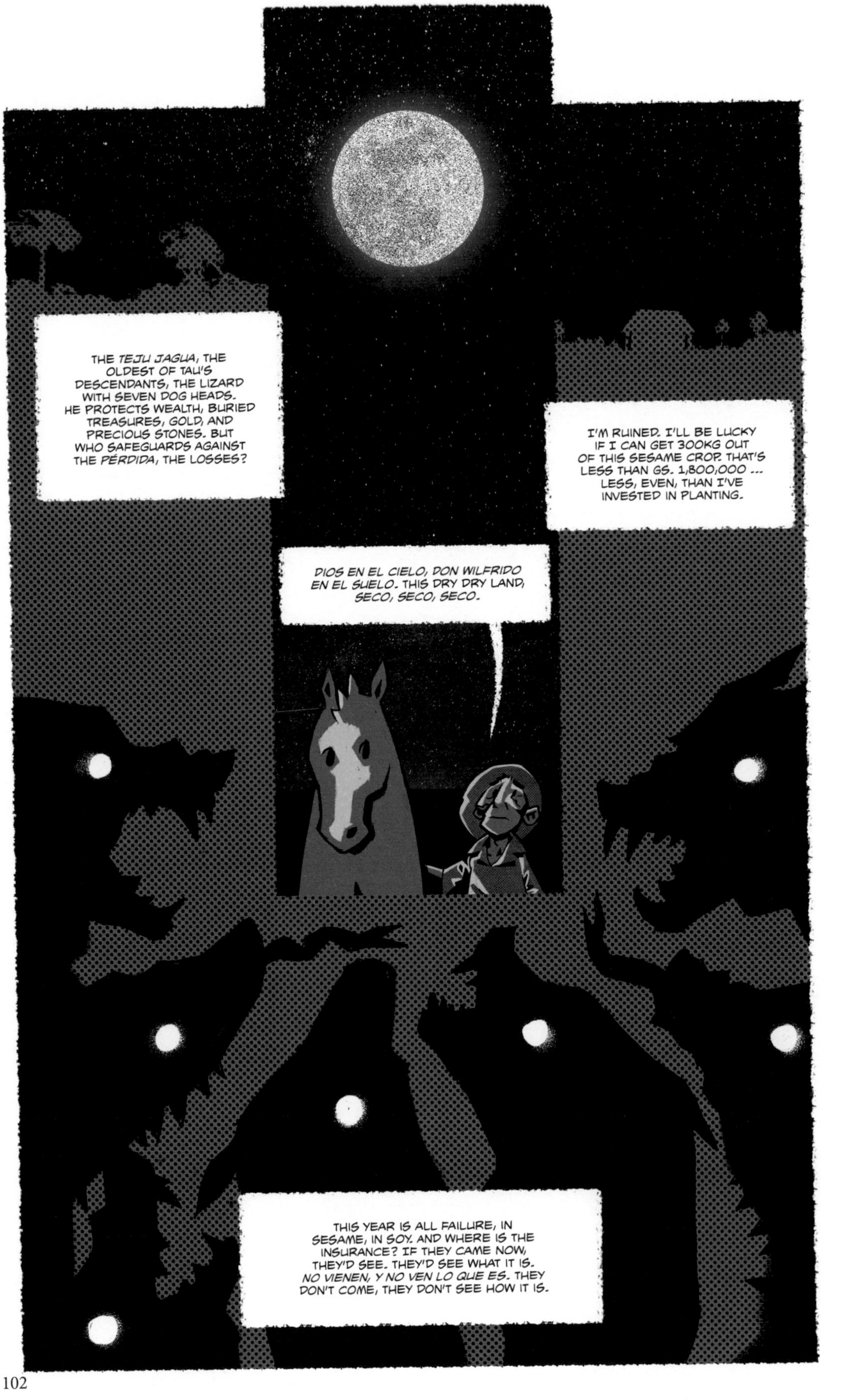
THE *TEJU JAGUA*, THE OLDEST OF TAU'S DESCENDANTS, THE LIZARD WITH SEVEN DOG HEADS. HE PROTECTS WEALTH, BURIED TREASURES, GOLD, AND PRECIOUS STONES. BUT WHO SAFEGUARDS AGAINST THE *PÉRDIDA*, THE LOSSES?
I'M RUINED. I'LL BE LUCKY IF I CAN GET 300KG OUT OF THIS SESAME CROP. THAT'S LESS THAN GS. 1,800,000 ... LESS, EVEN, THAN I'VE INVESTED IN PLANTING.
DIOS EN EL CIELO, DON WILFRIDO EN EL SUELO. THIS DRY DRY LAND, *SECO, SECO, SECO.*
THIS YEAR IS ALL FAILURE, IN SESAME, IN SOY. AND WHERE IS THE INSURANCE? IF THEY CAME NOW, THEY'D SEE. THEY'D SEE WHAT IT IS. *NO VIENEN, Y NO VEN LO QUE ES.* THEY DON'T COME, THEY DON'T SEE HOW IT IS.

IN ANOTHER VERSION OF THIS STORY...

IN ONE VERSION OF THIS STORY, THE DROUGHT INSURANCE COVERED WILFRIDO'S LOSSES WHEN "HYDROLOGICAL STRESS" FOR THIS GRID-SQUARE IN SAN PEDRO SURPASSED THE INDEX AND TRIGGERED AN INSURANCE PAYOUT OF GS. 1,500,000.

BUT IN THIS VERSION OF THE STORY, THE INDEX FELL 18% SHORT OF TRIGGERING. BECAUSE THE SATELLITE RAINFALL DATA REGISTERED JUST A BIT MORE MOISTURE THAN THE WEATHER CONDITIONS WRITTEN INTO THE DERIVATIVE CONTRACT.

INSURTECH NEVER CAME TO SEE HOW IT IS - IN FACT, THIS IS BY DESIGN. IT'S NOT THE CROP THAT IS INSURED, IT'S THE WEATHER ITSELF. THE SATELLITE DATA AND THE WEATHER STATIONS ARE ENGINEERED TO "SEE" THAT REMOTELY. IN FACT, FAITH IN THE QUALITY OF THE WEATHER INDEX, THE DATA, AND THE MODEL IS THE REASON WHY SWISS RE LOWERED THE PREMIUM, WHY FINTECH IS HOPED TO BE THE FUTURE OF FINANCE.

WILFRIDO FEARED THAT HE'D SPENT MORE TO PLANT HIS CROPS THAN WHAT HE'D MAKE FROM HIS HARVEST...

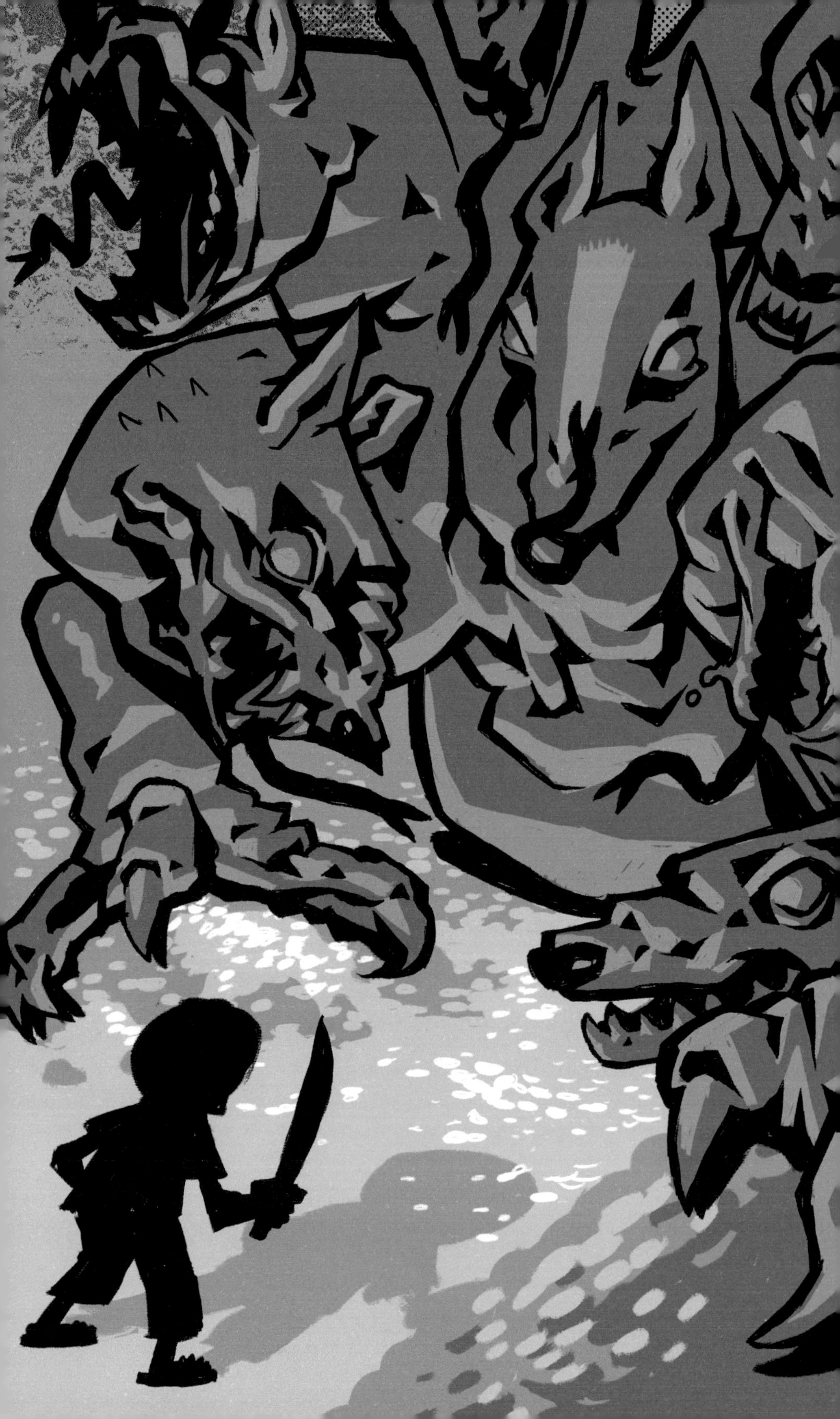

BUT HE SET HIS WORRIES ASIDE BECAUSE THERE WAS CAUSE TO CELEBRATE. AT THE VERY END OF THE HARVEST, WILFRIDO'S DAUGHTER BLANCA ARRIVED FOR A VISIT. IT'S A LONG JOURNEY FROM BUENOS AIRES.

THESE EUCALYPTUS ARE TERRIBLE SHADE TREES. THE SUN KEEPS MOVING, BUT I CAN'T MOVE THE HAMMOCK.

THEY ARE MY INSURANCE POLICY. I CAN SELL THE TIMBER IF EVER THERE IS A REAL NEED. YOUR MOTHER KEEPS NAGGING ME TO CHOP THEM DOWN AND PUT IN SOMETHING WITH REAL SHADE, A NICE MANGO. EH, WE'LL SEE.

SHE HAS A POINT.

SHHHH! QUIET. PROFESSOR ENRIQUE SABIO! I NEVER MISS HIS SHOW.

NOW THE HOROSCOPES FOR TODAY, THE LAST DAY IN JANUARY. <CRACKLE CRACKLE> FOR LIBRAS, MIND YOUR DEBTS, THEY CAN SNOWBALL. YOU MUST BE FINANCIALLY PRUDENT. DON'T LEAVE YOUR ACCOUNTS UNPAID. FOR SCORPIOS...<CRACKLE CRACKLE>

DID YOU HEAR THAT? MIND MY DEBTS. I'D BETTER PAY OFF MY LAST INSTALMENT AT THE COOPERATIVE.

AND YOU CAN COME CONSULT IN PERSON IN SANTANÍ, TUESDAYS FROM 8AM... <CRACKLE>

PAPA, YOU ARE AWFULLY WORRIED ABOUT YOUR SESAME HARVEST.

WE SHOULD GO CONSULT PROF. SABIO THIS WEEK.

CONSULTATIONS WITH PROF. SABIO

SO WHAT DID HE TELL YOU?

I AM SO HAPPY, EVERYTHING WILL BE ALL RIGHT. THE FARM IS FINE.

JUST A SMALL CLEANSE, THAT'S WHAT HE SAYS IS NEEDED. HE PERFORMS THESE CLEANINGS, *LIMPIEZAS*. I MIGHT DO IT, JUST TO BE SURE. DEPENDS ON HOW MUCH MONEY WE HAVE AFTER THE HARVEST. HE SAID GS. 200,000 SHOULD COVER THE EXPENSES. FOR THE MATERIALS. TO DO PROPER WORK.

DO YOU KNOW WHO IS DOING UN *TRABAJO ARTIFICIAL*, DOING WORK AGAINST YOU? WHO HAS PERFORMED *BRUJERÍA*, WITCHCRAFT?

YES. LET ME TELL YOU A STORY. YOU WERE JUST A LITTLE GIRL...

PEOPLE CAME FROM OUTSIDE FOR THE HARVEST, AND A WOMAN CAME WITH THEM. A WOMAN WHO KNOWS HOW TO DO THINGS, *SABE COMO HACER.*

BACK WHEN WE USED TO PLANT COTTON, THERE WAS A MAN WHO LIVED NEXT DOOR, AND HE HAD FIVE SONS. *ESTABAN ENTRE MUCHOS,* THERE WAS HARDLY ROOM FOR ALL OF THEM.

AND THE MAN NEXT DOOR, HE ASKED HER TO PLACE A FILTHY THING HERE, ON OUR LAND, SO THAT WE WOULD LEAVE THE HOUSE. AND SHE WOULD DO HER FILTHY WORK, HER *MACUMBA,* FOR MONEY. AND HE PAID HER GS. 50,000, WHICH WAS A FORTUNE AT THE TIME.

BUT LATER SHE CAME TO US, SHE TOLD US WHAT SHE HAD DONE. THAT SHE HADN'T KNOWN US, WHEN SHE DID THAT THING. BUT NOW SHE HAD SEEN US AND SAW THAT WE WERE GOOD PEOPLE. AND SO SHE TOLD US HOW SHE BURIED IT UNDER A TREE. AND HOW TO GET RID OF IT. SO I DID, AND TOSSED IT OVER ONTO THE NEIGHBOR'S PLOT OF LAND.

FROM ENVY, HE LOST EVERYTHING. BUT YOU KNOW WHAT IS STRANGE? THAT TREE WHERE THE FILTH WAS BURIED, THAT TREE DRIED UP AND DIED.

AND THE NEIGHBOR AND ALL HIS SONS, THEY PACKED UP AND LEFT. WHAT HE WANTED OF US – THAT WE LEAVE SO HE CAN HAVE OUR LAND FOR HIS SONS – HAPPENED TO HIM. AND HE NEVER CAME BACK.

YOU SEE, THAT'S WHY I NEED TO DO THE CLEANSE. THERE'S STILL A BLOCKAGE. AFTER ALL THESE YEARS AND IT WILL MEAN MORE LOSSES IF WE DON'T, *MÁS PÉRDIDAS.*

OK, LET'S GO HOME. WE CAN PAY YOUR LAST DEBT INSTALMENT AT THE COOPERATIVE ON THE WAY...

...JUST LIKE PROF. SABIO SAID.

BAD LUCK, ALCOHOL, PROBLEMS WITH LOVE, PROJECTS THAT FAIL; THIS ALL HAS A SOLUTION. THERE IS A SOLUTION IN THIS CASE TOO; *HAY SOLUCIÓN PARA TODO ESO...* FOR THE SPECIAL PRICE OF GS. 200,000...

IN ANOTHER VERSION OF THIS STORY, THE SESAME CROPS
NEVER WERE PLANTED BECAUSE WILFRIDO AND HIS FAMILY
RODE AWAY IN AN OX CART AND NEVER CAME BACK. AND
IN THAT VERSION OF THE STORY A TREE GREW ON THE
EDGE OF THE FARM, TALL AND BROAD AND SHADY, EVEN IN
THE WORST YEARS WITH THE WORST WEATHER AND THE
MOST TERRIBLE DROUGHT. BUT IT GREW AND GREW.

IN THIS VERSION OF THE STORY, A TREE HAS
DRIED UP AND DIED. YET DROUGHT
INSURANCE FOR WILFRIDO'S FARM IS
CALIBRATED TO WEATHER SATELLITES AND A
HYDROLOGICAL INDEX. NOT OTHER
FORECASTS, OTHER RISKS, OTHER *PÉRDIDA*.

WHICH LOOK TO SIGNS
OTHER THAN CLIMATE
SCIENCE.

INSURANCE, LIKE PROF. SABIO, OFFERS
SECURITY - *HAY SOLUCIÓN PARA TODO ESO.*
DOES PROF. SABIO OFFER ANSWERS FOR THE
EL NIÑO WEATHER PATTERN? DOES INSURTECH
INSURE AGAINST POMBEROS? IS THERE A
VERSION OF THIS STORY THAT HAS A CERTAIN
ANSWER?

I ADVOCATED FOR THIS INSURANCE, BUT NOW I HAVE DOUBTS. INSURTECH AGENTS SAID IT WOULD SURELY TRIGGER WITH 15 DAYS OF NO RAIN. WE ALL COUNTED, THE FARMERS COUNTED, 23 DAYS WITHOUT RAIN. THE FARMERS WILL THINK THAT SOMEBODY ATE THE MONEY – THAT I DID BECAUSE I WAS PUSHING FOR INSURANCE, OR THAT THE COOPERATIVE POCKETED THE PAYOUTS. WE'VE LOST THEIR TRUST, AND FRANKLY I CAN'T BLAME THEM.

WE DON'T KNOW IF THIS PROJECT WILL BE RENEWED, IF THE FUNDS FROM AID PROJECTS WILL KEEP FLOWING. IT'S A REALLY INNOVATIVE PROJECT, WE HAVE TO START OFF BY EXPERIMENTING. IT HAS SO MANY IDIOSYNCRASIES THAT WE HAVE TO GAIN THEIR CONFIDENCE.

EXPERTS AREN'T EVEN IN AGREEMENT ABOUT WHETHER THE *EL NIÑO* PHENOMENON IS AN ANNUAL VARIATION, AND TO WHAT EXTENT IT IS CLIMATE CHANGE. WITHIN THAT DISAGREEMENT, IT'S REALLY DIFFICULT TO MODEL THE WIDER RISKS. MEANWHILE, WE ARE AN INSURANCE COMPANY.

PROFITABILITY AND MASS MARKET ARE KEY TO ITS SUSTAINABILITY.

I CAN EVEN PLAY TRICKS ON THE MODERN FARM OWNED BY THE BANK. WITH THE CORN GROWING TALL, I WHISTLED TO WILFRIDO'S GRANDDAUGHTER. I ALMOST TRICKED HER BY CALLING IN THE VOICE OF HER FATHER. PERHAPS NEXT TIME I'LL HAVE BETTER LUCK.

TWO GRID SQUARES OF SAN PEDRO DISTRICT DID TRIGGER FROM HYDROLOGICAL STRESS. IT WASN'T A TOTAL CROP LOSS, BUT A DIMINISHED YIELD. MY SESAME INDEX DEPENDED NOT JUST ON THE WEATHER, BUT THE DATE OF PLANTING AND THE VARIETY OF SESAME. EACH FARM IS DIFFERENT – IT'S A QUESTION OF *NIVELES DE PÉRDIDA.*

JALE JALE JALE. ONE MORE YEAR OF PLOUGHING THE SESAME FIELDS. WILFRIDO SAYS HE'LL PLANT SESAME UNTIL THE DAY HE DIES. SO WILL I.

THIS YEAR THE PRICE IS GOOD! GS. 8,500 PER KILO. WORD WILL SPREAD. NEXT YEAR, EVERY SPARE CORNER OF THE DISTRICT WILL BE COVERED IN SESAME. WHO KNOWS THE PRICE; IT MAY BE GS. 3,000. BUT PEOPLE ARE ALREADY TALKING...

ON DON WILFRIDO'S FARM WE HARVESTED 900KG FROM 0.7 HECTARES. ALL IN ALL, THIS IS A REMARKABLE YIELD, CONSIDERING THE ADVERSE WEATHER THIS YEAR.

BUT WILFRIDO WAS UNHAPPY IN THE END. THE YIELDS WERE NOT AS HIGH AS THEY SHOULD HAVE BEEN, IF THERE HADN'T BEEN A DROUGHT. HE TURNED A PROFIT ON HIS SESAME BUT DREAMED OF A VERSION OF THE HARVEST WHERE THERE HADN'T BEEN 23 DAYS WITHOUT RAIN. PERHAPS NEXT YEAR....

CYCLES AND HARVESTS. I WANT TO BE RID OF THIS SESAME ALREADY, *OPA LA PLEITO*, THERE'S NO MORE DISCUSSION, CASE CLOSED. IT'S TAKING TOO LONG AND I NEED TO MOVE ON. I WANT TO PLANT MY CORN ALREADY. I NEED TO CLOSE THIS CYCLE, AND START THE NEXT CROP.

ASI ESTAMOS – UNO CANTA, UNO LLORA. SOME SING, SOME CRY. I JUST WANT TO BE DONE.

THE VILLAGE CELEBRATED THE END OF THE HARVEST WITH A HORSE RACE. WILFRIDO RACED A LOT OF HORSES IN HIS DAY, OR SO HE SAID. THIS TIME I FOUND MYSELF IN THE SADDLE...

I APPRECIATE THE NOVELTY OF A HORSE RACE WITH WOMEN JOCKEYS. BUT I'M SURE TO LOSE!

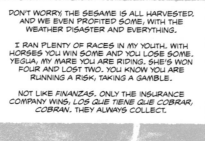

DON'T WORRY, THE SESAME IS ALL HARVESTED. AND WE EVEN PROFITED SOME, WITH THE WEATHER DISASTER AND EVERYTHING.

I RAN PLENTY OF RACES IN MY YOUTH. WITH HORSES YOU WIN SOME AND YOU LOSE SOME. YEGUA, MY MARE YOU ARE RIDING. SHE'S WON FOUR AND LOST TWO. YOU KNOW YOU ARE RUNNING A RISK, TAKING A GAMBLE.

NOT LIKE *FINANZAS*. ONLY THE INSURANCE COMPANY WINS, *LOS QUE TIENE QUE COBRAR, COBRAN.* THEY ALWAYS COLLECT.

I CAN'T BELIEVE YOU BET ON THIS!

OPORTUNAMENTE, BY CHANCE THIS LADY JOCKEY CAME, WHO EVERYBODY THINKS IS A MENNONITE, EH? HA! WHAT A GOOD TRICK. LIKE THAT TIME I "BORROWED" THE NEIGHBOR'S HORSE AND PAINTED ON A BLAZE WITH WHITEWASH SO IT WOULD LOOK LIKE MINE.

WELL, DON WILFRIDO IS SURE TO HAVE GOOD LUCK, AND IF NOT, IT'S STILL GOOD FUN.

I'M SO SORRY DON WILFRIDO. I HOPE YOUR LOSSES WEREN'T TOO BAD. THE MARE GAVE IT HER ALL. *JA'UMA ULE.*

NO NO NO! THIS ISN'T LIKE THE SESAME. WITH THE RACES I'VE ALWAYS BEEN *TRAMPOSO.** WE'LL RUN AGAIN AND I'LL SHOW YOU HOW TO USE YOUR WHIP TO TRIP THE STRING AT THE FINISH LINE, EVEN IF YOU ARE BEHIND. HA! DON WILFRIDO IS FULL OF PRANKS.

*A TRICKSTER

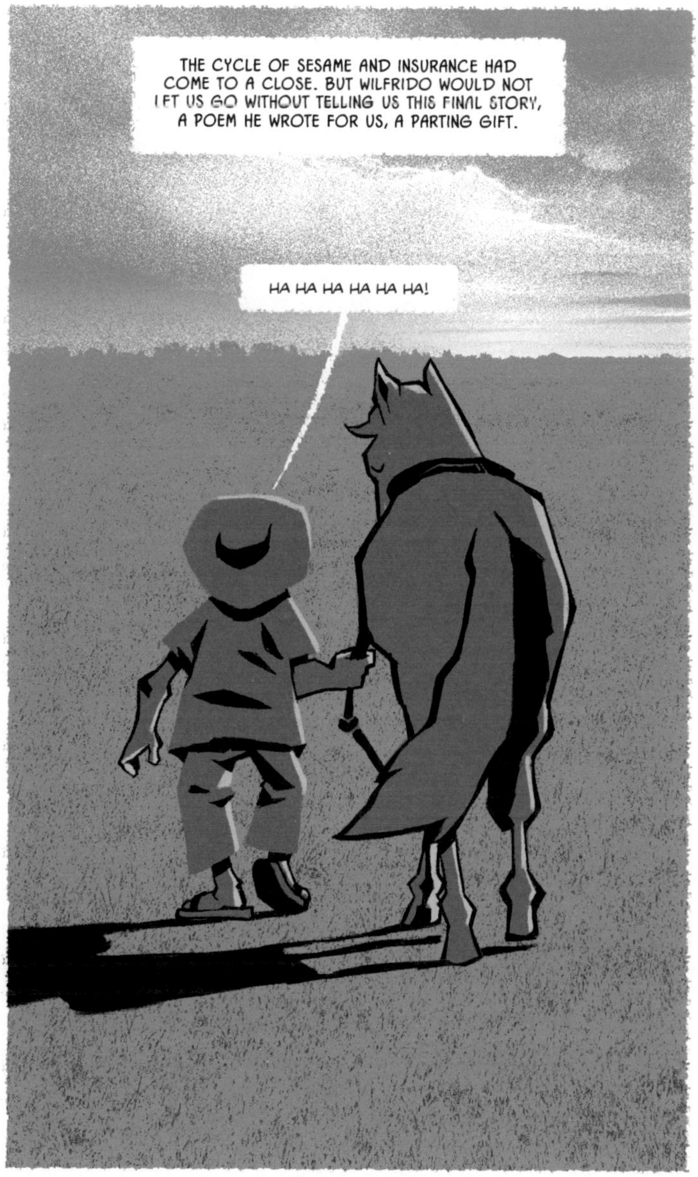
THE CYCLE OF SESAME AND INSURANCE HAD COME TO A CLOSE. BUT WILFRIDO WOULD NOT LET US GO WITHOUT TELLING US THIS FINAL STORY, A POEM HE WROTE FOR US, A PARTING GIFT.
HA HA HA HA HA HA!

AGUAPY SAPY'AMI,
EN AMABLE CONCURRENCIA
AÑAPY LA INTELIGENCIA
EN EL DULCE GUARANÍ

POHECHÁTAMA RUPI AJERUREMI
AHAKUÉVO PEHENDUMI AÑE'ĒVO
EN POESÍA GUARANIMI

CHE KORASÕ NDAHENDÁI
OĨ YPYPE AÑANDÚVA KYSÉICHANGA
CHEIKUTŨA CHEJOPÍKO HA CHE KARÃI
AVAVÉNTE NDOIKUAÁI KIRIRIHÁRE
CHEASUFRÍVA

HA CHE POHOHAYHU'ETEREÍVA

SITTING FOR A BRIEF MOMENT,
BEFORE THIS KIND AUDIENCE
I APPEAL TO THE WISDOM
OF SWEET GUARANÍ

SINCE I AM GOING TO LEAVE YOU,
I ASK YOU BEFORE GOING
LISTEN AS I SPEAK THIS
GUARANÍ POETRY

MY HEART IS RESTLESS
THERE IS SOMETHING THAT I FEEL
LIKE A KNIFE THAT PIERCES,
ITCHES, SCRATCHES ME
NOBODY KNOWS THAT I SUFFER
IN SILENCE AND THAT I CARE
FOR YOU VERY MUCH...

WE DO NOT SEPARATE,
I CANNOT BELIEVE IT.

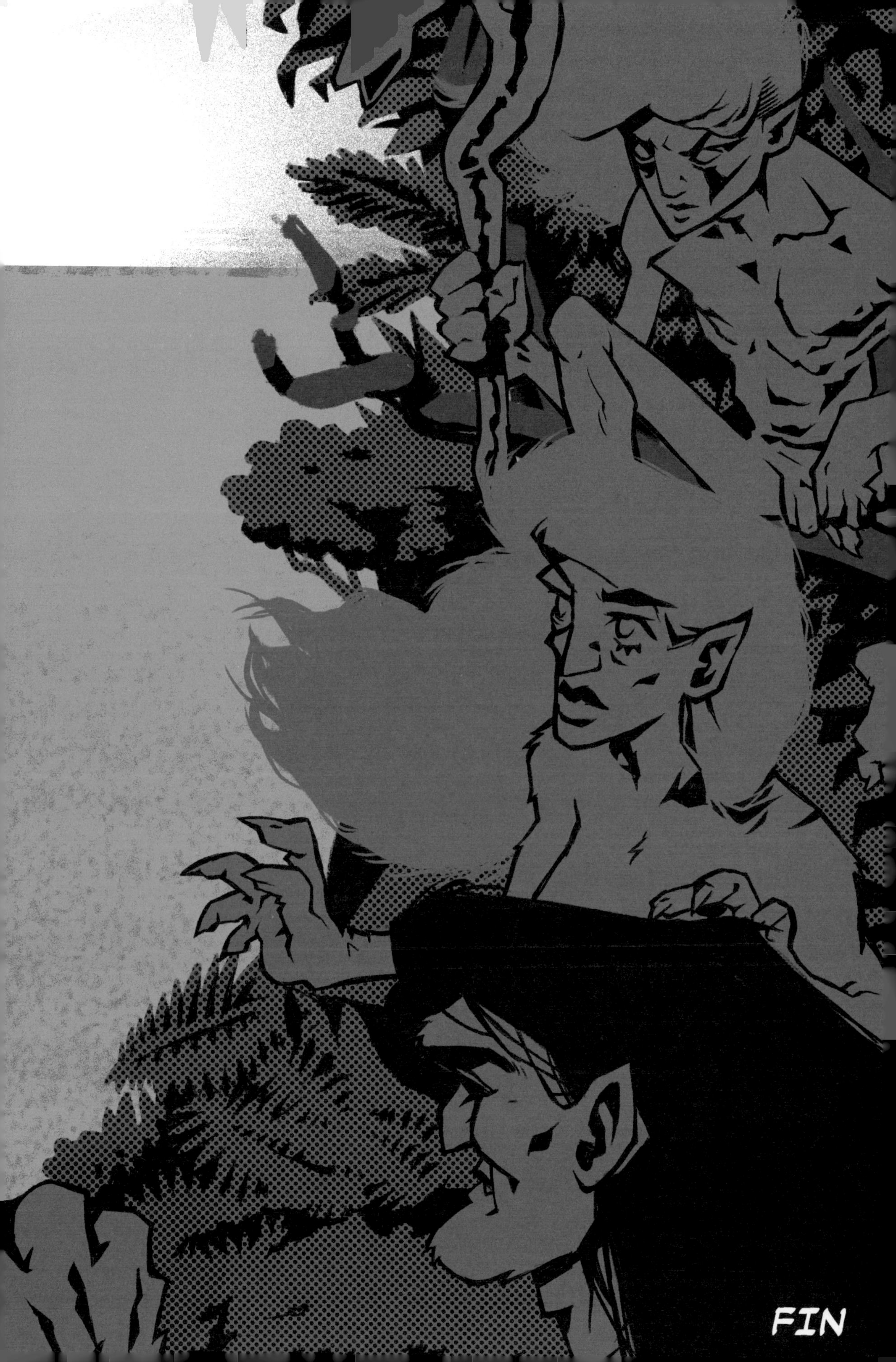
FIN

Appendix A

BESTIARY

ILLUSTRATIONS BY DAVID BUENO
TEXT BY ENRIQUE BERNARDOU

For many Paraguayans, animals – and particularly birds – serve as powerful portends. Their appearance at crucial moments can provide forecasts of what is to come through good and bad omens, and also reveal hidden connections to the past. In their illustrations, Enrique and David drew on the rich symbolism of birds and other critters to foreshadow the plot and fate of key characters. This bestiary is a field guide to the social significance of this multispecies community.

Mbói Chini / Cascavel (*Crotalus durissus*), p. 13
Rattlesnakes are venomous snakes that inhabit dry zones across all of Paraguay. Snake bites can cause the loss of a limb. In popular culture they are strongly associated with danger, both in Paraguay and globally. If Carly (Caroline Schuster's nickname) were to have encountered one in her travels, it would have been a big problem (even more so than the flaming Land Rover).

Urukure'a Chichi / Lechucita Vizcachera (*Athene cunicularia*), p. 23
In any pasture, especially near cattle, if you have a sharp eye to discern its expert camouflage you can spot these little owls perched on an old log or fence. Because of the way they blend in with the wood, they are silent observers of the events that take place in the countryside. If there are things that roam the hinterlands that human eyes cannot see, assuredly the owls have witnessed them.

Pitogüé / Benteveo (*Pitangus sulphuratus*), p. 23
Due to its distinctive song, it bears the name Benteveo, although in Paraguay it is much more common to hear the name Pitogüé. Like the Lechucita, this bird is also a witness. The name "Benteveo," or "I saw you well," refers to the popular belief that it witnesses lovemaking. Listening to "Pi-to-güé" on the patio at your house, for many, is a sure sign that a woman fell pregnant there. In the countryside, they are the pregnancy test par excellence.

Piririta (*Guira guira*), p. 39
The Piririta thrives in grasslands, scrub, and even urban areas. They prey on small animals, so they are always perched on low branches, poles, and bushes. They tend to gather in large flocks, which makes them masters of the landscape and everything that moves on it. If a snake were to appear in Wilfrido's path, the Piririta on his farm would be the first to know.
P.S.: Its scientific name comes from the word *guyra,* which means bird in Guaraní!

Mbói Chumbe / Serpiente de Coral
(*Micrurus corallinus*), p. 39
Another danger that menaces the grass-lands and farms. The coral snake is es-pecially deceptive due to its similarity to another species, called "False Coral" (*Lampropeltis triangulum*), which is harm-less. More than one unsuspecting person has met their end by striding confidently through the fields. Unlike many animals that appear in these pages as symbolic ele-ments, the ethnographic vignette with the Coral actually described a real danger to Wilfrido, Carly, and Kavajú Tuja during the field research for *Forecasts*.

Kururú Guasu / Sapo Toro (*Rhinella diptycha*), p. 55
A common visitor to rural houses, in-cluding the one Carly shared with Rocío. On a visit to their grandparents' house in the country, many Paraguayan urban-ites have been startled when they find a Kururú in the toilet (or the outdoor la-trine, which is still common in the coun-tryside). They come out in the rain, and their song (along with other amphibians) announces the arrival of storms. It is not entirely clear to me if this is the reason why so many people find them unpleasant, or if they simply disgust them a bit.
P.S.: The Kururú is related to the infamous "cane toad" that is an invasive plague in Australia.

Anó (*Crotophaga ani*), pp. 58, 74
Without a doubt, my favorite bird. It has a horned beak, which gives it a certain resemblance to a dinosaur. I typically see him sharing territory with the Piriritas on a path in Asunción where I usually go for a walk with my girlfriend. I am not aware of any negative symbolism in popular Paraguayan imaginaries, but in this story, he is a stand-in for crows (which are not native to Paraguay). Every time the Anó appears in the story, he is a bad omen.

Lembu Toro / Escarabajo Toro (*Megasoma acteon janus*), p. 61
These beetles are the largest species in Paraguay, reaching up to 11 cm. Their larvae, which inhabit tree trunks such as the samu'u (*Ceiba chodatii*), are a food source for Indigenous Aché people. In this story, he is one of the many creatures affected by pesticides, agrochemicals, and deforestation. For some, they are a pest that prevents farmers from producing the crops they sell; for others, they are the food.

Ypekú Akã Pytã / Carpintero Lomo Blanco (*Campephilus leucopogon*), p. 62
In Paraguay there are many species of woodpeckers. Toward the central region of the capital you can see species such as Ypekú Ñu (*Colaptes campestris*) or the Ypekú "La Novia" (*Melanerpes candidus*), but we decided to use this species because of its iconic place in Paraguayan popular culture. The red-headed Ypekú Akã Pytã is rare outside of northern zones.

Káva Mainumby / Avispa Verdugo (*Polistes carnifex*), p. 66
When it comes to working in the fields, countless problems can plague any technology more advanced than a burro and a manual sugar mill. A wasp nest in a switchbox would have been a perfectly common occurrence. And a nuisance that would have been easy to deal with if Freddy and the technician had something on hand to smoke out and ward off these relatively docile wasps.

Jarará Chica (*Bothrops diporus*), p. 85
Another of the feared and venomous specimens that haunt Wilfrido's farm. Its closeness to the sesame plants in the comic may herald a bad omen for the future of his family. What will the sesame harvest bring this year? Only God knows (and Professor Enrique Sabio, of course).

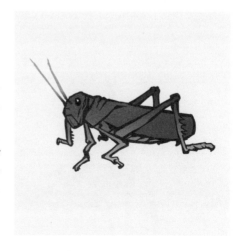

Chopĩ Estero / Pechoamarillo Grande (*Pseudoleistes guirahuro*), p. 86
This is another common bird in the capital, where I live. From afar I usually think it is a Pitogüé when I see it (because of the yellow breast), which is why it often comes to mind. I am not aware of any popular associations, but in our comic it acts as a Pájaro Burlón (mockingbird). There is a species called a "Chalk-browned Mockingbird" in English, and that we call "Calandria" (*Mimus saturninus*), but, honestly, I just discovered that when I was doing background research for this section. You can see that not everything in comics is meticulously planned.

Tuku Guasu / Langosta (*Tropidacris collaris*), p. 91
This pest is universally known as a destroyer of crops (of biblical proportions); even in Paraguay it is not uncommon to get news of vast plantations decimated by these insects. In the years it took us to produce this book, they appeared in large swarms, especially in the departments of Alto Paraguay and Boquerón. Like many other animals in our story, its presence does not bode well.

Karakará / Carancho (*Caracara plancus*), p. 94

It is very common to see this majestic eagle feasting on the remains of dead animals, especially those that were run over on the roads. They are opportunistic scavengers though they also hunt for live prey. Recently, they have even been sighted in urban areas. The first time I saw one was while I spoke to a professor at the National University of Asunción (UNA) campus. The Karakará was perched on the window of a building and I was amazed to think of this massive bird hanging around town.

P.S.: This is Carly's favorite Paraguayan bird! (And she says Paraguayan … because the Australian sulphur-crested cockatoo is the hands-down winner.)

Tatú Mulita / Armadillo de nueve bandas (*Dasypus novemcinctus*), p. 94

An animal that once was quite common across Paraguay, but recently has suffered significant decreases to its population, largely due to hunting. In Paraguayan barbecue, its meat is considered a rare delicacy. Personally, I have never dared to try – I find it far too cute to be on my plate. Another reason for its disappearance is the extreme drought in the Chaco region, one of its main habitats. I recently saw the Paraguayan film *Apenas El Sol* by Aramí Ullón (an excellent movie, by the way), and one scene shows several desiccated animal corpses, dried out by the relentless Chaco sun, and among them was a poor Tatú.

Akãngo / Hormiga Cortadora (*Atta laevigata*), p. 98

This ant was a nightmare of Enrique's childhood. It has a ferocious bite, which was traditionally used as a method to suture wounds and cuts. The children of my neighborhood used them to sow terror among other youth – I have traumatic memories of running away to avoid being bitten by one of these ants, wielded by a vicious playmate. If they did get you, the pain was excruciating. The cruelty of children knows no bounds.

Appendix B

ANTHROPOLOGY OF FINANCE CAPITAL AND CLIMATE CHANGE

At the time of writing, Don Wilfrido Medina is an 80-year-old farmer in Paraguay's rural sesame belt. At first glance, his life is completely disconnected from highflying centers of global finance: He struggles to get small loans from an agricultural cooperative to plant his crops, the family's only bank account is with the state's welfare system for the elderly poor, his ancient mobile phone does not support Paraguay's popular mobile money apps, and remittances are hand delivered by his children in cash when they come to visit. Yet for somebody so apparently "outside" of global capitalism, the fate of Wilfrido's farm is surprisingly entangled with the "techno-legal devices" (Ballestero 2019) of modern finance. And his primary commercial crops – niche export cereals including chia and sesame – are thoroughly financialized forms of life that couldn't survive in Paraguay without a complex economic support system, including nurturance from credit and insurance instruments. To understand value systems in the rural Paraguayan countryside, then, we must pay attention to a parallel story about commercial agriculture, the global reinsurance industry, weather data for the El Niño Southern Oscillation (ENSO), and investment in risk management systems by multinational development organizations. Global financial circuits are *generated* (Bear et al. 2015) out of the life projects and misadventures of people like Don Wilfrido.

All too often, these are connections that remain invisible. Poor farmers struggling with their sesame harvests appear to live in a separate world from European bankers or from satellite data or from climate change models. *Forecasts: A Story of Weather and Finance at the Edge of Disaster* is an effort to draw these crucial connections. It is a visual narrative that places disparate processes of financial capture and conversion in the same frame while juxtaposing their effects. And rather than depicting financial actors as shadowy comic book villains, it tells a people-centered story about the engineers who see progress in technical advances of modern commercial farming, of Paraguayan development experts who see democratic promise in "financial inclusion" for the poor, and of bankers who grasp the moral and social threat of planetary climate change.

The Anthropological Argument

According to Sigma, the research arm of Swiss Re[1] (a company that is among the largest global reinsurers), in 2020 the world suffered US$202 billion worth of economic losses due to natural and human-made catastrophes, with the insurance industry covering about US$89 billion of these costs.[2] However, this was not from a handful of major disasters. Many small events quickly add up. Surprisingly, the Swiss Re loss calculations suggest that 70 per cent of the insured losses in 2020 from natural catastrophes resulted from so-called secondary perils – that is, high-frequency, low-to-medium severity events such as thunderstorms, hail, wildfires, drought, flash floods, and landslides. While the wildfires in Australia and the United States certainly made news headlines globally, many of these secondary perils go unnoticed, both because they occur in remote areas and because they lack the sensationalism of large-scale events. Despite this, the industry expects secondary perils to become even more severe in the coming years as climate change produces ever more extreme weather patterns.

By the industry's own reckoning, weather peril is a growing concern, but we have an incomplete picture of how climate change contributes. Since events tend to be relatively small, granular data is often lacking and there isn't consistent monitoring. From the perspective of climate finance and global insurance systems, this is the technical promise of "financing for the future" – contracts literally written onto unpredictable future weather patterns, and that seek to anticipate the conditions under which, for instance, sesame plants live or perish. Meanwhile, global insurers and reinsurers have amassed staggering portfolios of financial assets, which in turn are vulnerable to climate risks. For instance, microfinance institutions (MFIs) are seeking ways to insure their loan portfolios against the effects of El Niño, since higher default rates can reduce the capital ratio, and they may be unable to find investors willing to recapitalize them during a crisis (Collier and Skees 2012, 57). The risk of portfolio-level losses has opened a wider conversation about Environmental, Social, and Governance (ESG) risks among the assets held by insurance companies, and where they should invest. In green bond markets to finance more resilient infrastructures (e.g., Tripathy 2017)? In sovereign risk facilities and catastrophe bonds (e.g., Johnson 2013a; Grove 2021; Collier and Cox 2021)? When discussions of "resilience" come up around climate risks, often these are directed toward ensuring the resilience of the companies themselves in the face of climate risks (Elliott 2021a).

Amidst this wider discussion of insurance and climate risks, index-based agricultural insurance (IBAI) has been heralded by international development agencies and humanitarian advocates as a crucial mechanism for bringing protection to vulnerable communities most impacted by weather disasters. If you are interested in reading more about IBAI, I suggest that you start with scholarship by Leigh Johnson (2013b; 2021), Sarah Aguiton (2019; 2021), and Nick Bernards (2018; 2019). Other helpful resources include Barry Barnett, Christopher Barrett, and Jerry Skees (2008), Nicole Peterson (2012), and Marcus Taylor (2016). From the angle of development policy, the World Bank (2011) has published important guidance for practitioners as well.

Much of the political economy debate about agricultural micro-insurance and rural development policy has focused on how risk is "governed" through insurance.[3] In the neoliberal era, this is strongly linked to the myriad ways risk has been devolved to individuals using market mechanisms like private insurance coverage to turn people into highly self-reliant subjects who feel intensely responsible for monitoring their own behavior and seeking out protection accordingly (Baker and Simon 2010; Ericson, Barry, and Doyle 2000). However, while classic debates about neoliberal governance took insurance as an exemplary case, the looming unknowns of large-scale and highly politicized planetary climate change suggest that we need to widen our view beyond individual risk-bearing subjects and their technologies of self-reliance. Many of these scholarly efforts to "zoom out" look at multi-scalar processes that bring together climate science, political institutions, advocacy groups, and property owners. For example, insurance is entangled in efforts to reassess the state's capacity to finance post-disaster recovery (Grove 2021) or urban planning and public policy (Elliott 2021b; Collier and Cox 2021). We can also appreciate the ambivalence of regulators and homeowners about new climate models in insurance markets (Gray 2021; Elliott 2021a).

In sum, insurance for climate risks has been forced to confront the vast uncertainty of global warming. For many in the industry, climate risks allow them to imagine unprecedented business opportunities and position themselves as "financial first responders" by "estimating and 'pricing in' risk, incentivizing mitigation, and unlocking recovery funds" (Collier, Elliott, and Lehtonen 2021, 162). And at an even larger scale, the global reinsurance industry has set itself out as a "thought leader" that's providing valuable planetary data that can help the world better understand climate risks, thus serving as "a mediating body that gives climate change a shape and presence; it objectifies and commodifies climate change as an uncertain phenomenon, yet presents it as manageable, at least to an extent" (Lehtonen 2017, 33). The role of insurance in climate financing, then, raises important questions about speculation – both speculation as a set of economic practices, as well as wider efforts to understand and control the future.

There has been a resurgent interest in speculation from social science researchers troubled by the effects of financialization. Looking through the lens of finance and securitization,[4] speculation often appears sinister. Lisa Adkins, for example, explores how "profit is yielded by finance capital from the non-chronological and indeterminate movements of speculative time" (2017, 450), which leaves debtors scrambling to constantly respond to recalibrations of pasts, presents, and futures as schedules of securitized debt adjust to their "possibles of payment." I am still paying a relatively modest student loan that I contracted in the early 2000s – the terms have changed so many times as it's been repackaged and resold, I've lost count. I still owe almost the entire principal – so this is an insight that hits close to home for many of us.

Scholars in the social studies of finance view this as a radical shift – the evolution of *homo speculans* from our ancestor, the rational and calculative *homo economicus* (Komporozos-Athanasiou 2022, 4–6). The efflorescence of speculative uncertainty and financial volatility, blooming wildly from neoliberalism's austere risk management, has profoundly reshaped the political, economic, and cultural order. For scholars studying financialization, the consequences are far-reaching: "faced with the perpetual domino of collapsing promises, from housing and healthcare to work security and family, the translation from fiction to facts is now all but sidestepped. More and more, *homo speculans* lingers in the space of fictions, not irrationally, but because fictions become the most reliable ordering principle in a protean reality" (26). The rise of speculative communities – collectivities bound by financialized relations, new technologies, and the uncertainties catalyzed by the failures of the neoliberal settlement – brings new attention to shared imaginings of the future. As Komporozos-Athanasiou suggests, "imagination is an act from which new meanings, rationalities, myths, narratives, and images of capitalism may always spring forth" (37). Working in the tradition of Benedict Anderson's classic *Imagined Communities* (2016), he calls for a more detailed account of how speculative communities construct collective imaginaries amidst extraordinary uncertainty and volatility.

Similarly, Laura Bear's recent work on speculation sets a research agenda centered on a political economy of *technologies* of imagination – "control of the means of speculation is governed by the distribution of contracts and credit in society" (Bear 2020, 2), which in turn hinges on ethical and moral evaluations of social difference. For feminist anthropologists like Bear, specific arrangements like contracts, collateral, insurance policies, and debts work powerfully to determine who has the right to buy the future. Importantly, these are technologies that can be traced ethnographically by anthropologists when they are put to use in social practice. Rather than simply a euphemism for "bad" or extractive finance, speculation does some hard work for these scholars by refocusing them on its operationalization through specific techno-legal devices (e.g., Ballestero 2019) such as indices and formulas, and which incite particular forms of labor, shared commitments, and social relations.

While speculation appears as the zeitgeist of our modern financialized way of life, it bears remembering that derivatives are not the only means of forecasting the future. This is a point made most forcefully by feminist and queer scholars of color such as Aimee Bahng (2018), who calls for decolonizing speculation by denying capitalism a monopoly on our imaginative faculties. Crucially, while the broken promises of the neoliberal compact and the collapse of risk logics may indeed manifest in digital practices like imagining endless possible partners or lifestyles while scrolling through Tinder or TikTok, those particular speculative imaginaries (rooted, broadly, in the Global North) reveal much less about the people and places that have experienced histories of empire and exclusion. By writing a story about speculation – financial and otherwise – from the perspective of Don Wilfrido, his family, and his agrarian community, we can appreciate how other forms of imagination are possible, indeed, how they are already happening. Bhang suggests that just this sort of subaltern politics presents radical alternatives to financial logics that "attempt to pull [the] horizon of the future into the present for profit" (2018, 7). A "queer speculation" can offer alternatives: departing from "the point at which one is pushed out of what could be called straight time, settler time, or the profitable time of compound interest – [one] can glimpse the horizon of the not yet, where not yet manifests itself not as a decree of foreclosure but as an embrace of the unknown" (7). For this reason, we conjugate *forecasts* (*pronósticos*) as plural. Wilfrido considers registers of speculation ranging from prophecy to gambling, insurance to horoscopes, loans to witchcraft. Those cultural logics of forecasting resist the financial colonization of the future while also grappling with the preexisting disparities of wealth that allocate heightened vulnerability and uncertainty to places such as rural San Pedro.

Our ethnographic exploration of forecasting resonates with research in "speculative anthropologies" (Anderson et al. 2018), a research area that focuses on the generative similarities between ethnography and science fiction. While these are genres of writing that might seem diametrically opposed – one focused on the organization of society in the here-and-now, the other on futuristic spaceships and alien forms of life – anthropology and science fiction are grounded in the same cultural relativism that seeks out alternative perspectives and worldviews. They also share common ancestry such as the work of Ursula K. Le Guin, daughter of famous anthropologists Theodora and Alfred Kroeber. Le Guin's novels about societies set among the stars influenced researchers like Donna Haraway, who explores science and technology in the contemporary United States. Anthropologists and speculative fiction writers share concerns around issues of alterity, which push both genres to "confront our world's inclusions and exclusions from across imaginaries of difference and thereby challenge the taken-for-granted by pushing boundaries of the individual and society, the human and alien, the planet, and life itself" (Anderson et al. 2018). Like Bhang's "queer speculation," speculative anthropologies offer alternative horizons of possibility that have not been immediately captured by financial value.

My point here is that speculation sits at the intersection of two value schemas: as an extractive mode of financial accumulation *and* a conceptual resource linked to ethnography – a toolkit to deal with the damage wrought by precisely those modes of accumulation in our troubled capitalist landscapes. Scholars of finance critique the deployment of technologies of imagination within financial arrangements that seek "to anticipate the future; to stimulate its emergence; and to control it" (Bear 2020, 8). Anthropologists of speculation imagine the weird, transgressive, and alien as excessive forms of life that escape the impulse to control.

I think this is a generative tension, and one that guided my approach to writing *Forecasts*.

Building on the anthropological debates about responsibility, risk, speculation, and technologies of imagination discussed here, the graphic novel is guided by the following orienting perspectives:

- **Temporalities of speculation matter**. Past grievance, debt, and loss needs to be accounted for in any imaginings of the future (that is, "technologies of imagination") – these are deeply social processes of rendering accounts of social difference, exclusion, violence, and peril. An ethnographic perspective offers tools to pay better attention to how different technologies of imagination account for "how we got here," the temporal shallowness or depth at which interdependency or obligation is understood to rest, and future accounts of "who owes what to whom."

- **Responsibility matters**. Some forms of loss demand active remediation and repair while others appear to be located "outside" of those more complex ethical and historical contexts, and are figured in terms of market mechanics, financing, and price. The same can be observed of wealth and profit. We need to pay careful attention to those maneuvers, because they are sites where privilege and social difference are enacted.
- **Loss matters**. Speculating about loss is as important as speculating about gain. Making loss manageable is not just a technical dimension of distributing risks and financing recovery. Rather than assuming that social understandings of grief, trauma, and hopefulness are "less sophisticated" accounts of the peril and economic costs of damaged environments, we must resist efforts to objectify and commodify climate change and seek out more nuanced and socially grounded perspectives.

Speculation and Loss in Practice

It was not until I found myself lining up for a 300-meter head-to-head race on horseback that I realized how profoundly I had misunderstood the complex social meanings of speculation in rural Paraguay. This was after nearly a year of studying insurance – an industry that prices risk professionally through actuarial sciences. I certainly felt *insecure* with my legs wrapped around what amounted to an airline flotation device that had been casually strapped to the back of Cohete (Rocket), the fierce little Quarter Horse that would – my *patron*, Don Wilfrido, hoped – carry me to victory. In this, *Forecasts* deviated from reality. Wilfrido's spirited mare, Yegua, had come up lame with a foot injury a week before the race. So, I found myself riding an unfamiliar mount, in addition to racing by unfamiliar rules. When it dawned on me that these local horse races were customarily ridden bareback not for functional reasons of enhanced speed, but rather for the thrilling spectacle of masculine bravado and horsemanship, my heart sank. No amount of reasoned debate about efficiency and velocity would afford me a set of stirrups or a helmet; the fun was in the riskiness of the venture, after all. At least for the spectators. After getting my adrenaline in check, I could appreciate the thrill of galloping headlong through fields, clutching the strap around Cohete's neck, eyes fixed on the finish line. And though I dreamed of losing many times (this was the ending that appears in *Forecasts*), Cohete and I actually won by a length. But I think Wilfrido would have enjoyed the spectacle either way.

After the race, the monies that had been distributed as payouts in the event's low-stakes betting were immediately redistributed again as we all bought cases of cold beer from the village grocery kiosk and gathered to recount the highlights of the day. Standing in a close circle under the shade trees, about a dozen local farmers took turns toasting the winners and consoling the losers (both jockeys and bettors) while debating the finer details of strategy, training, horse breeding, luck, and riding prowess. The amicable nature of the gathering supports anthropological research suggesting that, in some ritual contexts, gambling isn't about winning at all. In fact, a wager can pay off spiritual debts or recognize reciprocal obligations of kinship; it can even be "good" to lose (Klima 2002). While the farmers who had bet on the slower horse weren't exactly happy about their losses, their willingness to speculate on the outcome of a very uncertain venture was linked to shared community values that made the risks and rewards about so much more than just money changing hands.

And this is what spurred me to consider how I had misunderstood the collective enthusiasm for wagering on a horse race and the devil-may-care swagger of its jockeys. I had become accustomed to thinking about individual risks and the calculative logics of economic decision-making, and thus fixated on the profit/loss calculus of money changing hands. I was aghast when I learned Wilfrido had wagered Gs. 200,000 (US$40) on the race, which was more than the premium for the crop insurance I'd been tracking across the whole season. Global risk management, that is, "the ability to transform losses into opportunities" (Soederberg 2016, 2) by constantly optimizing cost/benefit analyses, is the guiding principle of both financial markets and disaster planning. I too had settled into the well-worn mental patterns and grooves of risk management frameworks, which worked relentlessly to individualize blame and responsibility (Lavinas 2013) while also placing great faith in entrepreneurial ability to make the most of that instability.

Cohete shook me out of that habitual thinking. The race was about so much more than a wager on individual risk and reward. It was about reaffirming community-wide normative expectations of masculinity; it was about recognizing the multispecies interdependency between horses and humans at the heart of this rural economy; it was about the thrill of a collective spectacle amidst endless bad news of crop failures and family hardship. Crucially, the social embedding of risk within a wider agrarian setting meant that participating in a speculative venture like wagering on the race actually reinforced bonds of reciprocal obligation that, while not clearly defined, would certainly prove useful in the future. This complexity made bounded, individualized accounting for risks, losses, and gains not only futile, but profoundly misdirected.

That is why *Forecasts* is about financial mechanisms that rearrange risk and vulnerability, but it is also about horoscopes and horse races, deadly snakes and devious Pomberos. Good ethnography – and particularly a graphic narrative – can be many things at once and offer multiple, sometimes contradictory points of view. It can breathe life into these diverse accounts of speculation and risk while allowing them to unfold across a complex and multi-perspectival story. This ethnography is about how the financial system is reimagining uncertainty using novel financial tools like weather insurance, and how centering risk management crowds out alternative forecasts and speculative imaginaries that organize life in the Paraguayan countryside. The anthropological argument of the book is that, rather than a limited site of expertise, organization, and control, speculation is socially embedded and takes many shapes. And this is true for financial arrangements too! Speculation manifests in the mischief of more-than-human monsters, in the fragility of kinship ties rendered tenuous by migration, and in ever-more-unusual weather patterns.

This requires a conceptual and analytic shift that reframes how speculation is experienced and who profits from it. Financial speculation is just as thoroughly socially embedded, as we can see from the moral quandaries faced by financial agents like Mario and Freddy and their almost millenarian faith in fintech to deliver its promised prosperity. Contract and credit propagate in Wilfrido's account too – they work on the world in and through the care and concern materialized in kinship and connection to land, and his cohabitation with sesame (a thoroughly financialized form of life). Contract and credit buy a "cleanse" to repair a long-ago and nearly forgotten evil, thereby animating renewed obligations of debt service. Anthropology has an important role to play in helping us understand these multiple points of view as well as their contingent alignments. Through long-term fieldwork in settings where many valuation practices comingle, an anthropological analysis can question the taken-for-granted naturalness of certain economic behaviors while rendering other seemingly strange value systems familiar.

Insurance is a financial technology that pools risk – the premium payments of the fortunate majority indemnify the unlucky few – and yet still translates those obligations into individual, technical, and contractual terms. For Wilfrido and other farmers working on commercial farms in San Pedro, speculation is what social anthropologists might call a "total social fact" that organizes all manner of interdependencies and is embedded in multiple social institutions: kinship, collective labor, religion, political affiliation, land management, and so on. Social losses like the absence of his family members to migration interact in complex ways with economic losses such as lack of field hands for the harvest. And the imponderabilia of these everyday commonplace losses present a direct challenge to the approach that seeks to *manage* risk in order to mitigate negative impacts and exploit positive opportunities. A running theme of the book, *pérdidas* – losses in Spanish – builds outward from farmers' challenges to the conventional approaches to financial risk and lays the groundwork for developing new social theories of economic interdependency based on alternative speculative imaginaries.

Crucially, the uninsured risks of environmental disasters are allocated to marginalized and racialized places such as rural Paraguay even while sites like Wilfrido's farm are remade into the experimental terrain where financial systems are adapted to the turbulence of climate change. Visually, the book focuses on the Paraguayan agro-industrial landscape and the characters who populate it. However, Wilfrido's field (*chacra*) of sesame is more than simply a setting. His *chacra*, a 3-hectare parcel of land, serves as a visual frame for the story. But the landscape of the *chacra* is co-constituted with the two sources of risk – weather and finance – that drive the narrative of *Forecasts*. Weather moves visually through the illustrations: darkening the sky, flooding the fields, and withering the sesame. Various characters also provide alternative (and sometimes competing) visual idioms for the weather, from screen shots of AccuWeather, to dream sequences imagining disaster-stricken landscapes, to technical models of the ENSO weather pattern. Meanwhile, finance also moves across the landscape. Political economy approaches to the study of capitalism have long emphasized the abstraction of finance and its untethering from the "real economy" (Appadurai 2015; LiPuma 2017). By illustrating the story, financial products are emplaced visually into the agro-industrial setting via their material infrastructures like weather stations that generate the data for insurance, money that changes hands to pay debts or make purchases, and cell phones that connect farmers to both the weather index and their kids. The landscapes of finance are given a visual identity that connects them to Wilfrido's fields by making explicit the sites and scales at which accumulation and speculation take place, whether in Asunción or the Multiactiva or the orbital trajectories of satellites.

However, this book is not a "follow the money" story of exploitation that uncovers the shadowy workings of a complex financial conspiracy. There isn't a *The Big Short* cinematic moment that reveals the sinister inner workings of derivatives markets via metaphorical champagne towers. That is because these derivatives work precisely as depicted in the graphic narrative: through glitchy weather stations that need wasp nests cleared out, through harried brokers leaving home at 4 a.m. to make the rounds to rural farms, through decades of development policy that has pushed for commercial export crops, through snazzy networking events that raise enthusiasm for fintech, and through credit-based financing arrangements that fund agrochemicals. This story tells a more complex truth: that Wilfrido would be the last to romanticize his agrarian way of life, and that his financial backers struggle with the moral quandaries of profiting from disasters. In the best tradition of comics, the protagonists of *Forecasts* develop in painful, intimate, and complicit connection with one another. And, crucially, these are the very people that *make* this financial system work. The visual medium of graphic ethnography reveals both their internal thoughts and motivations, as well as complex interactions and discussions between key characters. The following section will explore those visual conventions in further depth.

What Comics Can Teach Us about Life in the Anthropological "Multiverse"

"We are not in the worst of all possible timelines," wrote *Atlantic* magazine journalist Yascha Mounk (2020) early on in the US response to the novel coronavirus. "And yet, our hopes for the pandemic's quick resolution should clearly be shelved … We need to start to prepare for a darker reality." Writing in May of 2020, Mounk could not have foreseen just how deep the crisis would become. Throughout the COVID-19 pandemic, the public has been updated daily on public health models and seemingly ubiquitous references to "flattening the curve," epidemiological forecasts, infection rates, and so on, all of which imply other versions of reality where the COVID-19 response might have unfolded differently. We are invited to imagine possible futures and alternative worlds: where hospitals are not overrun with sick patients, where generalized quarantine measures are eased, where travel can resume.

This notion of "the worst of all possible timelines" – alternative hopeful or dark realities – is commonsensical even while *also* being imbued with the outlandish narrative conventions of science fiction. It is a narrative device used throughout this book. Readers of *Forecasts* may have initially been perplexed by the "in another version …" stories at the end of several sections of the graphic novel, but perhaps also recognized the recurring trope of "the worst of all possible timelines." These alternative accounts of "another version of this story" speculate on other possible directions that events might have taken. And since it is an anthropological multiverse, they are plausible alternatives – ethnographic stories of other, divergent Don Wilfridos. The first time we jump to an alternate ending, we confront the terrible risks of injury and illness from farming accidents in a timeline where Wilfrido is bitten by a coral snake while planting sesame. Other crises take shape in "alternate endings," from crop failure to witchcraft. This *ethnographic speculation* is not a flight of fancy – these scenarios actually arose from fieldwork.[5] As ethnographic speculation, they are nonfictional because they (1) were drawn directly from local discussions and preoccupations with "what if?," and represent an effort to document and take seriously those imaginative repertoires, and (2) in many cases, charted events that actually did befall members of the community. The anthropological multiverse presented by *Forecasts* offers a concrete proposal for ethnographic speculation that is grounded and empirical while also being committed to a particular point of view: "An empiricism that admits that one never gets to the bottom of things, yet also accepts and even celebrates the disavowals required of us given a world that forces us to act" (Rutherford 2012, 2). I think that an anthropological multiverse as both theory and method has a powerful role to play as we consider how to live through multiple overlapping crises. This book is our incipient effort to sketch how that might be done.[6]

I will address research methods in Appendix D and discuss the challenges of presenting the "true story" of empirical data as graphic narrative nonfiction. However, a separate discussion of the narrative structure of multiple timelines will address the intersecting logics of financial speculation and comics storytelling.

What is particularly uncanny for me about the constant stream of alternatives, models, and scenarios that characterize climate-based disaster risk management and the COVID-19 pandemic is the sense that I've been here before, that is, in the global climate change timelines anticipated by the financial actors that have been at the center of my ethnographic research program. In the course of the fieldwork at the heart of this book, I found myself sitting in a hotel conference room at the Hilton in Bogotá, in the center of Colombia's financial district. I was an academic delegate for an industry meeting sponsored by Fasecolda, Colombia's peak commercial body for insurance. They were leading a regional conference on *microinsurance* – insurance products aimed at low-income people traditionally excluded from financial services. The meeting wrapped up with a scenario modeling exercise where groups of conference attendees were engaged in a role-playing exercise. Think *Dungeons & Dragons* for bankers and policy wonks. We were faced with a series of potential environmental catastrophes and each group had to imagine and narrate a set of possible responses based on the "character" they were allocated. These, in turn, were iterative and interactive. When the local government team presented their policy responses to widespread flooding, the team tasked with representing the agricultural cooperative had to decide if they would make weather-indexed insurance compulsory for members, or if the cooperative itself would use its capital to purchase weather-linked bonds as part of their investment portfolio, thereby transferring the financial exposure holistically. It was an exercise in collective storytelling, of conjuring multiple timelines and divining their key features. It was an effort to buy the future by envisioning alternative worlds and investing in the most profitable one.

While the financial system has often been analyzed in terms of apparently technical "calculative agencies" (Callon and Muniesa 2005) of pricing models and yield curves (Zaloom 2009), recent scholarship in the anthropology of finance has taken a different approach to the combined financial and climate crises. As the economy has re-geared to manage and price risk, a range of political and economic actors have looked for new techniques to forecast the future. Rather than a threat to global capitalism, "when uncertainty is standardized, homogenized and made calculable, it can be given a price and it can be bought and sold. Not only has it been economized, but also it has been made into an essential commodity of the current capitalism" (Lehtonen and Hoyweghen 2014, 532). This process of "economizing" uncertainty depends in part on "hard data," but also on the creativity of imagining the future.

An important technique for engineering financial markets that can absorb emergent risks is *scenario planning* for incalculable, uncertain contexts: "a forecasting technique which attempts to divine not this or that aspect of the future but the *multiple future worlds* attendant on alternative actions in the present" (Cooper 2010, 170). Scenario modeling combines formal game-theory modeling and mathematical rigor with affective and "prospective" orientations to the future (e.g., wishfulness, belief, confidence, and trust). In the hands of energy companies like Shell and ELF, which were concerned about the effects of energy crises on the long-term profitability of their industry in the 1970s, the imaginative impulse at the heart of scenario modeling was far from benign. As Melinda Cooper reminds us, it is "too closely invested in the operations of power to reflect on its constitutive idealism, an idealism that blinds it to the intimate relationship between imperialism in the speculative mode and the preemptive form of political violence" (2010, 171). By preemptive political violence, Cooper is calling attention to the deployment of force – including wealth, influence, and so on – to engineer the future by aligning it with the desires and values of certain actors. Some futures are stillborn so that others can thrive (e.g., Haraway 2018; Murphy 2018).

Scenario modeling is not the only economic tool to anticipate the future. Probabilistic statistical approaches are a mainstay of economics, and use tools such as structural equations, time-series analysis in econometrics, dynamical simulation models such as climate and policy impact analysis, and so on. These are all based on historical data to make projections, with future states of the world having a specific probability of being realized (Tuomi 2019, 5). By contrast, scenario modeling was popularized after the Royal Dutch/Shell Company deployed it in response to the oil crisis of the 1970s. What is notable about the "gold standard" model propagated by the Global Business Network (known as the GBN/Schwartz scenario approach) is that uncertainty is used methodologically to generate alternative future states of the system (Tuomi 2019, 8). As Tuomi (2019, 8) suggests

The aim is to generate surprising, novel and relevant stories about possible futures, and these are then explained as causal consequences of events that could lead to the imagined outcome. Scenarios can therefore generate images of the future that are considerably richer than those provided by probabilistic approaches.

As I found in the scenario modeling exercise that took shape at the microinsurance summit in Bogotá, the organizing principle of "plausibility" meant that a narrow set of stories could be collectively imagined. As Tuomi suggests, "some narratives are inherently believable, diffuse virally, and are recreated whenever imaginary visions of the future are produced" (8). Speculation as viral financial memes.

The "Plausible" Multiverse

Does this style of reasoning remind you of anything? For comic book fans, imaginary visions of the future and alternate realities are a familiar conceptual terrain. Comics have a rich tradition of experimenting with sequential narratives that time-jump (Kukkonen 2010): visually juxtaposing timeframes, slowing down and speeding up the plot, creatively deploying flash forward and flash back to aid character development, and so on. The storyworlds of classic superhero comics like Superman, Batman, or The Avengers have been penned by a rotating lineup of authors and artists, resulting in narrative inconsistencies. Comic book nerds out there will recall that the DC Universe was especially plagued by this incoherence (e.g., Morrison 2015). Fans are challenged to navigate the continuity problems of stories and characters that develop in a fragmented and often-contradictory reality. A narrative work-around emerged in the 1980s: "Superhero comics made a virtue out of necessity and presented their storyworlds as part of a larger 'multiverse,' in which a variety of mutually incompatible narrative worlds existed as parallel realities. Villains aim to turn the entire multiverse into their dominion, and superheroes unite to maintain the status quo across storyworlds" (Kukkonen 2010, 40).

In superhero comics, the multiworld model of reality is an ontological given. These mutually incompatible realities feature not only distinctive perspectives, styles, and storylines; they also often develop "counterfactual scenarios involving alternative developments of the story" (Kukkonen 2010, 41). Classic examples such as Marv Wolfman's (2018) *Crisis on Infinite Earths* (1985–86) see the heroes of the DC publishing house team up to face a universe-wide threat, while also encountering alternate versions of themselves. Later examples such as Alan Moore's (2009) *Tom Strong* (1996–2006) and Warren Ellis's (2014) *Planetary* (1999–2009) offer meta-commentary on the superhero genre. *Tom Strong* depicts the titular hero incarnated as a character in myriad pop-culture styles from the twentieth century, including styles popularized by pulp fiction and superhero comics, while *Planetary* offers a meta-reflection on sequential art and comics storytelling itself.

The interplay between the constitutive idealism of scenario planning and preemptive deployment of force (whether buying the future or co-opting political actors) shares some commonalities with multiverse storytelling in comics. The politics of pre-emption (De Goede and Randalls 2009) – that is, a preemptive strike on undesirable futures – is a technology to make the future actionable for crises perceived as "total threats." Scenario planning promises to deliver a world without surprises, since all unexpected risks have been foretold and foreclosed. It is *also* the animating logic of multiverse stories like *Crisis on Infinite Earths.* The narrative device of total threats (whether villainous antimatter plot, or energy crisis, or climate change) deploys a speculative imagination of multiple future worlds in order to confirm a normatively white heterocapitalist patriarchal existence for the heroes of Earth-One … or multinational corporations like Shell and Enron. Saving the day means conserving the current way of life, no matter how unjust or inequitable it is. Put another way, the idealism at the heart of multiverse storyworlds can be profoundly conservative if aimed at confirming the status quo distributional order. A similar critique has been leveled at climate financing, which sees climate change as manageable, and is committed to conserving the comfort and lifestyle of the current distributional order.

Comic genres in Latin America have experimented with other chronotopes that challenge the conservatism of a "politics of preemption" at the heart of multiverse narratives. For a sweeping overview of distinctive Latino symbolization, narrative conventions, and comics creators, see Aldama and González (2016). One of the most important works of graphic fiction (*historietas*) produced in Latin America, *El Eternauta* (1957–59) or *The Eternaut* (meaning "eternal traveler"), was authored by Argentinean writer Héctor Germán Oesterheld and drawn by Francisco Solano López. While *The Eternaut* was situated within the genre conventions of adventure comics, the narrative follows the "sad and desolate condition as a time pilgrim" of the protagonist, Juan Salvo (cited in Haywood Ferreira 2010, 281), thus recasting the heroic tropes of space explorers. After an alien invasion decimates the planet, an intrepid group of scientists invent a time travel mechanism to try to defeat the colonizing force and bring about an alternate future. The frame story in which the figure of the *guionista* (writer of comics) records the Eternaut's tale subverts the continuity of linear time and positionality, as Juan Salvo is doomed to search through time and space for his lost family. The multiverse is a setting of iterative experiences of loss, pain, and grief rather than conquest and heroic triumph (Foster 2013).

Oesterheld became increasingly active in politics, particularly as a member of the Montonero guerrilla group that supported popular revolution against Latin America's repressive authoritarian regimes in the 1970s (Foster 2016). For this, along with more radical scripts for later instalments of *Eternautas,* Oesterheld was "disappeared" – detained, tortured, and killed – by the Argentine military in 1977 along with his four daughters. A forceful critique of the intimate relationship between imperialist expansion and preemptive political violence (to recall Melinda Cooper's framing) was a constitutive feature of radical Latin American comic book storytelling. Indeed, Argentina's internationally acclaimed humorous comic strip *Mafalda* shows how the comedically rebellious middle-class youth of the 1970s were reframed as politically subversive under the dictatorship, where "state terrorism would brutally demonstrate just how little space there was in Argentina for the young, antiestablishment generation depicted in the strip" (Cosse 2014, 35). Politically pointed critique of the status quo was a vital narrative component of Latin America's graphic tradition, for which comics creators paid a deadly high price.

Contemporary Latin American comics continue to experiment with nonlinear narratives as part of an explicit decolonial agenda. For this, a touchstone volume is *Graphic Indigeneity* (Aldama 2020). Javier García Liendo (2020, 146) analyzes the fractured and multidimensional narrative of memory in the Peruvian comic *Nuestros Muertos* (*Our Dead*). He argues that the comic represents the history of Peru's violent past in a manner deliberately fractured and confusing, and that it further uses "categories of Indigenous thought as a way to introduce forms of the production of meaning that serve as alternatives to the linear discourse of History" (146). This style of narration is demanding. It requires a "detective-reader capable not only of connecting and reconstructing the pieces and narratives of memory, but also of putting down the comic book in order to research Peru's political and cultural past" (146). Eisner Award–winning comics scholar Frederick Luis Aldama (2017) has designated this process "co-creation," whereby the reader is so emotionally and cognitively involved in the work that they become its co-author. Challenging conventions of historical narrative is key in contemporary Latin American comics. Daniel Parada's comic series *Zotz,* which tells an alternate history of Mesoamerica, begins by directly addressing the reader, which is a "gesture typical of the meta-cooperative aspects of graphic narrative storytelling" (Santos 2020, 182). Jorge Santos, a scholar of Latinx comics, argues that *Zotz* makes use of oral tradition and graphic methods, both of which are central to Indigenous cultural traditions and challenge status quo multicultural politics that erases Indigenous sovereignty and self-determination (Santos 2020; see also Rutherford 2020). On history, national identity, and comics in the Americas, see L'Hoeste and Poblete (2009). For a further discussion of posthumanism and science fiction in Latin American graphic novels, see Edward King and Joanna Page (2017).

By calling attention to the synergies between scenario modeling and the comics multiverse, my argument throughout is that finance is an idiom and practical mechanism for editing out and erasing stories that don't contribute to accumulation. Seen as such, new and alternative models to explain the causal consequences of events are both subversive and generative – they conjure new worlds while casting doubt on who has the right to buy the future.

Ethnographic Speculation

After engaging with anthropological theories of finance and speculation, we can look at Don Wilfrido's entanglement with IBAI insurance with greater nuance. Use the anthropological concepts presented here to discuss the following questions.

Discussion Questions

1. Are there heroes and villains in *Forecasts*? Why or why not? What does your answer reveal about the social, economic, and environmental injustices propagated by modern financial arrangements and how we might organize to confront them?
2. Feminist scholars of finance have argued that capitalism is *generated* out of diverse life projects, often by capturing and converting the value created through kinship, care, intimacy, cultivation, and sustenance (Bear et al. 2015). What do we learn about masculinity, domestic labor, and kinship in *Forecasts*? How is kinship presented as a gendered set of relations? Discuss how gender takes shape in the financial arrangement and economies depicted in the graphic ethnography. Consider what this reveals about what sorts of people and activities are classified in the realm of the "properly economic," and what's pushed out of or erased from that definition.
3. Make a list of the speculative imaginaries in *Forecasts* and compare these to the debates about financial speculation surveyed in this appendix. Compare and contrast.
4. Consider how the multiverse is depicted in popular media (movies, TV shows, comics, literature). Choose some examples and use the key themes from this chapter to analyze and interpret them.

Essay Topics

1. Using examples from *Forecasts* and from this review essay, define and evaluate alternative theories of "loss" within the value systems of insurance,

development, kinship, and agriculture. Use specific examples to support your claims.

Research-based option: Based on these insights, develop a case study related to environmental damage and climate risks.

Reflective essay option: Use the three "Rs" of reflective essay writing to apply these insights to your own experience of loss. (1) **Retell** an example of loss or losses that you explore through autoethnographic self-study. (2) **Relate** your example to the anthropological discussion of value systems developed above. (3) **Reflect** on how you've deepened and/or reevaluated your understanding of social theories of loss and losses through this exercise.

2. In discussions of Latin American agrarian livelihoods, the category of "peasant" (*campesino*) has often been defined as a class status – that is, a relation to a particular mode of agrarian production. Read Jane Collins's classic essay on how the household figures in subsistence agriculture, wage labor, and the shifting political economy of agrarian settings. (Collins, Jane L. 1986. "The Household and Relations of Production in Southern Peru." *Comparative Studies in Society and History* 28 (4): 651–71.)

   How would you update Collins's analysis in light of the integration of Wilfrido and members of his community into wider financial systems? How does the household shift as a socioeconomic unit when it becomes financialized?

Activities

1. *Unpacking your wallet*: Take stock of all the financial products, services, and relationships that you carry around with you – often invisibly – every day. This can include credit and debit cards, cash, but also loyalty cards with cash-back bonuses, vouchers, coupons, airline miles, and so on. Also take stock of your phone and all the apps related to financial services. Do any of these include secret insurance policies (e.g., debt cancellation insurance, life insurance, property insurance, travel insurance, health coverage, and so on)? How would you find out? Lead a wider discussion of the "financialization of everyday life."

2. *Develop a glossary*: Using *Forecasts* and this appendix, develop a glossary of unfamiliar terms related to finance and climate change. Start with the obvious candidates, like index-based agricultural insurance (IBAI), agricultural credit, reinsurance, weather derivatives, basis risk, and so on. Then branch out. You may need to do more research to develop your definitions.

3. Write a short story from the point of view of any of the characters *except* for Wilfrido or Caroline. Consider the moral dilemmas they face when grappling with the future, speculation, loss, and peril. What personal and social resources

do they have to resolve these dilemmas? What value frameworks do they use to make sense of their situation?

Optional graphic exercise: Write this as a script and perhaps storyboard it as sequential art.

Optional research exercise: Develop an annotated bibliography of background research that will support the story/scriptwriting.

4. Choose an environmental issue facing your community and do some background research. In groups, create "characters" to represent different points of view and stakeholders involved. Run through a scenario planning activity to role-play how your community is going to respond. What different scenarios do you come up with, based on different perils? In the wrap-up discussion, consider the "plausibility" of different scenarios and from what point of view they are reasonable and believable. Which perspectives are left out of the modeling activity? What temporalities are mobilized to make your decisions and act?

Appendix C

AGRARIAN TRANSFORMATIONS

ILLUSTRATIONS BY GUILLAUME MOLLE

The scene in *Forecasts* set in the rooftop "after-office" networking event on fintech (11–12) epitomizes the buzz surrounding and enthusiasm for techno-solutionism in development – that is, the promise that technological innovations will fix social problems like poverty, gender discrimination, racial bias, and so on. Daniel Greene dubs this the *access doctrine*, which decrees that "the problem of poverty can be solved through the provision of new technologies and technical skills, giving those left out of the information economy the chance to catch up and compete" (Greene 2021, 5). This is the revolutionary and optimistic future promised by fintech. Greene suggests that even though techno-solutionism doesn't actually offer up a better life or more opportunities for any but a handful of adopters, the magical simplicity of the access doctrine is a feature, not a bug. The simple solution of technological skills and access allows organizations – in this case, development NGOs, policy teams, and financial specialists – to reimagine themselves as a conduit for innovation and social uplift. Even though many are aware that the issue of poverty and inequality is much more complicated, the techno-solutionism narrative is so appealing (and fundable!) that nobody can give it up. Rather than simply describing predetermined and inevitable social and technological progress, the access doctrine is a form of social engineering.

One important feature of fintech is its self-described newness. This is a key reason why the technology and skills training at the core of the access doctrine have such a powerful hold. Many of my Paraguayan fintech interlocutors adopted language that would be right at home in the tech world: "disrupting" traditional banking practices, innovating, platforming, creating app ecologies, integrating, and so on. And brand-new digital and financial skills would be summoned to adapt to this new technology.

To contextualize the narrative of techno-solutionism at the heart of fintech within longer histories of development and interventionism in Latin America, I am going to go back in time to the archaeological record of migration of Tupi-Guaraní speaking people from the central Amazonian region, to the incorporation of Guaraní people into the Spanish Empire in the sixteenth century, and to major post-independence nineteenth-century financial upheavals that reshaped life in the territory that has now become Paraguay.[7] Fintech is far from the first technological innovation that has promised to mitigate inequality and lift agrarian communities out of poverty. Romanticized narratives of tropical forests and "innocent" Guaraní "natives" recur in European writing about the early colonial period. To understand the succession of political and social experiments that profoundly reshaped agrarian society along the Paraná River and its Atlantic forests, we must dispense with both the romantic image of life in the jungle, as well as simplistic understandings of social and technological change since the sixteenth century. Looking at the long history of social engineering on the southeastern coast of the Americas challenges many of the underlying assumptions that feed into the fintech narrative.

Amazonian Horticulturalists

This agrarian history begins with the large-scale human movements of Tupi-Guaraní languages speakers, who expanded their territory throughout eastern South America about 2,000 years ago (Noelli 1998). For a long time, history and ethnography greatly influenced the deterministic and evolutionist theories on the Tupi migrations. Historical linguistics and archaeology, and more recently genetic studies, have now provided new insights on the origins, expansion routes, and cultures of the Tupi-Guaraní groups. Archaeologists heavily rely on the ceramic markers of the Guaraní groups, especially the Amazonian Polychrome Ceramic Tradition (with a white background and various geometric designs) attesting for human movements out of central Amazonia. Various models of expansion have been proposed since the 1970s, including patterns of migration along the largest branches of the Amazon River (Lathrap 1970). Continued works by Brochado (1984) and others have refined the expansion routes southward including the Paraná and Uruguay rivers (Bonomo et al. 2015; Noelli 1998; Noelli 2004; Noelli, Brochado, and Corrêa 2018) while more nuanced approaches to ceramic typologies further building on ethnographic data came to consider "ethnicity as an identifiable process in the observable patterns of the material culture," in an effort to characterize this episode of

Funerary urn from the site ACH-LP-07, Santa Catarina, Brasil (After Castro 2019)

Yapepó (storage container) from the Salto Grande area, Entre Ríos, Argentina (After Castro 2019)

human dispersion (López Mazz and López Cabral 2020). Additionally, radiocarbon dates obtained from a series of sites in Brazil, Paraguay, and Argentina refuted early ethnographers' view of a quick migration close to European contact, and rather pushed the Tupian expansion back in time to 2,000 years ago, and maybe earlier. Tupi groups were certainly present on the coast of Rio de Janeiro in about AD 300, with only few dates available from Paraguay later than the tenth century. Antiquity and processes of human movement still require more work, but archaeology significantly increased our understanding of traditional Guaraní cultures, especially with regards to settlement patterns and subsistence practices.

Guaraní archaeology reveals interesting patterns around settlement, hunting, and landscape management. López Mazz and López Cabral (2020) suggest that, in addition to characteristic ceramics traditions, "at an archaeological level, the Guaraní can also be defined as a singular way of occupying space." Drawing on ethnohistorical data, Noelli et al. (2019) and Milheira (2014) suggest that the Teko á, sometimes referred to as *tekoha* (Chase-Sardi 1989) – that is, a well-designed settlement with main villages connected to secondary settlements with specific use – was a defining feature of Guaraní groups dispersed over long distances and connected as a lowland world-system. Some research attributes this settlement pattern to the advantages afforded by proximity to the Paraná and Uruguay rivers, drawing on theoretical frameworks of ecological niche construction and environmental risk condition (Loponte and Carbonera 2017, 5). However, zooarchaeological data analyzing skeletal parts present in several assemblages suggest a more nuanced approach, where river access is not the only functionalist driver of settlement patterns. Subsistence strategies with broader biodiversity is "a particular signature of these

Nivaclé grater, piece of Stetsonia coryne (?) wood with toothed metal plate. From a site on the Pilcomayo River, Paraguay. Museo Etnográfico 'Juan B. Ambrosetti' (Buenos Aires) (After Kamienkowski and Arena 2017)

horticulturalists" (Acosta, Carbonera, and Loponte 2019, 1006): they not only relied on fishing but also on hunting small and larger preys in areas surrounding the villages while they further invested in crop management and plant gathering. Thus, they progressively transformed the primary forest into productive areas. Landscape management was complexly related to other settlement patterns, including the relocation of villages every three or four years, which allowed abandoned fields to be used as "hunting gardens" (1008).

Ethnohistorians focusing on the colonial encounter between Guaraní people and Spanish colonists draw on archaeological and historical accounts to understand precolonial Guaraní society. Ganson, for instance, describes a strict gender-based division of labor. Men were allocated intermittent activities like hunting, fishing, and clearing fields, as well as traveling to other villages and preparing for conflict. Women's work included planting and harvesting manioc, corn, beans, squashes, and sweet potatoes. They also engaged in a range of productive tasks such as gathering honey and palm hearts, transporting water, producing pottery and cotton weavings (blankets and hammocks), and preparing food (Ganson 2005, 18). Both men and women harvested tree branches and straw to build long houses. Multiple families resided under one roof, as "settlements of five or six long houses usually had two or three hundred inhabitants" (18).

The evidence suggests that Guaraní people were adept "Amazonian horticulturalists" (Acosta, Carbonera, and Loponte 2019) with a deep relationship to human landscapes developed through complex mobility patterns.

The Jesuit Reductions

By the early sixteenth century, Spanish invaders (explorers, settlers, missionaries, and conquistadores) began to arrive on the southeastern coast of the Americas.

When Juan Díaz de Solís made his way to the area in 1516, Indigenous people residing near the river that Guaraní people named Paraná-guazú (later renamed Río de la Plata by the invaders) killed him using clubs, bows and arrows (Ganson 2005, 23). After a further series of expeditions in which the Spanish were repelled, in 1537 Juan de Ayolas made a more than 1,000-mile journey upriver, arriving at a large Cario-Guaraní settlement (with a population of as many as 24,000 people). After violently subjugating the Guaraní warriors, the Spanish established a settlement that they called Nuestra Señora de Santa María de Asunción – which later became the capital of the Spanish colony and, later still, the capital city of Paraguay. This was not a peaceful intercultural encounter – violence characterized many colonial situations in the Americas. After a revolt was brutally put down, the Spanish Crown directed the governor to "establish a more formal mechanism to extract tribute (a head tax) from male Indians between the ages of eighteen and fifty in the form of forced labor, the *encomienda* (a grant usually given to a Spaniard of the right to receive tribute and/or labor from a group of Indians; it carried the obligation to Christianise the Indians)" (Ganson 2005, 23). In 1556, some 20,000 Cario-Guaraní were allocated to 320 Spanish *encomenderos*. By 1580, most lived in Franciscan villages that tied mobile Amazonian horticulturalists to settlements through forced labor (*mitayo*).

The Jesuits arrived relatively late in Paraguay (1609–1768; see Wilde 2011); their order was only established in 1540 during the Counter-Reformation in Europe. The Jesuits set about creating *reducciones* – that is, organized settlements that missionized Indigenous Guaraní people and were self-sustaining social, economic, and cultural orders.[8] However, while the *reducciones* have been described in both colonial documents and later by historians as rigidly organized and bounded settlements – some went as far as to call them utopian communities (Cunninghame Graham 1901; see also Wilde 2017) – they were both internally quite diverse and also much more porous than the strict separation between "*indios reducidos*" and "*indios infieles*" ("reduced *indios*" vs "infidel *indios*") would suggest (Wilde 2011). Despite the complex sociopolitical landscape composed of multiple Indigenous communities, the *reducciones* certainly sought to impose European and Christian beliefs and values. In her history of *The Guaraní Under Spanish Rule*, Ganson notes that the Jesuit beliefs about the Guaraní were patronizing for the duration of their missionization. "[They] approached their missionary work from a standpoint of cultural superiority. This perceived superiority was based on their [self-described] advanced education, technical skills, knowledge of the arts and sciences, and strong sense of moral rightness. They were entirely convinced that their intentions were good and that the Guaraní needed their protection and guidance" (34). Through their *reducciones*, the Jesuits profoundly reshaped the daily life, social roles, and

Map of the Jesuit Reductions

Paraguay

Santa Maria de Fe
San Ignacio Guazu
Santa Rosa
Jesus
Trinidad
Corpus
San Cosme
Itapua
San Ignacio Mini
Santiago
Loreto
Candelaria
Santa Ana
Martires
San Jose
San Carlos
San Javier
Apostoles
Santa Maria la Mayor
Argentina
Conception
Sao Nicolau
Santo Angelo
Santo Tome
San Luis
Sao Joao
Sao Borja
Sao Laurencio
San Miguel
Brasil
La cruz
Yapeyu

A Jesuit father,
Brazil, 18th century

political organization of the Guaraní living in the mission system (Susnik 2017). At their height, the population of the Jesuit *reducciones* on the Paraná and Uruguay rivers reached 141,182 people, far exceeding the populations of other missions in the Americas (52–3).

Key to the success of the Jesuit *reducciones* was the priests' tactical incorporation of certain Guaraní cultural practices. Ganson suggests that "to make the missions function properly and prosper economically, the Jesuits utilized the political, social, and economic structures in Guaraní society to ensure continuity and stability" (2005, 58). For instance, they maintained important political roles such as *cacicazgos* (i.e., the leadership of *caciques*), where traditionally Guaraní warriors and elders selected their *caciques* on the basis of talents like bravery, knowledge, and oratory skills. The Jesuits maintained the social status of *caciques* but converted the role into a hereditary chiefdom. This political structure – where *caciques* were the delegated leaders on an "Indian *cabildo*" (where Jesuit-authorized Guaraní chiefs oversaw their subjects) and were responsible for the recruitment of Indigenous labor – generated a system of indirect rule that was crucial to the stability and economic success of the missions (Susnik 2017).

And they were indeed very successful by the standards of eighteenth-century agrarian production and burgeoning global mercantilist trade. The *reducciones'* economic activities – agriculture, livestock, and artisanal products – depended on profound alterations in the division of labor and settlement patterns of Guaraní people. Surrounding the central church and living quarters for Guaraní families were extensive workshops and gardens, and beyond that, large pastures for herds of cattle, sheep, oxen, horses, goats, mules, and burros (Ganson 2005; McNaspy 1987). The large estates produced commercial exports, especially of yerba mate and cotton, through which the Jesuits raised capital for their churches and for the wider settlement.

This system of economic production depended on reformatting normative gender roles, kinship and family relations, and conceptions of property. For instance, "the Jesuits required the vast majority of men to work as farmers and day laborers, rather than hunters and warriors. Men, women, and children worked as horticulturalists on plots of land that belonged to their families and were called *abambaé* (men's possession), and also on communal land, called *Tupambaé* (God's possession)" (Ganson 2005, 63), such that the pre-Colombian agricultural pattern of communal land was tactically redeployed to sustain community members cut out of the new Christian European kinship structure organized around the heteronuclear family. Ganson speculates that men may have resented being forced to perform agricultural labor, which had conventionally been allocated to women, and that "the Jesuit's depictions of them as 'lazy' perhaps was a sign of their resistance to this change in gender roles" (2005, 63). However, the profound transformation of the division of labor and of daily economic activity did not entirely abandon Guaraní agricultural practices. New agricultural technologies like iron farm tools were readily adopted. But the material culture excavated by historical archaeologists in several mission sites suggests that "these European iron tools, certain types of ceramics produced in workshops, and ornaments were utilized in addition to, rather than in replacement of, aboriginal items" (63). These findings, along with extensive analysis of the colonial archive, suggest Guaraní in the Jesuit missions "not only helped shape the formation of Paraguay's hybrid culture but also were active

Jesuit Mission of San Ignacio Mini, Argentina

participants in the historical processes of the Río de la Plata" (6). They were active political agents frequently petitioning the Spanish Crown while also persisting with their value systems and material culture.

Against this historical and archaeological evidence of complex adaptive processes under Spanish and Christian domination, it is remarkable to examine the persistent stereotypes that recur in European literature about the missions and their "native people." My first encounter with this romanticized view was reading early twentieth-century British travel writer R.B. Cunninghame Graham's classic idealization of the Jesuit *reducciones* in *A Vanished Arcadia* (1901). Cunninghame Graham was mostly interested in supporting his political agenda – he went on to found the socialist party in his native Scotland – and portrayed the missions as something of a proto-socialist state. Indeed, this habit of looking through the lens of European political and social preoccupations goes all the way back to the eighteenth century. Voltaire's masterpiece *Candide* sees the title character make a fictitious visit to the Paraguayan *reducciones*. The text serves as a meditation on power and corruption. Montaigne and Voltaire, too, were among "the notable writers whose portrayals of the Tupi-Guaraní as innocent children of nature, noble savages, or animals often revealed more about the nature of Western culture itself than about the original beliefs and cultural traditions of these 'others'" (Ganson 2005, 6). My point here is that an ethnohistorical approach based on archaeological and archival evidence challenges us to consider the historical roles that Guaraní people played in the rise of the Jesuit missions. Indeed, without the complex interrelations of incorporation and resistance between "Amazonian horticulturalists" and novel forms of social organization geared to creating vast productive estates, "the Spanish would not have had much of a presence in the Upper Plata region" (9).

The Jesuit *reducciones* were a massive social engineering experiment – one that was profoundly coercive and violent. It was an experiment undertaken under the mantle of benevolent Christian uplift, as well as a profound philosophical commitment to the belief that mercantilist global trade brought mutual benefit, peace, and prosperity. We can continue to trace the effects of this mode of production and form of political organization, as they are an important reminder that any story of Paraguay's "development" necessarily engages the histories of colonialism and racial capitalism at its root.

Expulsion of the Jesuits and Paraguayan Independence

On February 27, 1767, the King of Spain, Charles III, issued a decree expelling the Jesuits from Spain and all of its overseas colonies. The decree also confiscated all of the Order's properties. The complex relationship between the Catholic Church and the Spanish State is too nuanced to fully cover here. For more in-depth reading see Guillermo Wilde (2017). For the purposes of this schematic history of Paraguayan agrarian transformation, suffice it to say that Guaraní people were incorporated into colonial society as many migrated from the missions into areas of Paraguay and throughout the Río de la Plata region. The missions, meanwhile, continued to function, though they now depended politically on the Spanish colonial government whose seat had shifted south to the newly created Viceroyalty of the Río de la Plata (later, Buenos Aires). These political relations changed again in 1811 when Paraguay declared itself independent from Spain under the rule of Dr. José Gaspar Rodriguez de Francia. Francia's dictatorship was famous for its isolationism. Under his rule, Paraguay closed itself off, a move responding to Argentina's refusal to recognize the newly independent republic and blockading of river trade, and Brazil's imperialism.

Francia's land reforms were especially consequential, as they transformed yet again the pattern of settlement and agrarian labor. In September 1825, he decreed that all Paraguayans were to produce satisfactory proof of their land ownership rights via documentary evidence within three months. If they were unable to do this, the land would revert to the state. The land under state ownership also increased dramatically as Francia seized all properties that had belonged to the Spanish Crown, land belonging to political opponents, and the lands of any foreigners who did not have native-born heirs (Kleinpenning 1987, 75). With these vast land holdings, the state established a number of large *"estancias"* (vast estates) in areas that were deemed suitable for livestock; many of these were the site of the former Jesuit *reducciones*. Guaraní and other Indigenous groups were also stripped of their land rights, which devolved to state control.

After the death of Francia in 1840, and as foreign relations became less fraught, the regime of Carlos Antonio López began to pursue industrialization and new production methods. Foreign technicians and other experts were welcome but carried out their work under direct state supervision. The preeminent human geographer of Paraguay, Jan Kleinpenning (1987; 2009), noted that "no facilities were given to private foreign investors, nor were loans raised abroad or foreigners allowed to purchase land" (Kleinpenning 1987, 77). By the 1860s, almost all of the land in Paraguay was owned by the state, and "de facto" access to land either via labor on *estancias* or through small holdings was the norm. In fact, it was only after the disastrous War of the Triple Alliance (1864–70) that "the Paraguayan rural population would experience the negative effects of the absence of well-defined and officially recognized private land ownership rights" (84).

There has been a great deal of scholarship on the politically, socially, and demographically ruinous conflict that Paraguayans call the Great War. The Triple Alliance consisting of Argentina, Brazil, and Uruguay invaded and defeated Paraguay. In the process, it is estimated that up to two-thirds of the prewar Paraguayan population perished (Whigham and Potthast 1999; Reber 2002; Kleinpenning 2002; Whigham and Potthast 2002), and at its conclusion, women outnumbered adult men by ten to one. If you are interested in this period of Latin American history, I suggest that you read Hendrik Kraay and Thomas Whigham (2004).

For the narrative that I am developing about fintech and the faith in markets that we see so strongly in *Forecasts*, the war's aftermath is especially consequential (Warren and Warren 1978; Warren 1989). That is because it saw the vast state-owned *estancias* converted into global financial assets and a strong ideological commitment to foreign speculative finance (see Schuster 2015). The story begins with two loans floated on the British Stock Exchange in London in 1870 and 1871, partly to finance reconstruction but also to pay "war debts" to the occupying caretaker governments of Brazil and Argentina (Schuster 2021a). Paraguay had been ravaged by war and was in no condition to begin making regular interest payments to British bondholders. Members of the ruling junta pocketed most of the funds, and the loans entered into default in 1874. But the story doesn't end there. Years

Ilex paraguariensis

later, when the debt was refinanced, large tracts of land were converted into speculative financial assets under the aegis of land warrants attached to the renegotiated debt. These warrants were created to indemnify bondholders for interest in arrears. Vast tracts of land were sold to foreigners in an effort to raise capital to service the large foreign loans. The period between 1870 to the early twentieth century saw the wholesale liquidation of state-owned land, as well as its financialization (Abente 1989; Warren and Warren 1985). Few of those estates were ever occupied by their owners and absenteeism was a major problem. In fact, for decades the art of cultivating yerba mate was lost (Reber 1985; Folch 2010), as the Jesuit agricultural estates fell to ruin, and the technique of germinating seeds to grow new trees was lost to popular knowledge. Meanwhile, Paraguay found itself newly tied to international financial markets.

Twentieth-Century Transformations

An early twentieth-century Paraguayan statistical encyclopedia estimated that, between 1881 and 1914, more than 25 million hectares of grazing land and *yerbales* (areas of dense semi-domesticated yerba mate) had passed into private hands. Some, like the Barthe Estate, took over lands that had previously been part of the Jesuit *reducciones*, with their extensive yerba mate groves (Ocampos 2016). Kleinpenning's review of this period suggests that "a payment order issued in Europe was all that was needed to become a large landowner in Paraguay" (Kleinpenning 1987, 93, citing Frutos 1974). This had grave consequences for Paraguayan agricultural production. Many Paraguayan producers had to abandon their cattle, yerba mate, and timber enterprises because they lost their leases. The dominant form of land tenure became the *latifundia*, with barbed wire fences to enclose those vast pastures. Even small villages that remained – including many of the colonial era settlements that had been attached to the Spanish *encomiendas* – found themselves completely surrounded by *latifundia* land. Meanwhile, a small group of urban Paraguayan elites who established close connections to large landowners emerged. They were highly dependent on the import and export trade (Abente 1989). This, in turn, made land even more valuable as an asset class and site of financial speculation. In fact, "a number of consortia were formed at the time for the sale and resale of land purely as a speculation" (Kleinpenning 1987, 94, citing Herken Krauer 1989; Pastore 1972).

The early twentieth century was politically and socially unstable, as this small group of elites vied for political control. Another major military conflict – the Chaco War (1932–5) – saw Paraguay go to war again, this time against Bolivia, its neighbor to the west. If you are interested in economic and social policy during this period, see Kleinpenning (2009), Diego Abente (1993), and Juan Carlos Herken Krauer (1984). The political schisms that wracked the country through the first half of the twentieth century culminated in the rise in 1954 of Alfredo Stroessner, who ruled Paraguay under his brutal authoritarian regime until 1989. It was Latin America's longest running dictatorship. For an anthropological analysis of Stroessner's embrace of development and modernization, often with the enthusiastic support of the United States, see Christine Folch's anthropological research on the "archive of terror" and political control of eastern Paraguay (Folch 2013).

Recent activist work by a collective of independent investigative journalists in Paraguay called El Surti (*el surtidor*, the petrol station, is the best stop for fuel and local news) has highlighted the environmental impacts of Stroessner's economic policies.[9] Stroessner's policies had two aims: first, maintaining his political coalition of supporters by rewarding loyalty with vast estates, industrial monopolies, state contracts, and judicial impunity; and second, close relations with the Alliance for Progress in the United States, which sought to mechanize and industrialize the countryside in a political strategy to head off the perceived threat of Cuban socialism in the hemisphere. A veritable firehouse of aid moneys in the form of US-backed loans built a road network and "experimental stations" for Green Revolution agribusiness (Hetherington 2019; 2020). Wide-scale deforestation of the Atlantic rainforest in eastern Paraguay was a consequence of mechanized agriculture and commodity-export monocropping. By 1975, the National University of Asunción opened the College of Agronomy (now called the College of Agrarian

Sciences); five years later a forestry degree (Ingenería Forestal) was created to support the highly lucrative timber industry. Agronomy and agricultural sciences were closely tied to the interests of big agribusiness, and linked to major global chemical and seed companies.

While Stroessner's regime took aim at enriching his cronies among the wealthy landed elite,[10] his political strategy also sought to assert territorial control over the countryside. His right-hand man in the early days of the regime, Edgar Ynsfrán, orchestrated the "March to the East" in response to the perceived threat of Brazilian imperialism on the border (Ynsfrán 1990). It should be noted that Ynsfrán was the powerful minister of the interior – the same office that was in charge of the regime's terrifying and violent campaign of surveillance, disappearances, and state-sanctioned torture, which were characteristic of Stroessner's political rule. The 1960s, then, were an era of "colonization" in addition to *latifundismo*. In fact, the predominance of *latifundias* meant that there were significant population pressures around the more densely populated central region (Asunción and its surrounds). The Instituto de Bienestar Rural (IBR) established a framework for *colonias* in the heavily forested sections of the east on residual state-owned lands (*tierras fiscales*) that had not passed into private control. These in turn were subdivided into very small *lotes*. Colonists were faced with the daunting task of building their own houses, drilling wells, cutting their own roads, and so on. Virtually no help, save for the *lote*, was offered by the state. Colonists undertook the arduous work of clearing virgin forest to plant labor-intensive cash crops (cotton, tobacco, citrus) and subsistence crops. Few farmers managed to bring more than about 4 hectares into active production.

In *Forecasts*, this would have been around the time when Wilfrido bought his first 25 hectares of land (mentioned by his son on page 90). In the story, he cleared his parcel for cotton production and subsequently had a run-in with his neighbor's witchcraft (pages 106–8). The isolation of *colonias* was the reason why personnel for the harvest came looking for seasonal work – there simply weren't enough resources in the countryside to undertake the task themselves. Homesteads were so isolated that hardly any families could make use of basic educational or medical facilities. In the 1970s there was only one agricultural technician per 2,500 farmers (Kleinpenning 1987, 168). Tellingly, the IBR generally did not help farmers transport their equipment or their export products to market. For decades this meant that *colonias* depended on brokers or larger trading companies (*silos, acopiadores*). Agricultural cooperatives were discouraged – often violently – by the Stroessner regime, as it feared that the farmers would become too organized.

The fall of the Stroessner regime in 1989 left hundreds of thousands of hectares of *tierras malhabidas*, that is, estates owned by the disgraced members of his junta. Near Wilfrido's farm, a large overgrown paddock is whispered about quietly by locals – it had been the property of Pastor Coronel, Stroessner's powerful spymaster and engineer of the regime's apparatus of torture and disappearances. He was a native of San Pedro and had been granted several estates in the area. Coronel had been known for detaining political prisoners using his red Cadillac, dubbed *Caperucita roja*, or "Little Red Riding Hood," and his infamously brutal tactics won him favor with the regime for his political loyalty, for which he was rewarded with land and wealth. The *tierras malhabidas* have been a juridico-political quagmire since the fall of Stroessner and the disgrace of his inner circle. Subsequent democratic administrations have failed to make much progress in redistributing land, in part due to the enduring power of agribusiness interests and the Colorado Party (Stroessner's political machine), which has dominated the so-called return to democracy. The last *censo agrícola* (agrarian census) in 2008 indicated that Paraguay has among the most unequal distribution of land in the world.

In Fintech We Trust?

After engaging the long history of agrarian transformation in Paraguay, we can look at the arrival of development interventions like organic sesame and chia, or index-based agricultural insurance (IBAI), in new light. Use the archaeological, ethnohistorical, and political economy perspectives presented here to discuss the following questions.

Discussion Questions

1. What is novel about the arrival of fintech in rural San Pedro? In what ways does it resemble past economic experiments and projects of social engineering? How does it differ?
2. Make a list of the plants and foods that were adopted, consumed, and/or commercialized over the years. How was the arrival of sesame similar to or different from these other crops?

Essay Topics

1. How does Wilfrido and his family relate to land in *Forecasts*, and how is this relationship shaped by other principal actors and institutions such as the Multiactiva, agronomists, USAID, and the financial system? How does the cosmology of Guaraní myth shape his relation to the land? Incorporate references and materials from this chapter as you respond.

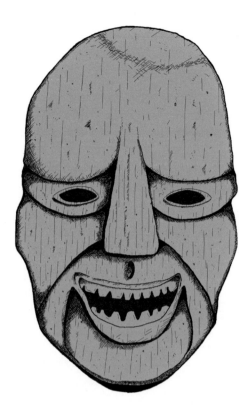

Activities

1. Using a sketchpad or photo collage, create a series of panels that narrate your relationship to the land you are on. After you finish your sketches and/or photos, assemble a list of scholarly resources that would help you better understand the long history of this land from an archaeological, historical, and anthropological perspective. Alongside this bibliography, consider writing down histories that have been passed to you from your family and community. If you are in a settler-colonial context, pay particular attention to the perspectives that have been erased from standard histories.

Notes on Illustrations

The drawings of ceramics are based on photographs published in Castro (2019). The nivaclé grater derives from a specimen in the Ethnographic Museum Juan B. Ambrosetti (Buenos Aires) reproduced in Kamienkowski and Arenas (2017).

The representation of the Jesuit father is inspired from a drawing by an unknown author, in public domain (https://commons.wikimedia.org/wiki/File:Brazil_18thc _JesuitFather.jpg).

The representation of the church façade at San Ignacio Miní, Argentina, builds on a series of virtual reconstructions developed by Trexel Animation in collaboration with historians (https://www.behance.net/gallery/14280247/San -Ignacio-Mini). This digital material was part of an audio-visual show for the visitors of the site. The *reducción* of San Ignacio Miní was founded in 1610. The ruins of the mission are among the best-preserved in the territory, and were listed as a UNESCO World Heritage site in 1984. For more information, including the spatial organization of the reductions, you can visit https://revista.drclas.harvard .edu/imagining-guaranis-and-jesuits/.

The *Ilex paraguariensis* plant was drawn after a botanical plate by Franz Eugen Köhler published in *Köhler's Medizinal-Pflanzen* in 1887; the yerba mate bowl, cup, and bombilla are inspired from a photograph by LarisaBlinova / Getty Images.

The illustration of the mask is inspired by a photo reproduced in a book of photography, *La luz sobre el rostro: Algunos elementos sobre el Kamba Ra'anga* (Colombino and Allen 2013, 50–1).

Appendix D

ANTHROPOLOGICAL METHODS FOR *FORECASTS*

Anthropological fieldwork tends to involve a long-term and immersive study of a small sector of the population. Field studies have been the basis for anthropology's characteristic methodology – ethnography – and are the inspiration for this book series, ethnoGRAPHIC. However, "the field" has been reframed and reconceptualized by scholars who are critical of the bounded and geographically delimited archetype (see Gupta and Ferguson 1997; Seizer 1995) that the discipline inherited from early twentieth-century anthropologists such as Bronislaw Malinowski, who famously set his ethnographic scene by describing being set down on a beach surrounded by all of his gear and watching the ship sail off toward the horizon (Malinowski 1984). This archetype of mud-between-the-toes "village ethnography" has been stubbornly durable (Passaro 1997), even as the discipline has shifted to urban contexts, "studying up" focused on elites, online worlds, and so on. The process of decoupling "the field" of fieldwork from assumptions that are not particularly helpful about geographically and temporally distant "others" who can be accessed only through vigorous, masculine, rugged expeditions remains incomplete and ongoing. For a discussion as well as a practical guide for research methods that explore novel "experiments" with ethnography, see Ballestero and Winthereik (2021). Much of the critical impetus comes from feminist, Black, and Indigenous anthropologists, many from the Global South (e.g., George et al. 2020; Heinze 2020; Bedi et al. 2021). Their critical engagement with anthropology's complex history as a field science has revealed the overlapping ethnocentric, colonial, racist, and gendered imaginaries that animated the fantasy of "real" fieldwork. I am deeply indebted to their critical insights and ongoing efforts to re-imagine the discipline's characteristic methodology.

A "Village Ethnography" of Complex Global Finance?

One of the reasons that I have spent such a long time thinking about the boundaries, composition, and geographies of "the field" is because I study financial systems. These are often quite difficult to conceptualize in terms of community-based research or classical "village ethnography." People interact with financial products and services every day. And importantly, the assumptions, values, and logics of financial systems have reorganized many aspects of our daily lives in powerful but often invisible ways, from how we experience our homes, often the most valuable financial asset we own (e.g., Cooper 2017; Stout 2019; Allon 2015), to how universities conceptualize the knowledge that we produce, too often geared toward seeking "efficiencies" and commercialization of research (e.g., Connell 2019; Strathern 2000). Yet for a set of durable dispositions and embodied practices that take center stage in many different facets of social life, finance is maddeningly difficult to pin down in "a place," at least in the classic geographic imaginaries of the anthropological "field." Where would ethnographers locate themselves if they wanted to "see" the operations of finance? If we stop trying to generate numbers to describe the unequal effects of financialization, what alternative approach might we have as ethnographers?

The first step is to "people" financial systems rather than describing the abstract movement of money and markets. Along those lines, my first instinct for this project was to replicate the research methods that I had developed to study microcredit programs in Paraguay (Schuster 2015). For that earlier research, I lived in Ciudad del Este, the commercial hub and Free Trade Zone on the Paraguayan side of the Triple Frontier with Argentina and Brazil (see Rabossi 2003; Folch 2019; Tucker 2020). I arrived for fieldwork in February of 2008, just as the Global Financial Crisis (GFC) was beginning to ripple outwards from mortgage markets in the United States to shake credit systems globally. For my doctoral research, I was interested in how anti-poverty group-based microcredit loans for committees of women entrepreneurs (e.g., Elyachar 2005; Karim 2011; Kar 2018) interacted with the wider smuggling economy and commercial society that made Ciudad del Este famous as a bottleneck for trade in the region (Schuster 2019). I didn't know it at the time, but I was also tracking a story about how financial interdependency articulated across scales, from the tiny neighborhood associations up to the "too big to fail" US banks at the heart of the GFC. These were connections that I didn't anticipate when I first envisioned the research; they were a coincidence of the timing of my doctoral degree. Neither economists nor everyday homeowners could foresee how the collapse of the US housing market would soon catalyze a global crisis (see Schuster and Kar 2021).

In this midst of a rapidly changing global economic landscape, I began with the branch office of a local microcredit NGO (non-government organization). To understand local credit systems and build outward toward their global connections, I set about immersing myself in the life cycles of their loans. My primary method was *participant observation*. I shadowed credit counselors and loan officers as they made their sales pitches and tried to enroll new clients in the microcredit program (e.g., Krause-Jensen 2013). I rode along in buses as they crisscrossed the city to visit groups that were behind in their payments (e.g., Kusenbach 2003). And I was on hand for the bureaucratic process of closing out one cycle and renewing loans for the next round of borrowing. I attended plenty of policy meetings at the organization's head office (e.g., Thedvall 2013). It was through this constant interaction with credit that I came to appreciate what borrowers called *bicicleando*, that is, paying off one loan with the next and thereby turning the pedals of the credit bicycle (see James 2014). So, in addition to following the daily financial labor of making and managing financial products, I also spent a great deal of time in a handful of neighborhoods that were saturated with microcredit loans. I used my decrepit 1960s Volkswagen Beetle to give the women I worked with rides (e.g., Black 2017) as they bought and sold wholesale beauty products or used clothes, as neighborhood associations raised funds through community bake sales, and as we all fretted about making ends meet. I found that my own research schedule became tightly coupled to the banking cycles of loan payments. Dealing with debt was a constant concern (Han 2011; Han 2012). Microloans incited flurries of movement within households and neighborhoods, and animated circuits of trade across the city.

When I started planning this project about microinsurance, which I began in 2017 with support from an Australian Research Council fellowship, I thought I would follow a similar methodology. I expected to track the financial labor of advertising insurance and seeking new clients by hitching my schedule to the itineraries of insurance agents. I hoped to develop relationships with different firms so that I could shadow their fintech teams through various stages of development, sales, and claims. In short, I assumed that insurance followed a similar financial lifecycle to credit, and that I would be able to use participant observation to track it. I was very wrong.

The first thing that I found out about insurance is that it is experienced as an expense, not as a financial service; most people buy a policy and then forget about it. It didn't incite the flurry of activity and worry that the rigid repayment schedule of microcredit loans always seemed to create in the daily lives of borrowers. In fact, the insurance team touted the policies as "peace of mind" – the point, quite literally, was for it to provide an invisible safety net. Buy it and forget about it.

Second, and even more methodologically problematic, was the fact that much of the negotiation between the fintech sales teams and their prospective clients actually hinged on enrolling agricultural cooperatives, which meant that their real task was to get the agronomists and general managers onside; if the cooperative saw the value of crop insurance, then they would simply make the policy a requirement for lines of agricultural credit for their members. You can see a glimpse of this on pages 14–15, where Mario and the InsurTech team are trying to persuade agronomists to make IBAI insurance a requirement for their cooperative members. And many did, since the policies were touted as peace of mind for the cooperatives too. If many members lost their crops and defaulted on their agricultural loans, the cooperative might run into financial trouble itself. Insurance was a safety net for the lender as much as for the borrower. And it was invisible to me as a researcher, since these arrangements were mostly in place before I began fieldwork in rural San Pedro in 2018. The scene in *Forecasts* reconstructs what happened based on conversations that I later had with Freddy and Mario.

And finally, the novelty of IBAI for sesame farmers hinged on its remote sensing and climate modeling. The whole point was that the insurance company would never have to send an adjuster out to remote farms, since the policy triggered (or didn't) based on the data gathered by satellites and calibrated to weather stations (Johnson 2013b; Aguiton 2019). The business model hinged on "depopulating" the whole process.

In sum, insurance was invisible and unremarkable. Hardly anybody even thought about it until I brought it up.

The Fintech Assemblage

So, my research plan – which aimed to follow the financial labor of making, marketing, and managing insurance – was a bust. I had to seek out other avenues to understand how fintech was quietly reshaping life in the rural communities that enrolled in the IBAI pilot project. Much to my surprise, starting back at square one turned out to be an unexpected opportunity. As I trained myself in the specifics of the insurance market in Paraguay, I found myself making contact with a loose network of specialists working in development aid, agricultural policy, financial services, and community projects. Schwittay (2011) describes financial inclusion as an "assemblage,"[11] and I found myself sketching the contours and connections of this assemblage. Methodologically, this meant starting in the capital city, Asunción. Much of my time was spent in the unglamorous pursuit of LinkedIn contacts operating in the fintech space and cold-emailing organizations in the network. I scoured policy documents and websites for their content as well as for hints about the key players who were active in setting the "financial inclusion" agenda in Paraguay. This led me to the company I call InsurTech, the firm that was developing a pilot project for drought insurance aimed at sesame farmers in the District of San Pedro. This was the first I had ever heard of sesame – I had no idea that it was a commercial export crop in Paraguay. I also made contact with a development consultancy with connections to the Paraguayan National Financial Inclusion Strategy (ENIF, Estrategia Nacional de Inclusión Financiera Paraguay), and I learned a great deal about the policy framework pushing for the expansion of insurance markets. This in turn brought me to a very helpful public servant in Treasury who was working on insurance and social policy and considering what these market-based solutions mean for the national budget. From there, I made contact with the Central Bank of Paraguay, and the team that oversaw regulations for the insurance market. All of this information is in the background of *Forecasts*, but was just as ethnographically rich as the research on Wilfrido's farm.

My meetings with all these contacts in the financial and public sector started off embarrassingly basic – no sophisticated interviewing or deep probes into the complex cultural dynamics of financialization. I was literally just trying to get my head around how insurance markets and regulation work, and how this complicated policy landscape fits together. From August to November 2017, I made myself a menace by showing up to every training, roundtable, workshop, forum, and meeting that I could talk my way into. One research contact joked that he and his colleagues got together to gossip about the introductory letter that I had blasted out to all of them, unaware of the connections they shared – laughingly, they agreed that "Dra. Caroline seemed to be everywhere at once." And I met one-on-one with anybody who would speak to me about crop insurance, from the consultant who developed the project for FOMIN (an Inter-American Development Bank fund also known as MIF or Multilateral Investment Arm), to the World Bank's representative who came to do monitoring and evaluation for a related scheme, to the teams involved in an earlier study of the market potential of insurance funded by the Japanese aid agency JICA.

If I had stopped there, I would have had a fairly comprehensive grasp of the policy landscape that generated insurance as a site of intervention and value production for various actors in Paraguay and globally. I learned a great deal about how development is "rendered technical" through the logics and techniques of finance (Johnson 2014; Johnson 2013b). And I gathered granular data about the push to financialize Paraguayan public policy, specifically social protection for its most vulnerable citizens (Lavinas 2018). It would have been a study of the "in-betweenness of finance," and especially the labor that stitched finance together at the margins (Schuster and Kar 2021). It was only through happenstance that I found myself transported out of the buzz and excitement of start-up culture and fintech in Asunción, and re-settled among the sesame farms in San Pedro.

Following Weather Insurance to the Sesame Farms

My journey to southern San Pedro began with a coincidence that is characteristic of the serendipity of ethnographic fieldwork. Contacts in InsurTech had mentioned that they were developing weather insurance for sesame farmers in San Pedro, but I had scanty information about where these farms might be located. In retrospect, I think this was partly due to the fact that this team of insurance specialists were working on weather models and underwriting, and they had little contact with field operatives. I contacted the academic meteorologist who had consulted for InsurTech and built the weather models, and whom I had met at an industry conference in the early stages of fieldwork; he knew where all of the stations were located. He was interested in my research, but hesitant to disclose confidential client information and suspicious about what an outsider was doing poking around in their project. With little to go on, I realized San Pedro is a big state and I hardly knew where to start.

In preparation to make some scoping visits to San Pedro, I put out a call for a research assistant, since my Guaraní language skills were woefully deficient even after years of study and fieldwork in Paraguay. I also was eager to develop a collaboration with a Paraguayan social scientist as a co-researcher for team-based ethnography. Through personal networks I was referred to Rocío Silvero, a political sociologist who happened to be from Ciudad del Este (where I had done the previous study on microcredit) and who was in San Pedro as part of a Paraguayan youth volunteer program that drew inspiration from the Peace Corps. It just so happened that Rocío was based in a town not far from one of the agricultural cooperatives that, it turned out, had most readily adopted the sesame insurance (something I didn't know at the time). And even better – she had a spare room in her rented house and was eager for a roommate. I bought an ancient 4WD Land Rover with gremlins in its electrical systems. It immediately broke down, and I spent nearly two months struggling to rebuild its engine and retrofit the brake servos (going and stopping being the two key criteria for a functioning vehicle). Finally, I relocated from Asunción to southern San Pedro.

My collaboration with Rocío was fascinating and generative in part because we were both "outsiders." If anything, I had more experience with rural life, having grown up in an agricultural area in California before moving to Australia. I knew my way around horses and livestock, could drive a truck on treacherous dirt roads, and felt an affinity for cowboy culture. Rocío, despite being a city girl and fish out of water in agrarian San Pedro, brought a deep understanding of Paraguayan politics, history, and society. And we shared an interest in feminist movement politics and gender justice. From June 2018 to April 2019 (with a few interruptions for travel back to Australia), we lived together in her little house. Rocío adopted Betty, a goofy, gangly, mischievous mutt who promptly had a litter of puppies under my bed. We shared countless debriefing sessions over cold *tereré* or icy beers on the patio under the mango tree as we processed our ethnographic data.

With the help of the Land Rover, Rocío and I began working closely with the Multiactiva, the cooperative that had been an early adopter of the InsurTech sesame insurance. The Multiactiva's office was overseen by an overbearing and mercurial general manager who was a member of the nearby Mennonite colony (Canova 2020a; Canova 2020b; Canova 2021; Kleinpenning 1987). He supervised the flow of aid and technology from the large and prosperous Mennonite farms to the tiny *chacras* where small parcels of sesame were grown by Paraguayan *campesinos*. This flow was racially and class marked, as the wealthy white German-Paraguayan financiers and scions of agribusiness considered their role in supporting Guaraní-speaking mestizo peasants in terms of Christian charity and help for the poor. Farmers were by turns resentful of the patronizing relationship and grateful for the assistance.

At the heart of the technology transfer was a financing model that redistributed climate risks using everything from agrochemicals, to resilient GMO seed varieties, to weather insurance (e.g., Flachs 2019). Under the general manager's direction, a team of agronomists and technicians looked after the farms and fields of their members. Freddy was the lead agronomist at the Multiactiva and was diligent about supporting its members with his technical skills and expertise. He was a native of the area but had studied agronomy in Asunción before returning home to start a family. He bought a parcel of land to raise cattle while his wife was an expert in horticulture. In addition to being a small-scale producer himself, he had worked as a field officer troubleshooting farm issues for members of the Multiactiva for over 10 years. So, we began following Freddy on his visits to local farms. We also worked at Multiactiva's experimental station (Centro de Investigación Regional, or CIR) as staff planned out the planting strategy for the year's sesame crop. Our work at the CIR opened a window onto the agricultural economy of the region. And we dealt with the rain, which, in an El Niño year, was unrelenting.

All winter (June–September) we worked closely with Freddy as he crisscrossed the region, often using his in-depth knowledge of the local area to serve as intermediary for the team from InsurTech that made the journey from Asunción to train local farmers in the specifics of their sesame insurance. For the narrative of *Forecasts* I followed the ethnographic convention of creating a synthetic character, Mario, out of a composite of the several insurance agents who regularly visited the area.[12] This is partly to protect their identities, but also underscores the empirical reality that this was a very small team, and the sesame insurance was a relatively marginal pilot project within a much larger organization. The Asunción-based InsurTech specialists often teamed up with a project manager for USAID, Ingeniero (Engineer) Francisco, who made field visits to sesame farmers and helped troubleshoot the unfamiliar commercial crop (as seen on page 79). We would gather under cover in the big sheds that housed farm equipment or on the large covered patios of the more prosperous households in the area. And as the rain belted down, we would listen to Mario, Freddy, and Francisco struggle to explain how a weather derivative works to an audience of skeptical farmers. They often brought a portable laptop and projector to show complicated diagrams and models – blurry images projected against the whitewashed cement wall of a shed or grain silo. Most farmers had grown accustomed to a landing pattern of aid workers who came, season after season, with a new pilot project meant to raise income and improve living standards in the impoverished countryside (see Hetherington 2014). Many complained that insurance was even more out of touch than most programs, as it didn't even carry a tangible benefit (like agrochemicals, seeds, or tools). I was very grateful to the ancient 4WD Land Rover, which was one of the few vehicles – save for the flashy Toyota Hilux trucks that were popular with the Mennonite farmers and field teams for development organizations – that could navigate the treacherous roads in the pouring rain.

It was through our work with Freddy and the Multiactiva that we connected with Don Wilfrido. This is where the story of *Forecasts* picks up. We really did offer him a ride when he couldn't get the seeder into his neighbor's little sedan. From the very first visit to his *finca* (small farm), Wilfrido and his wife Ña Neca[13] were generous hosts and patient teachers. Wilfrido has a penchant for the dramatic and is a gifted poet and storyteller. We audio-recorded hours of interviews, most often during breaks in farm work as we were sitting in the shade and drinking *tereré*, in which he described his life spent as a farmer, his heartache for distant children who had migrated, and his struggles with the ever-more unpredictable weather. I carried a little notebook in my back pocket to take down scratch notes while we worked in the field, and then typed those up into fieldnotes at night (Emerson, Fretz, and Shaw 2011; Jackson 2016). Wilfrido introduced us to neighboring farmers and we spent time with other families that planted sesame and purchased IBAI weather insurance. But perhaps most importantly, we immersed ourselves in the daily rhythm of the sesame and the humans and other animals who tended it. This is how we learned that we had to pause at 3 p.m. on the dot each day to listen to Professor Enrique Sabio read out the daily horoscope and catch a glimpse into the future. We kept a watchful eye for Pomberos, as Wilfrido reminded us of the times the monsters sent his plans scattering akimbo. And we learned which birds were harbingers of luck, or storms, or sorrow.

I wrote the first draft of the script for *Forecasts* while I was working on Wilfrido's farm. Much of the dialogue is adapted directly from my fieldnotes. For example, one of the pages that I think exemplifies the key themes of the book, where Wilfrido vents his frustration at how "those who collect always get paid" interspersed with the WACK! of threshing sesame (page 100), is transcribed directly from my field diary. So too is his story of the nightmare where he dreamed of floods and ruin and suicide, and the story he told his daughter about the witchcraft worked on his farm when he was a young man. The script is as faithful as possible to the dialogue I reconstructed in my fieldnotes and transcribed from interviews. For the narrative flow of the sequential art to work, sometimes I combined scenes out of sequence. There are other instances where I constructed a scene out of a "patchwork" (Günel, Varma, and Watanabe 2020) of multiple perspectives and accounts from different participants. Overall, we maintained the guiding principle of adapting real-life conversation and events as closely as we could manage.

You may wonder, then, about Kavajú Tuja and ShooShoo. We had a close relationship, but I was not privy to their conversations. Instead, their dialogues are adapted from discussions that Wilfrido and Neca had about their *socios* (work colleagues). We lived in an animated world where all manner of creatures were entangled with the lives of humans and could communicate amongst themselves and with us. The conversation about mortadella as told by Don Wilfrido was voiced in such a way that animals had an unspoken but important part to play. Scholars such as Hartigan have made a compelling case for studying multispecies sociality on its own terms; that is, developing a "model for how multispecies research might synthesize ethnological expertise in an enhanced anthropological approach to other species," and thereby extend cultural analysis to other animals (Hartigan 2021, 847). In his research on wild horses in Galicia, Spain, he analyzes the results of his observations through anthropological frameworks such as Goffman's concepts of face, footing, and civil inattention, thereby putting horse sociality at the center of the analysis. On Wilfrido's farm, the relations among species were configured by the question posed by Besky and Blanchette (2019) about "how nature works." They suggest that seeing animals as workers "risks the projection of capital's fixation on the value of human labor onto all the planet's energies" (Besky and Blanchette 2019, 5). Just as anthropological studies of agriculture have pressed us to consider all the ways that farming is "performative," and not just an economic activity (Richards 1993; Batterbury 1996; Flachs 2019), so too can we consider the multiple and complex social roles that farm animals occupy on Wilfrido's *finca*. Indeed, "if acknowledging the agency of nonhumans is a key to survival on a damaged planet, we would argue that we also need to learn how to conceptualize those activities outside labor frames of creation, growth, and productivity" (Besky and Blanchette 2019, 5). The lively relationship between Kavajú Tuja and ShooShoo is my effort to conceptualize those activities with empathy and solidarity.

Curiously, the only protagonist who was not given a speaking role in the everyday life of the farm was, in fact, the weather. It never was accorded the agency that other more-than-human characters such as trees and Pomberos and farm animals were. While storms and drought and wind were central topics of discussion and sites of ongoing anxiety, they were not spoken about as beings, monsters, or spirits (see, e.g., Musharbash and Presterudstuen 2014). In this, farmers seemed to have adopted the worldview of agronomists such as Freddy (Valentine 2016). The title engineer (*ingeniero*) was no misnomer. Agronomists put their faith in models, data, and technology, which rendered storms and drought into technical indices of "hydrological stress." Freddy and his peers kept a sharp eye on AccuWeather and its forecasts. Their smartphones were loaded with several weather apps, which helped them make forecasts and advise farmers about when to plant, or spray, or harvest. Meanwhile, for farmers the weather was an occasion to think about time and movement. As Adams-Hutcheson suggests, dwelling with weather infuses us with a sense of place and the experience of motion: "Climate is fundamentally fluid and mobile, and weather is a narrative that we wish to tell and retell across time, over and over again. Weather mobilizes us to feel a connection to places and times, to remember seasons past and to feel the delicious anticipation of future weather" (Adams-Hutcheson 2020, 222). But while weathering was crucial to the rhythms and risks of farm life for Wilfrido, they were shaped by values and demands that connect weather to a rich sensorium of farm life (Ingold 2010; Ingold 2005). Though storms are certainly protagonists in the plot of *Forecasts*, they were most often experienced in sensory and meteorological rather than mythic terms.

Methods for Graphic Ethnography

A final word should be given to the ethnographic realism of *Forecasts*'s graphic style. Most of the key characters were developed by Enrique and David based on photos and videos that I shot during fieldwork in San Pedro. In fact, I found it quite disconcerting to face a comic book version of myself! However, they took creative license with characters that didn't feature prominently in my photo archive. Freddy, for example, took on a life of his own (that hair!) and bears little physical resemblance to Multiactiva's mild-mannered and hardworking agronomist. Similarly, my script described the street scene that opens the book, and they used their deep familiarity with urban life in Asunción to bring the narrative to life. In our weekly team meetings, I got in the habit of describing their illustration style as "Paraguayan gothic," since it is based on visual conventions of Paraguayan folklore and urban life, especially its monstrous and otherworldly styles. Thus, while a few characters might not be "true to life," they are certainly imbued with Paraguayan social and aesthetic sensibilities.

Working on the script for *Forecasts* while in Paraguay and conducting research on fintech was an interesting methodological decision itself. As I worked on the script and met with Enrique and David, I realized that I had to pay attention to the visual, material, and human dimensions of financial systems like never before.[14] Scenes would have to be storyboarded into panel layouts. The script needed to develop characters that were more than a hastily sketched cardboard cutout, reduced simply to a social type or role. When asked what the book was "about," the answer had to center plot and characters, not anthropological theories and debates. And crucially, the story had to be driven by its material and visual dynamics and not by expository writing that describes financial systems. My writing about finance often relied on the "God trick" of a view from 10,000 feet – that is, an overview that explains abstract concepts and processes. Producing a comic was a welcome change from writing conventions in economic anthropology, which often lavish descriptive detail onto the technical inner-workings of financial systems and devices at the expense of humans and their social dramas. My scriptwriting and fieldnotes began to converge in terms of my empirical observation and recording. I would be sure to include details about establishing shots, framing, and sequence in my written fieldnotes; this, in turn, trained my attention to notice the landscapes, lighting, mood, and pacing of my fieldwork sites. Before this project, my fieldnotes had a distinct "talk bias" – they mostly recorded conversations, with specific attention to the precise phrasing that people used to communicate about economic matters. Working on a graphic ethnography during fieldwork meant that my observations shifted toward world-building. I vastly expanded the scope of the beings and environments that I noticed.

This discussion of research methodology has been light on the formal study-design details that are conventional in some areas of qualitative research (e.g., enumeration of number and category of formal interviews, sampling approach, reliability of findings). This is in part to do with the bottom-up approach that characterizes anthropological ethnography. Despite the fact that this is not research that tests a hypothesis, nor does it seek to provide a predictive framework that can be applied cookie-cutter to other contexts, it *is*, I believe, rigorously empirical (Rutherford 2012). While *Forecasts* may be a graphic novel, it is narrative nonfiction based on solid ethnographic foundations. Like all ethnography, some details have been omitted, combined, or changed to protect the privacy and confidentiality of research participants. But Wilfrido's story is as true an account as we can render. If you don't believe him, you should ask Kavajú Tuja and ShooShoo.

Doing Ethnography?

Discussion Questions

1. What are some of the principal challenges of doing anthropological fieldwork on and in financial systems? How can these obstacles be overcome? Choose some important financial relationships or services that impact you (e.g., credit cards, student loans, wages, cryptocurrencies – you name it!) and debate how you would go about studying these financial tools from an anthropological perspective.

2. The landmark book *Writing Culture* (Clifford and Marcus 1986; see also Behar and Gordon 1995; Marcus 2002; Starn 2015) engaged anthropologists in ethical debates about the politics of representation (i.e., who has the power to write about and represent whom, and how did those arrangements emerge from long histories of power disparities?). Discuss the many different "communities" that are represented in *Forecasts*, and consider who typically has had the power to represent them. These groups might include financial professionals, development experts, farmers, labor migrants, nonhuman animals, social science researchers, and so on. How does *Forecasts* reinforce or subvert some of these conventional approaches to representation? Draw on both the graphic novel and this appendix about fieldwork methods to guide your discussion.

Activities

1. There has been a robust discussion of the subjective role of anthropologists as situated, engaged, and highly partial actors in a complex social field[15] – not detached objective observers! Certainly, we come to see the fieldworkers, Caroline and Rocío, as principal actors in the story in addition to the book's disembodied narrator.

First, develop a character profile for one or both ethnographers. What are her main motivations? Fears and hopes? Did her character develop over the course of the story?

Next, compose a short story where you write from the ethnographer's perspective. It could either be set in the world of *Forecasts* or in another time/place.

2. *Weather ethnography*: Keep a weather journal for a week. This could be in the form of a field journal (i.e., fieldnotes) and/or visual records such as photographs, screenshots from weather apps, drawings, maps, clothing inventories, and so on.

Looking back over your journal, consider how you might interpret your data. What do you notice about your experience of weather? What details do you record? How do these jottings mobilize connections to other times, places, memories, and anticipations?

Optional graphic activity: Use your weather journal to create a page of sequential art. First, define your characters and write your script. Next, storyboard your panels. Finally, using your own illustrations and/or photos, create your comic.

Optional ethnographic writing activity: Choose an anthropological theme (for example, temporality, place-making, multispecies, kinship, embodiment, self and personhood, ritual and religion, knowledge(s) and expertise, just to name a few). Review your data from a week of studying the weather. Write up an "ethnographic vignette" that you then interpret through the lens of your anthropological concept or theory.

Appendix E

AN INTERVIEW WITH THE CREATORS

Caroline [Carly]: I want to start with some history. Our first meeting in Café Consulado [which appears on page 16] in Asunción. In 2018, such a long time ago! And now we are finishing up the book in 2022. Could you share your first impressions of the project? What did you think, way back when? That here came this anthropologist with a crazy project? What was that moment like?

Enrique: Well, the first thing that struck me was that it came right after the exhibition that we did there with David – it was an exhibition of comics art right there at Café Consulado, and that would generate interest in a project. And what's more, a foreigner, right? And I don't know, for me it was like wow, I've never done this sort of work, and certainly not for an international market. And at the beginning we had this idea to make a "super team" of a whole bunch of illustrators. And at one point the team included mostly women, and we got together to do sample pages and everything. Well, the team dynamic didn't turn out quite as we'd hoped so we had to cut it way down and we ended up how we are now, right? And it was a really interesting process to present the ideas of all those artists who were candidates and make the sample pages. It was a bit of a long process there at the beginning, even with a period where we didn't even know if it would continue, and again when the pandemic hit. But if I draw any lessons out of this it would be that you have to show your work and everything that you can do, even beyond the internet and social media, if possible, everywhere you can. And opportunities come out of that.

What do you think David?

David: Well, I think that for me, the first impressions of the project – and I'm speaking for myself here. The proposal was super interesting and to think that it might actually *happen*, from a professional standpoint, was "amazing" – that's to say, incredible, that something fell into our lap like this because really, neither of us, we never tried to make a graphic novel before, definitely nothing of this length.

But apart from that, once everything got going, once we made the sample pages, and we got back in contact and it became apparent that the project definitely was going to go ahead, it felt like a bit of "a gamble." Knowing that you were going to face something that was going to be, that was going to require a ton of work and a ton of time, but that would result in something real, I think it was a mix – a threshold you pass through – from fear to "well, let's do it!" I really think that was my main impression, it was like *hijo de mil*, oh my gosh, I'm going to make a graphic novel of over a hundred pages, and up to now I've only made comics of max two pages, three pages. Right? And to go from that, at first it felt unreal, like, "Ok, we'll just make the sample pages, it depends if there's money or if there isn't money for the project." And I thought, well, as an experience this first stage was ok, I learned a lot. But once the project was approved it was like, wow. Fear, but also "time to work." And we got lucky that things turned out well.

Carly, you know, the themes, or the script, or everything that has to do with Don Wilfrido's life, or the commentaries that he has about life in the Paraguayan countryside, and everything that surrounds agriculture here, that's how it all is. Personally, I'm honored to know that I'm doing something good with my art, that we are creating something that is culturally relevant for the contemporary situation of the country. Art that is commenting on something that's been happening in this country for decades and that we urgently need to talk about now, and that we will need to keep discussing in the future.

Carly: And were you really connected to these themes at the beginning? Or was it something that you developed over the course of the project?

Enrique: To make a comics project it really wasn't the *first* thing that came to mind. But I am a bit familiar with projects with a social emphasis. I've spent a long time working with El Surtidor, with various non-government organizations (NGOs), so it was something constant in my work. But never in this format of a comic [more as an illustrator]. And never in anything this big and with such a long time frame. Because here in Paraguay, it's really difficult to get a big enough budget to develop a project of this scale. It's the reality, that long-term planning is hard, and nobody thinks about big investments.

With the specific themes of life in the countryside, it's something that we know only a bit about living in the city. We get closer to it with news reporting and trying to stay informed, but you realize that you're not quite as informed as you thought. Especially reading this script, which came from experience there *in situ*. I think that even more than being a comic about finance and all that, for me it's a comic with a lot of heart. It's about the life of this poor guy and all of his misadventures and his fears, his joys too, there's humor, there's a bit of everything. So, at the end I feel like it was an excuse to tell a more human story.

Carly: Speaking of comics telling a human story, I want to ask you about your inspiration and your background. And also about the challenges of creating comics here in Paraguay.

David: Inspirations first. Inspirations related to my "comics language" – lots of South American comics, especially reading lots of Argentinean comics. And graphically, apart from artists we'd all recognize like Mike Mignola, Ashley Wood, or reading Batman or Spawn, or graphic novels that are a bit more alternative. Also "watching movies," film, it's a huge influence on me, and a lot of the graphic language that I use personally, whether with my drawing or in final art or all that.

And the other part of the question?

Carly: The challenges. Because comics aren't your "day job."

David: From that perspective, as a comics artist I think that one of the biggest challenges is to be able to make a living doing comics. I think there are very few people, or really nobody, even the big-name artists in Paraguay, who can say that they live exclusively, or even almost exclusively, from the comics market. That is, making their own comics or working on final illustrations, or a colorist, or inking, or writing the script, or even teaching drawing or anything related to comics. It's something that's just really difficult in general. And at a global scale there are very few people who could say, "The only thing I do is create comics and with that I pay my rent, I can travel, pay my medical bills, and everything." And here more than most places, that's guaranteed. So, I think that we always were making comics more for personal artistic expression and a "hobby" – it's something that we like to do and that we want to do. But it's not, I never consider, I can't imagine how it's something that would be economically viable. That's certainly the case for me, and I think that for most Paraguayans who want to live off comics.

Enrique: Ok, starting with the theme of inspirations. I share a love of Mike Mignola with David – *Hellboy*, right? It's always very present in what I do, for my approach to composition especially, not so much from the drawing style, it's not a similar style. But it's an important reference for composition, the layout, what makes a comics page, I really look to what Mignola does.

Really for me, inspiration comes from lots of different sources. I play a lot of videogames, I love movies, I read a lot of comics – South American, European, *yanqui* (United States), a bit of everything. Maybe not quite so many superheroes in my case. A lot from Image – if it's *yanqui* it would have to be Image, not a single series but their general vibe.

And with regard to the challenges, I'm totally in agreement with everything that David said, and I would add one more thing, which is the lack of confidence from investors, or rather, the people with the means to make something like this happen. In this case it was the Australian National University, right? I doubt that the National University of Asunción would have the courage – I have to say, the *courage* more than anything right? – to invest in something like this. Even less a thesis, a research project, no way [laughing]. They just wouldn't accept something like this.

And I think that with a comics mindset, it wouldn't necessarily need to come out with a comics press, it could come out in a newspaper, or with an NGO, it could even come out through a university. There could be thousands of opportunities to make comics, but what's lacking is an understanding of comics, of confidence in the genre, and about its professionalism. And doubts about whether it would be worth it to invest and create a product like this one. And I have to be honest, for me – this project is the highest paid of my whole career up to this point. Most people would think it's crazy that in my whole career as an illustrator, it would be a comics project that was the best paid. It even allowed me to move house, it's made a big difference. So, thinking about that, lots of people don't pay enough attention to the financial part, but I think that you'll only get a quality product if the people involved in the process have the security – if they can live, and improve their lives, by being involved in the project.

David: Speaking of the funds and the process of creating a comic, or really anything that has to do with the academic side of things in general. Paraguay is passing through a major crisis right now because the government wants to cut absolutely everything – that is, 40 per cent of the education budget, which includes 100 per cent (all of it, *no más*) of the research and training programs called BECAL and FONDEC [which are the only national funding bodies for research]. One hundred per cent. That's to say, if it was hard to get funding for educational projects or projects that were related to comics before, now there will be absolutely nothing invested in scientific and academic research of any kind. That's to say, Paraguay is basically "doomed" if you want to be a researcher or if you want to dedicate yourself or know that you can make any kind of living with research.

Enrique: And cultural projects.

David: Right, and cultural projects too. And especially scientific. My brother, for example, he is fighting so hard for this right now. He's a biologist and does a lot of research. He also has his work as an assessor for all the people who do oversight for ecosystems management in the Chaco. And he also had projects that depended on research funds, which are essentially going to be cancelled, completely (100 per cent). There won't be anybody left who can do any type of academic or scientific research, it's done. And this leaves a whole bunch of people that – my brother still has work, but lots of people depended on income from grants, which wasn't very well paid to begin with, and what do those people do now? They don't have anything. Their only option if they still want to be scientists, to do any type of research, or anything that has to do with humanities and the arts, is to leave the country and migrate. There's no other way.

Carly: Or treat research like a hobby, which is not viable.

David: And if this is what you did for your university degree, and your professional career – if you started when you were twenty and now are in your mid-thirties. What do you do?

Carly: Disaster.

David: Absolutely. Am I going to start my life over? Or do I need to migrate and go somewhere else? Leaving isn't always an option for people, if they've got kids, or if they have bigger economic responsibilities. Basically, it's the destruction of education that's happening right now.

Carly: So, we have a double disadvantage. That comics are devalued as a cultural and academic product. And at the same time the destruction of the academic base of research, which can generate these alternative perspectives, ethnographic perspectives, in comics. That's to say, we wouldn't have *Forecasts*, the book, without a year, more than a year of field research. And that depended on the scientific resources of the university and the Australian Research Council.

David: Exactly. That's to say, nobody in Paraguay is going to be able to make *Forecasts*. If you were Paraguayan, Carly, this project would never have happened. Ever. And it's really sad knowing that because you are investing more in bringing recognition to aspects of Paraguayan culture than the country itself is willing to do. It's sad but true.

Carly: And for my part, I really want us to create a Paraguayan book. So, I wanted to ask you both how you are approaching that as illustrators. What are the elements that are totally from the perspective of Paraguay, from your point of view? In terms of the art, pacing, layout? What style have you developed that really brings that out?

Enrique: Well, I'm going to start with the obvious, which is the inclusion of the symbolism related to all the animals. Which has its own appendix in the book [see Appendix A: Bestiary]. I think that it's important to talk about the beliefs, about the spiritual elements of nature, you could say. It's a common joke to hear a Pitogüe and make fun of a girl who supposedly fell pregnant, you know, just to joke around. And when I read the script, it seemed like a more Paraguayan script than many Paraguayans would write, truly. And I'll tell you why. Unfortunately, sometimes Paraguayans are really insecure. And many Paraguayan writers try to be something they aren't and use language that isn't their own. They replace the *vos* tense with *tuteo*, for example. Because we consume foreign media that's dubbed into a generic fake Latino Spanish. If you read a Paraguayan story or novel or even comic, they aren't even speaking like Paraguayans. The greatest exception that comes to mind is Juan Moreno, and you could write a whole thesis about his qualities as a script writer, beyond even his drawings. Because even as a comics creator, I think he's the most Paraguayan writer there is. But that's a separate point. What I meant to say is that you, Carly, with your security, perhaps. With high self-esteem [laughing].

Carly: Anthropological confidence.

Enrique: Through that, you could depict what you saw with honesty.

Carly: The style that you developed. For example, the inking and coloring you did David, I'm describing it as "Paraguayan gothic" in reference to the visual style, separate from the writing. I had the great fortune of being able to work with Don Wilfrido, who is an incredible narrator. So much of the dialogue, I lifted it directly from interviews, from our conversations. In that sense, he is a gifted storyteller. So, my job as script writer was relatively easy, because his narration was such high quality. But on the illustration side, what came out for me, at least for me reading the comic, is a product that is quintessentially Paraguayan in its visual conventions. I don't even have words to describe its characteristics, the mood, what it does, what you captured. But it's excellent.

David: Well, it's our style, a combination of our styles, of Enrique's and mine. And it has to do with – well, I'll start by speaking about my own approach. I never was a person who was really involved in, or really paid much attention, even in my youth, I didn't have much interest in Paraguayan culture. But even despite that, there are so many things that are so organic or that are naturally part of me and of the country, that couldn't be reflected any other way in the comic. And I think the style is exactly that, that we know how to express certain things that we saw in the script. Because I suppose too that if we realized that the script had things in it that we thought had no connection with the visual language that we were using, and what we wanted to represent, then it would come out artificial or strange. So, I think there was such a great connection between the research, the script, which is so imbued with Paraguayan sensibilities, and with us, as Paraguayans. It's impossible to take it out of the style, and you can see it, for example, in how we illustrate the plants, or the way we represent the landscapes. How we draw the animals, the roads. Even the proportions of people. I think that all that, it's the little things that other people – from other countries, other cultures – would have represented differently. They simply wouldn't have been able to because they aren't in the context we are in, every day, here in Paraguay.

Enrique: I need to draw out the most iconic thing, which isn't even our style, it's *anything* that's made here in Paraguay. And that would be the horizon, not much elevation, with all the little plants like this, and the *pop!* a coconut that stands out over everything. That is *classic* Paraguay.

David: So Paraguay!

Carly: Yes! And the roads that go all the way to the horizon.

Enrique: To infinity.

Carly: In the script, it's impossible to describe these elements of the visual style. It comes out in the collaboration with you. Even with the pacing, sometimes the pause using *tereré*, as an idiom to show conflict or friendship between the characters. Which isn't in the script, but came out organically in the art.

David: Exactly.

Carly: Ok, last question. If you could – now, many years later – time travel back to the beginning of the project, what advice would you give yourselves, the Enrique and the David from back then?

Enrique: I have advice, but from this evening, which would be to set an alarm for 9 p.m. so I don't show up late to this meeting!

Carly: It's genuinely a miracle that we've managed to work across 14 time zones between Australia and Paraguay. And through the bushfire crisis in Australia [2019–20], the Amazon fires in Paraguay, and the drought. And now the pandemic. It has been a road full of potholes.

David: The magic of the internet.

Enrique: I don't know if it's advice, but something that I love about this project is how it demonstrates that with a bit of regularity, with constant contact, and always being in communication, a project *a la gran siete* can come out without having to be in the same place all the time. That's a parenthetical, now I'll think of some advice that I would give.

David: This is really interesting. That is, to make more of a comment about the state of everything around the world in relation to work. Working hours, office work, all that. That in a non-COVID world even if we lived in the same area, with all the investment that it entailed, it wouldn't be crazy to think of this in an office environment, doing a nine-to-five check-in. But I think it also speaks to good communication, coordination, good delegation of responsibilities, and dedication to make a super good project, over months and months. And the results are good. And we are all comfortable with our work situation and our physical spaces and the times that we manage in relation to that. Which is great.

And advice? To myself, it would simply be to draw more – if I could give myself advice it would have been to draw more. I always draw, but to have practiced certain specific things or even experiment with the software a bit, or Photoshop, or in my daily art. I think I would have reached certain conclusions, visually, before I actually did, so I wouldn't have needed to rework so many things. Because I reworked the art – really, I did a major redraw of the illustrations, and then various adjustments as we were working on the comic itself. So, I think that "not being lazy" about graphic experimentation. Which is obviously something you learn by undergoing this sort of experience of a big comic project.

Carly: Learning by doing, it's got to be our motto.

David: Yes! "I have no idea what I'm doing" there in the beginning. But if anybody ever hires me again to do another graphic novel of a hundred or more pages, I'll know exactly what to do. I'll know that first I need to really define my visual language. Do all the character design, draw them in certain poses so that I know that this is what I'll have to replicate across the whole comic. And grab all the assets I can to compose the panels in the most agile and satisfactory way possible. This is definitely a "lessoned learned."

Enrique: And I've been thinking and thinking and the only advice I'd give myself would be to try to get a head start on the work more. So that we wouldn't get to a point where one of us was really busy with other work, or there's no new work to pass over to the other. I think I could have done that better in this project. Even though you think there's plenty of time, it doesn't matter. If you can advance a bit, do it. But this is literally the only advice that I can think of because up to now, there was never a moment where I felt stressed about how it was going. I mean, sure there were times when timing was tight, but nothing about the project itself, that's just life, and misalignment with other stuff going on. But I should also say that out of all the work I've done, in addition to being the best remunerated, it's been the work I've enjoyed the most.

Carly: Well, I think that's our conclusion then. Thank you both.

Appendix F

MAKING OF *FORECASTS*

As with many collaborative projects, this began as a WhatsApp group. At the outset of the project, Enrique and I thought to bring together a comics collective that would gather all of the active young illustrators in Asunción. The "SúperEquipo" messenger group began planning an anthology project, with chapters divided up between the different artists. They worked on the draft of a script I'd written while based in San Pedro, and we met in person to plan the workflow. Each of the 10 illustrators – including Enrique as lead designer and producer, and David as contributing artist – produced a sample page based on a section of the script. You can see one of those sample pages on page 187. Sample page by Cielo Caballero.

We quickly realized that the story we wanted to tell in *Forecasts* had a clear and tightly scripted narrative arc based on principal characters that we follow across the whole story. It wasn't really suitable to an anthology format with distinctive art styles across multiple episodic chapters. The mental whiplash of seeing completely different versions of Don Wilfrido, Neca, and Kavajú Tuja from one chapter to the next was just too much. So, we regretfully disbanded the team, bid farewell to the WhatsApp "SúperEquipo," and reconceptualized the project.

Meanwhile, I finalized a draft of the script and Enrique negotiated availability and workflow with David. A new WhatsApp group was formed, "CómicsClub," to define a unified visual style for the graphic novel and develop its key characters. David took the lead on character design, as you can see from his early sketches on page 192. Enrique continued as lead designer, producing about three *bocetos* (sketches) of page layouts per week. David worked off those panel designs to do inking and coloring (i.e., the line art and greyscale shading) in Photoshop before handing the pages back to Enrique for lettering and final layouts (i.e., the "gutters" – black or white margins that cue the reader into the flashbacks) in InDesign. Throughout the bushfire crisis in Australia and the global pandemic, we still managed to meet weekly on Zoom to go over planning and editing.

Was this the final version of the graphic novel? Goodness, no. We undertook a major edit of the script after an intensive set of "walkthroughs" with Marc Parenteau, our wonderful series editor at ethnoGRAPHIC (and experienced illustrator/creator). The detailed feedback on how the story was coming together sent me back to Final Draft (the scriptwriting software I used to write *Forecasts*) to add some key scenes at the beginning, hone the role of the "narrator," and edit clunky dialogue. With a revamped script, Enrique and David set about incorporating those changes into the graphic novel.

In this making-of section, you can see David's early work sketching out Don Wilfrido, Mario, and Freddy (in fact, the iconic image of Wilfrido in profile that appears on the cover makes its first appearance here). These sketches were based on the section of the script that appears on pages 188–91. Compare those to our very early sample page from the "SúperEquipo," developed in a very different style (page 187; the early team consisted of Lira Gonzalez, Jimena Zaldivar, Cielo Caballero [artist for the page sample page included here], Belén Oporto, Karina Jiménez, and Sofía Amarilla). You can see how our lettering developed significantly over the course of the project too – in the early sample page, it's often difficult to tell who is speaking and in what order the dialogue should be read. Big learning curve there! Finally, you can see the evolution of Freddy and Wilfrido a few scenes later in Enrique's page layout for a scene at the Multiactiva cooperative. By the time we get to sketches of the battle with the deadly coral snake, Wilfrido has a very well-defined visual identity in the comic. Enrique and David have dialed in their characterization of the protagonist and developed the "Paraguayan gothic" style.

SO THIS MEANS THAT MY SESAME CROP IS INSURED? AND THROUGH THIS?
YOU GOT IT. IT'S FINTECH THIS IS THE FUTURE!
AH, DON WILFRIDO IS AN OLD MAN. HE JUST WANTS TO REST.
MAYBE HE'LL JUST TAKE A SIESTA AND CUDDLE UP WITH DOÑA ÑECA.
MAYBE HE'LL JUST WATCH SOME TELENOVELAS.
BUT THIS IS THE FUTURE YOU SAY?
THE FUTURE SOUNDS LIKE A LOT OF WORK TO ME IF I HAVE TO CARRY MY PHONE ALL THE TIME.
NOT ALL THE TIME. YOU'LL JUST GET WEEKLY UPDATES!
I'TS NOT REALLY MINE, YOU SEE.
IT'S MY WIFE'S PHONE.
ÑA ÑECA'S. SO SHE CAN COO AT OUR GRANDKIDS.
WE CAN ONLY AFFORD TO PAY AS-YOU-GO MINUTES, MINICARGA GS. 3000 AT A TIME.

Pink Rev. (mm/dd/yy)   14.

                    DON WILFRIDO (CONT'D)
            The Pombero sent me back home to   *
            the farm all those years ago. But   *
            now what do I do? I'm ruined.

            Maybe this is her nasty twin's last
            trick.

Full page of a young man entwined with the Pombero.

                    NARRATOR
            Wilfrido told me this story at the   *
            end of the harvest, when he thought   *
            that he would only make a pittance   *
            from his sesame crop.   *

            He might have been reminiscing on   *
            better times. We spoke often of   *
            luck and fortune.   *

            His story of the last trick of the   *
            Pomberos might be an exaggeration.   *
            He's a storyteller after all.
            Larger than life.

            But his fields and farm **do** hang by
            a gossamer strand -- a thread of
            hope and money. This is the story   *
            of how it all came unraveled.   *
                                                               *

3   - DAY, RURAL SAN PEDRO   3   *

    Establishing shot, wide-open landscape with palm trees and
    cattle pastures. A fire burns to clear brush for grazing.
    Columns of smoke dot the horizon.

    EDIT [Distribute these three captions across the top three *
    panels - the burning field, the three talking, and the phone. *
    Flip page layout so that the panel with the phone is on the *
    right]   *

                    CAPTION   *
            Wilfrido's farm, 2018. Farmers   *
            around the region burn off the last   *
            of the weeds and corn stalks to   *
            clear the fields for sesame.   *

            Wilfrido told me about the time   *
            *Ingeniero** Freddy, the agronomist   *
            from the Multiactiva Cooperative,   *
            came out to his farm to explain a   *
            new type of crop insurance.   *

                    (MORE)

Pink Rev. (mm/dd/yy)   15.

                    CAPTION (CONT'D)
        Freddy was guiding Mario, an   *
        insurance agent from Asunción,   *
        around to all the farms in the   *
        area, introducing him to members of   *
        Multiactiva that grew sesame.   *

[in bottom gutter] *Ingeniero* means Engineer, and is the   *
common title for agronomists. Freddy studied agronomy in   *
Asunción before moving back home to San Pedro, where he   *
purchased a property that he slowly built into a cattle   *
ranch. He had been the lead agronomist for Multiactiva for   *
ten years.   *

Close up of an old Nokia analog phone with SMS. Several lines *
of text with lots of numbers. Held in an old man's hand. EDIT *
— add a string of numbers to his phone   *

                    DON WILFRIDO
        So this means that my sesame crop
        is insured? And through this?   *

Don Wilfrido is talking with a member of the insurance team
and the engineer from his agricultural cooperative. Both men
are wearing office clothes. Mario is a tall, very well
groomed, fastidious man with curly hair. His loafers seem ill
suited to the field visits. The agronomist, Freddy, is
obviously much more at home on the farm (his floppy sun hat
is emblazoned with brands of companies selling seeds,
fertiliser, weed killer).

                    LIC. MARIO
        You got it. It's **FinTech** -- this is   *
        the future!

                    DON WILFRIDO
        (smiling and half joking).
        Ah, Don Wilfrido is an old man. He
        just wants to rest.

        Maybe he'll just take a siesta and
        cuddle up with Doña Neca. (winking)
        Maybe he'll just watch some
        telenovelas.

        But this is the future you say? The
        future sounds like a lot of work to
        me if I have to carry my phone all
        the time.

                    INGENIERO FREDDY
        Not all the time, you'll just get
        weekly updates.

                    DON WILFRIDO
                (ignoring Freddy)
            It's not even really mine, you see.
            It's my wife's phone. Ña Neca's, so
            she can coo at our grandkids.   *

            We can only afford to buy pay-as-
            you-go minutes, *minicarga*, Gs.
            3,000 at a time)

Wilfrido looks out over his fields -- an expanse of
grass/weeds waiting to be planted, with a few rows of
mandioca and maize to the right of his fields.

He turns back to the insurance salesman to talk.

                    DON WILFRIDO
            Are you sure it will work?

            I just have this old thing, my
            daughter has a new one but she is
            in Asunción.

            All of them are away. The other
            ones are in Argentina, working. I'm
            just an old man, here by myself.

                    INGENIERO FREDDY
            Sure sure Don Wilfrido. It really
            is just to contact you for updates.
            The insurance company has the high
            tech.

            Don't you worry.

Mario launches into an explanation -- intercut with images to
illustrate what he is talking about (eg satellite, weather
station, plants/seeds)

                    LIC. MARIO
            This is all for your protection,
            for your peace of mind, so that you
            don't have to worry for the next
            three months.

            Because of course you'd be worrying
            about the weather. Sesame is a crop
            that likes heat, right? It thrives
            in the sun.
                (panel of small sesame
                 plants)

                    (MORE)

```
                        Pink Rev. (mm/dd/yy)              17.
                        LIC. MARIO (CONT'D)
            But with drought -- actually not
            drought, we in the insurance
            industry have to be very careful
            about our words.

            Precise contracts, you know. Ha ha!
            So 'hydrological stress'. Yes,
            that's where you run into trouble.

            Drought is a catastrophe, total
            loss. Hydrological stress is a
            series of  weather events. 10-15
            days with no rain, your plants
            really are starting to suffer.
                    (panel of dry, withered
                     plants under a hot sun)


Wilfrido has lost interests. He turns away to his dog.

                        DON WILFRIDO                              *
            Dog! ShooShoo!

            Don't start chasing the neighbour's
            pig again!


                        LIC. MARIO
            So how do we know if your sesame is
            experiencing hydrological stress,
            you might ask? Good question!

Wilfrido turns back to him and stares quizzically at his
phone.


            See, first we have these weather
            stations that we have installed all
            over San Pedro.
                    (panel depicting weather
                     station)


Zoom out to show the field -- a dog and horse are  standing
slightly apart from the human conversation.

                        SHOOSHOO THE DOG
                    (speaking to Wilfrido's
                     horse)
            See!? I knew they were spying on
            us!

Meanwhile, the insurance salesman continues his monologue.
```

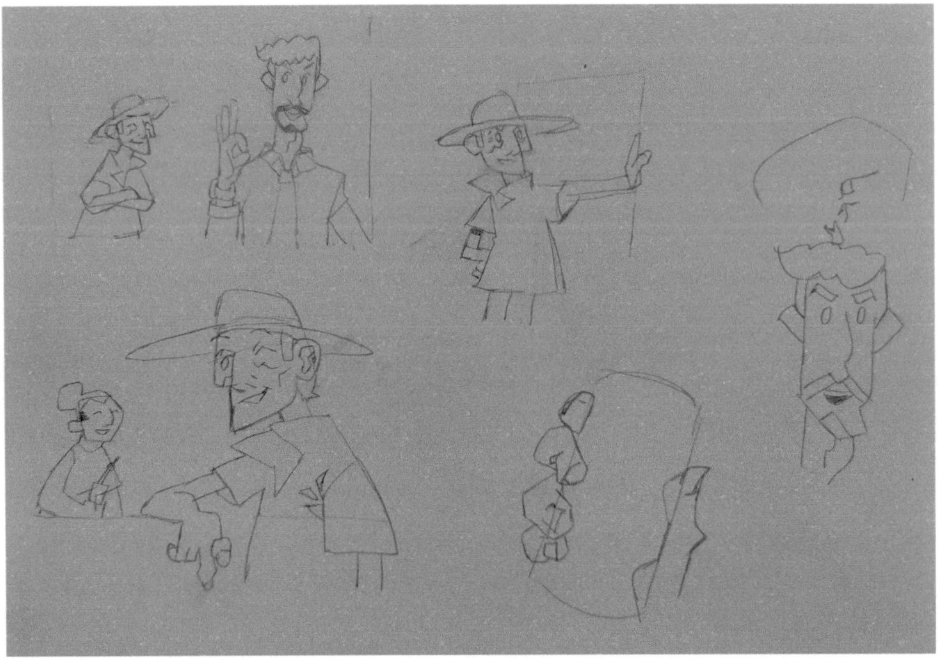

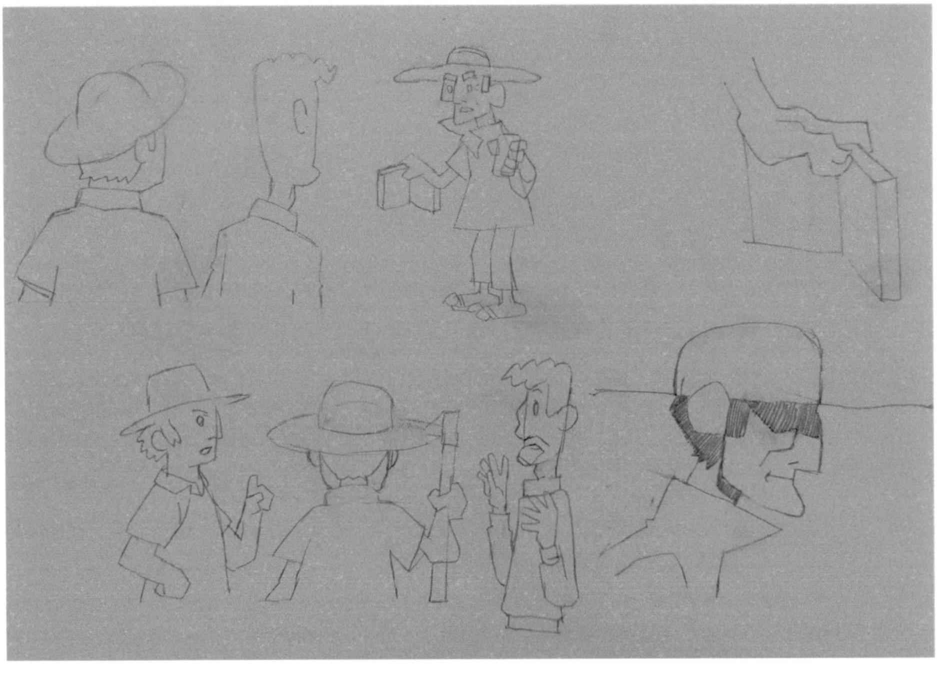

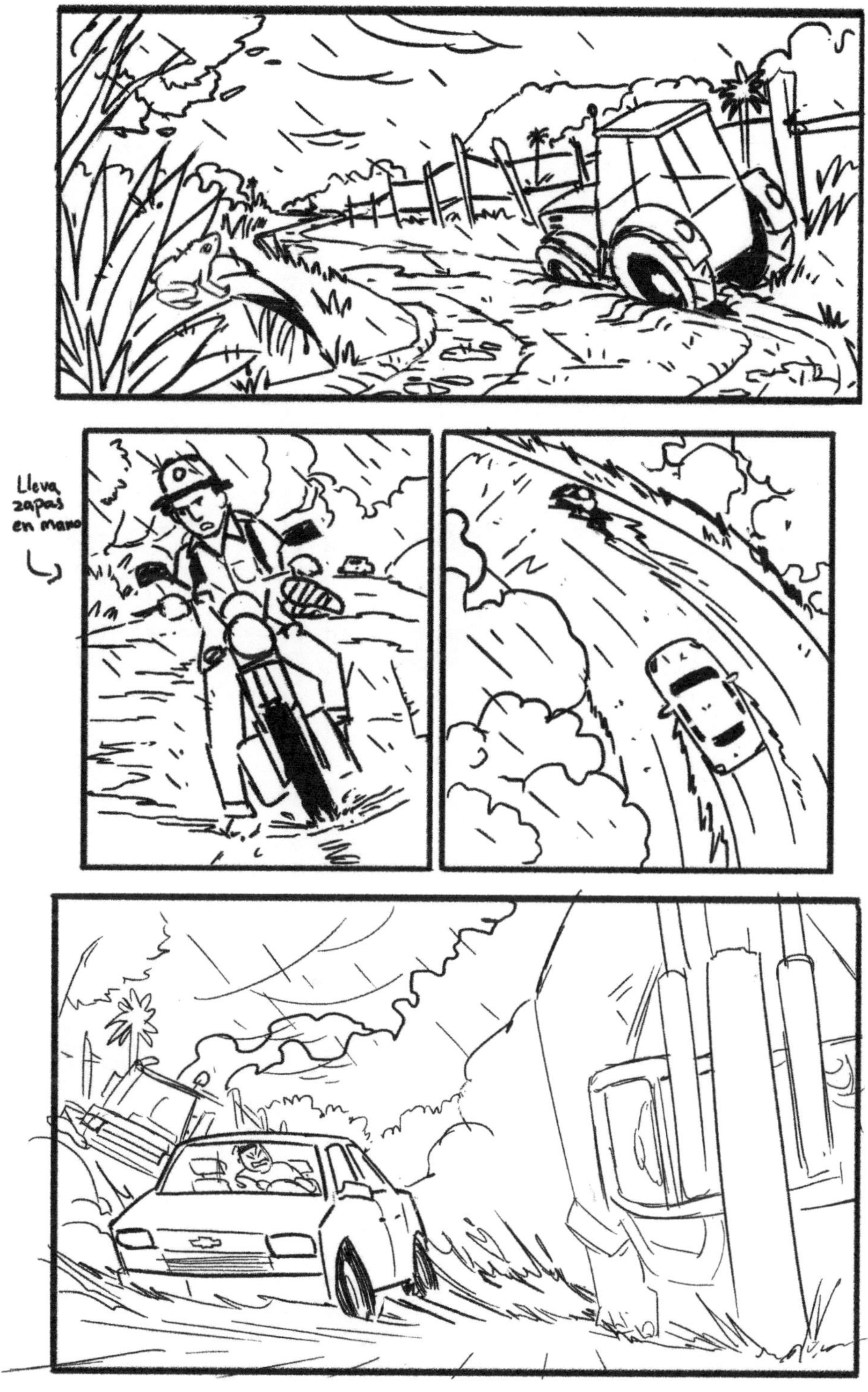
Lleva zapas en mano

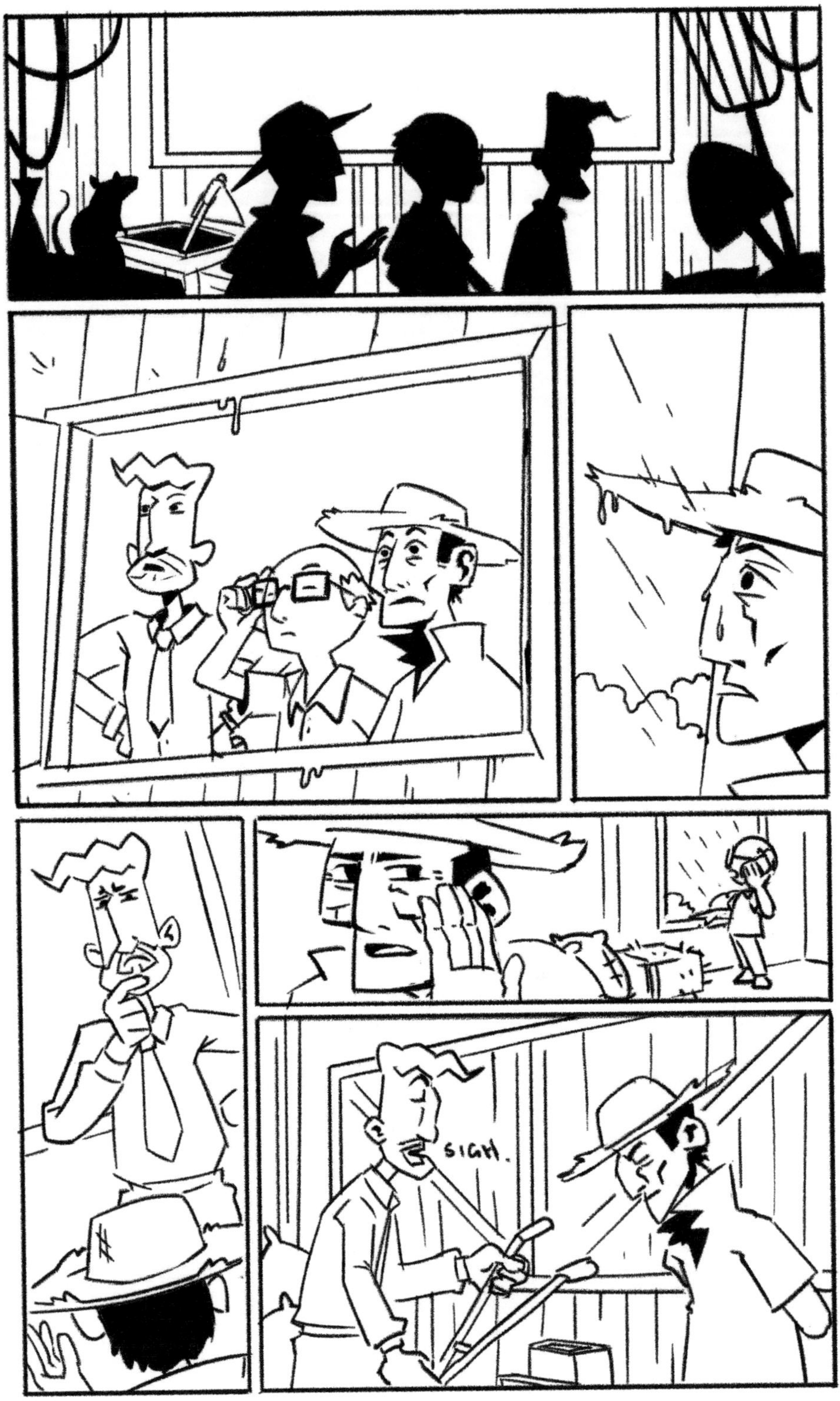
SIGH.

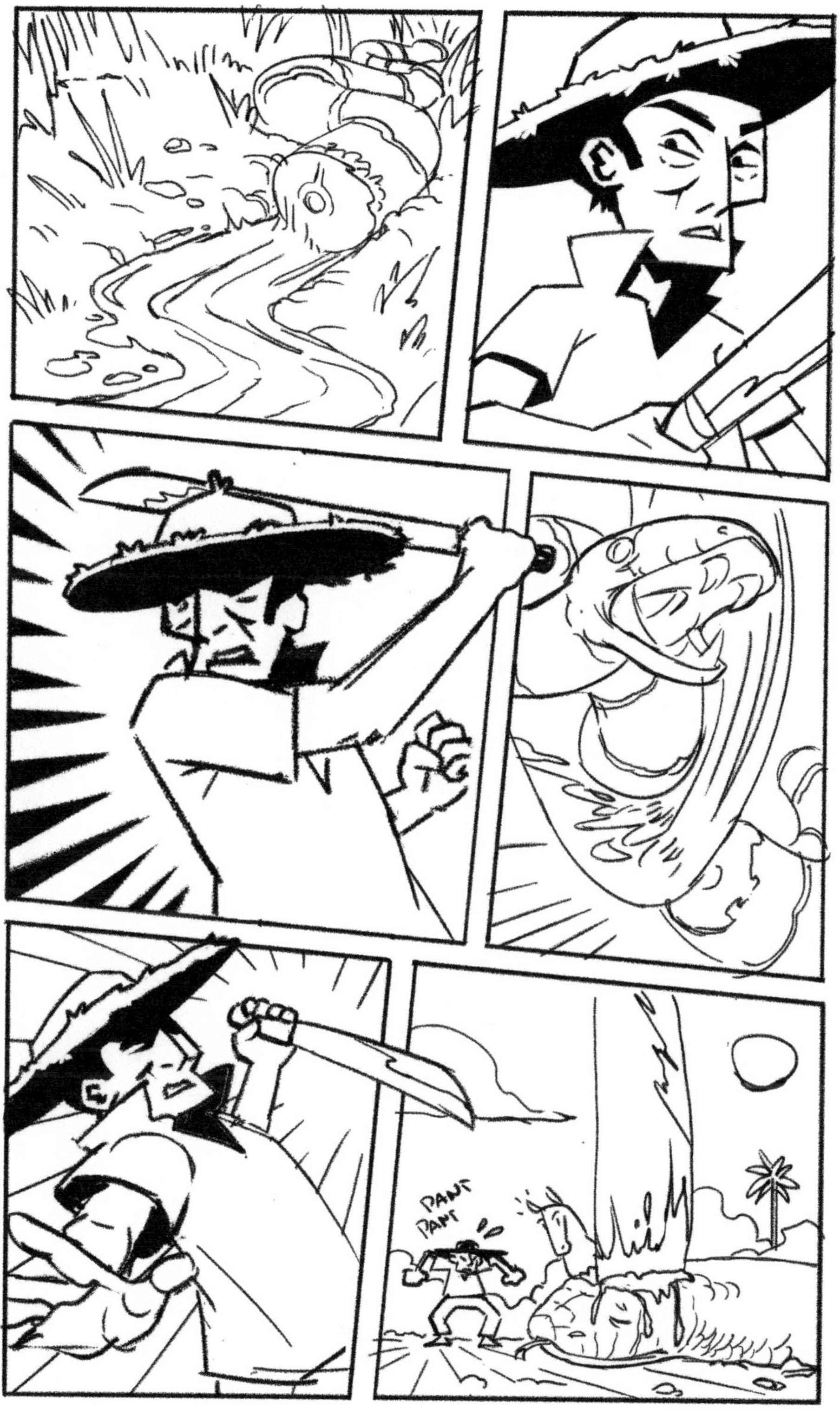
PANT
PANT

NOTES

1 For a history of Swiss Re and the rise of insurers for the insurance industry, see Borscheid, Gugerli, and Straumann (2013) and Rohland (2011). For contemporary discussions of disaster risk and reinsurance, see Lehtonen (2017) and Taylor and Weinkle (2020).

2 https://www.swissre.com/risk-knowledge/mitigating-climate-risk/we-must-learn-more-about-secondary-perils.html. The terminology "natural disasters" is favored by the industry. However, this framing has been questioned by scholars who see catastrophes not simply as something that just "happens," but rather as an effect of the complex entanglements of humans, ecologies, and ways of life (Weston 2017). Additionally, the political and scientific interventions aimed at controlling environments and minimizing the risk of so-called natural catastrophes can be even more damaging than disasters themselves (Zeiderman 2013; 2016).

3 For an excellent review of the difficulties of governing risk through insurance (and thus the limits of a Foucauldian approach centered on governmentality) see Johnson (2021, 253–4).

4 Securitization involves converting an asset – especially loans – into marketable securities so that they can be sold on secondary markets to other investors, usually with the purposes of raising cash ("liquidity" in the idiom of finance).

5 This framing resonates with Komporzos-Athanasiou's (2022, 120–43) analysis of "counter-speculations" – collective efforts to weaponize political and financial volatility, in some cases for insurgent or counter-hegemonic purposes. However, while an ethnographic speculation may also take place on the grounds afforded by speculative technologies, it has an anthropological agenda rather than collective political aims.

6 I would like to thank Andrea Ballestero for this remarkable insight – that this book offers a grounded framework for ethnographic speculation via an anthropological multiverse, and for pressing us to make a bolder methodological claim about ethnographic speculation.

7 Archaeologists, biological anthropologists, and ethnolinguists have all contributed to our understanding of human migration and settlement in lowland South America. Because we lack historical records that clearly define group identity on their own terms, different disciplines have developed alternative mechanisms for describing the cultural and linguistic groups and their expansions. Archaeologists refer to the "Guaraní matrix" when they speak of the typical material culture – particularly characteristic pottery and designs – that appears in specific areas; this material culture seems to indicate a geographic migration or expansion by the people who would have made these items. In archaeological studies as early as 1839, scholars combined linguistic, ethnographic, and material culture to identify Indigenous groups in Paraguay and Brazil, referring to them as Tupi, Brasilio-Guaraní, or simply Guaraní. Von den Steinden coined the term Tupi-Guaraní in 1886. Métraux was the first to combine ethnohistorical and archaeological methods to characterize Tupi-Guaraní migration in 1928. For an excellent review of these early debates, see Francisco Silva Noelli's (1998) paper. Alternatively, evolutionary anthropologists and paleo-linguists refer to the Tupi language group (see Walker et al. 2012), and seek to reconstruct Tupi homelands purely through linguistic phylogenies used to trace the dynamics of human population expansions, separate from the material culture. In summary, the alternate spellings and groupings in this chapter reflect a lively interdisciplinary debate about early human settlement and movement in lowland South America, using different types of data to reconstruct the past. These reconstructions of the past are in dynamic interaction with contemporary ethno-linguistic groups in both Tupi and Guaraní language families.

8 Only three *reducciones* have been investigated in Paraguay from an archaeological perspective (including only one UNESCO listed: Santisima Trinidad) (Roca 2019).

9 You can access their timeline of *el estronismo climático que no nos deja respirar* ("Stroessnerism's climate, which won't let us breathe") here: https://elsurti. com/futuros/culpables/especial/estronismo-climatico/.

10 For a list of the VIP "*invasores*" (invaders) who retain control over vast estates that were granted by the Stroessner regime, see further reporting from El Surti here: https://elsurti.com/oligarquia/especial/los-invasores-vip-del-paraguay/.

11 Based on her research on microfinance programs, Schwittay suggests that financial inclusion is a multi-scalar and multi-sited phenomenon that is not merely policy, and instead encompasses subjects, technics, and rationalities. She posits "financial inclusion as a global assemblage that constitutes materially poor people as fiscal subjects, financial consumers, and monetary innovators. To provide them with poor-appropriate microfinance services, including

loans products, savings mechanisms, and insurance policies, a wide variety of institutions, from multilateral development organizations and foundations to corporations and academic research institutes, have begun to regard financial inclusion as a development problem and a market opportunity" (Schwittay 2011, 382).

12 On the challenges of maintaining confidentiality in ethnographic writing, see especially Nancy Scheper-Hughes (2000) and her reflections on the pushback against her work among the rural Irish communities that she had studied. For further suggestions and exercises on ethnographic characterization and writing, see Narayan (2012; 1999). For a wider discussion of different anthropological approaches to writing it all up, see McGranahan (2020).

13 Unlike other characters in *Forecasts*, I use Wilfrido and Neca's real names at their request. This was one element of the ongoing reciprocity that bound us together with his family. On reciprocity as an ethic in anthropological fieldwork see Glowczewski, Henry, and Otto (2013), in contrast to institutional ethics protocols that prioritize doctrines of informed consent and privacy (Bell 2014).

14 I did not take visual fieldnotes, and instead used my scriptwriting to translate ethnographic writing and dialogue. For more on visual fieldnotes, see Hendrickson (2008).

15 If you'd like to review some of these discussions, I find Bornstein (2007), High (2011), Rutherford (2012), and Black (2017) especially helpful.

WORKS CITED

Abente, Diego. 1989. "Foreign Capital, Economic Elites and the State in Paraguay during the Liberal Republic (1870–1936)." *Journal of Latin American Studies* 21 (1): 61–88. https://doi.org/10.1017/S0022216X00014425.

Abente, Diego. 1993. *Paraguay en transición.* Caracas, Venezuela: Editorial Nuevo Sociedad.

Acosta, Alejandro, Mirian Carbonera, and Daniel Loponte. 2019. "Archaeological Hunting Patterns of Amazonian Horticulturists: The Guarani Example." *International Journal of Osteoarchaeology* 29 (6): 999–1012. https://doi.org/10.1002/oa.2813.

Adams-Hutcheson, Gail. 2020. "Dwelling and Weather: Farming in a Mobilised Climate." In *Weather: Spaces, Mobilities and Affects*, ed. Kaya Barry, Maria Borovnik, and Tim Edensor, pp. 222–35. Abingdon, UK: Routledge.

Adkins, Lisa. 2017. "Speculative Futures in the Time of Debt." *The Sociological Review* 65 (3): 448–62. https://doi.org/10.1111/1467-954X.12442.

Aguiton, Sara Angeli. 2019. "Fragile Transfers: Index Insurance and the Global Circuits of Climate Risks in Senegal." *Nature and Culture* 14 (3): 282–98. https://doi.org/10.3167/nc.2019.140305.

Aguiton, Sara Angeli. 2021. "A Market Infrastructure for Environmental Intangibles: The Materiality and Challenges of Index Insurance for Agriculture in Senegal." *Journal of Cultural Economy* 14 (5): 580–95. https://doi.org/10.1080/17530350.2020.1846590.

Aldama, Frederick Luis. 2017. *Latinx Superheroes in Mainstream Comics.* Tuscan, AZ: University of Arizona Press.

Aldama, Frederick Luis, ed. 2020. *Graphic Indigeneity: Comics in the Americas and Australasia.* Jackson, MS: University Press of Mississippi.

Aldama, Frederick Luis, and Christopher González. 2016. *Graphic Borders: Latino Comic Books Past, Present, and Future.* Austin, TX: University of Texas Press.

Allon, Fiona. 2015. "Everyday Leverage, or Leveraging the Everyday." *Cultural Studies* 29 (5–6): 687–706. https://doi.org/10.1080/09502386.2015.1017140.

Anderson, Benedict. 2016. *Imagined Communities: Reflections on the Origin and Spread of Nationalism.* Revised edition. London: Verso.

Anderson, Ryan, Emma Louise Backe, Taylor Nelms, Elizabeth Reddy, and Jeremy Trombley. 2018. "Introduction: Speculative Anthropologies." Fieldsights, Theorizing the Contemporary, December 18. https://culanth.org/fieldsights/introduction-speculative-anthropologies, accessed November 14, 2021.

Appadurai, Arjun. 2015. *Banking on Words: The Failure of Language in the Age of Derivative Finance.* Chicago, IL: University of Chicago Press.

Bahng, Aimee. 2018. *Migrant Futures: Decolonizing Speculation in Financial Times.* Durham, NC: Duke University Press.

Baker, Tom, and Jonathan Simon. 2010. *Embracing Risk: The Changing Culture of Insurance and Responsibility.* Chicago, IL: University of Chicago Press.

Ballestero, Andrea. 2019. *A Future History of Water.* Durhamn, NC: Duke University Press.

Ballestero, Andrea, and Brit Ross Winthereik. 2021. *Experimenting with Ethnography: A Companion to Analysis.* Durham, NC: Duke University Press.

Barnett, Barry J., Christopher B. Barrett, and Jerry R. Skees. 2008. "Poverty Traps and Index-Based Risk Transfer Products." *World Development* 36 (10): 1766–85. https://doi.org/10.1016/j.worlddev.2007.10.016.

Batterbury, Simon. 1996. "Planners or Performers? Reflections on Indigenous Dryland Farming in Northern Burkina Faso." *Agriculture and Human Values* 13 (3): 12–22. https://doi.org/10.1007/BF01538223.

Bear, Laura. 2020. "Speculation: A Political Economy of Technologies of Imagination." *Economy and Society* 49 (1): 1–15. https://doi.org/10.1080/03085147.2020.1715604.

Bear, Laura, Karen Ho, Anna Tsing, and Sylvia Yanagisako. 2015. "GENS: A Feminist Manifesto for the Study of Capitalism." Fieldsights, Theorizing the Contemporary, March 30. http://www.culanth.org/fieldsights/652-gens-a-feminist-manifesto-for-the-study-of-capitalism, accessed February 24, 2016.

Bedi, Tarini, Aditi Aggarwal, Josephine Chaet, and Lakshita Malik. 2021. "Feminist Pedagogy through the Small Fieldnote." *Feminist Anthropology* 2 (2): 199–223. https://doi.org/10.1002/fea2.12068.

Behar, Ruth, and Deborah A. Gordon, eds. 1995. *Women Writing Culture.* Berkeley, CA: University of California Press.

Bell, Kirsten. 2014. "Resisting Commensurability: Against Informed Consent as an Anthropological Virtue." *American Anthropologist* 116 (3): 511–22. https://doi.org/10.1111/aman.12122.

Bernards, Nick. 2018. "The Truncated Commercialization of Microinsurance and the Limits of Neoliberalism." *Development and Change* 49 (6): 1447–70. https://doi.org/10.1111/dech.12454.

Bernards, Nick. 2019. "'Latent' Surplus Populations and Colonial Histories of Drought, Groundnuts, and Finance in Senegal." *Geoforum* 126: 441–50. https://doi.org/10.1016/j.geoforum.2019.10.007.

Besky, Sarah, and Alex Blanchette. 2019. "Introduction: The Fragility of Work." In *How Nature Works: Rethinking Labor on a Troubled Planet*, ed. Sarah Besky and Alex Blanchette, pp. 1–22. Santa Fe, NM: University of New Mexico Press.

Black, Steven P. 2017. "Anthropological Ethics and the Communicative Affordances of Audio-Video Recorders in Ethnographic Fieldwork: Transduction as Theory." *American Anthropologist* 119 (1): 46–57. https://doi.org/10.1111/aman.12823.

Bonomo, Mariano, Rodrigo Costa Angrizani, Eduardo Apolinaire, and Francisco Silva Noelli. 2015. "A Model for the Guaraní Expansion in the La Plata Basin and Littoral Zone of Southern Brazil." *Quaternary International* 356: 54–73. https://doi.org/10.1016/j.quaint.2014.10.050.

Bornstein, Erica. 2007. "Harmonic Dissonance: Reflections on Dwelling in the Field." *Ethnos* 72 (4): 483–508. https://doi.org/10.1080/00141840701768292.

Borscheid, Peter, David Gugerli, and Tobias Straumann. 2013. *The Value of Risk: Swiss Re and the History of Reinsurance*. Oxford, UK: Oxford University Press.

Brochado, José Joaquim Justiniano Proenza. 1984. "An Ecological Model of the Spread of Pottery and Agriculture into Eastern South America." PhD Thesis, University of Illinois at Urbana-Champaign.

Callon, Michel, and Fabian Muniesa. 2005. "Peripheral Vision: Economic Markets as Calculative Collective Devices." *Organization Studies* 26 (8): 1229–50. https://doi.org/10.1177/0170840605056393.

Canova, Paola. 2020a. *Frontier Intimacies: Ayoreo Women and the Sexual Economy of the Paraguayan Chaco*. Austin, TX: University of Texas Press.

Canova, Paola. 2020b. "Negotiating Environmental Subjectivities: Charcoal Production and Mennonite–Ayoreo Relations in the Paraguayan Chaco." *Journal of Mennonite Studies* 38: 61–84.

Canova, Paola. 2021. "Intimate Sovereignty: Mennonite Self-Government in 'Green Hell' and the Politics of Belonging in Paraguay's Chaco." *The Journal of Latin American and Caribbean Anthropology* 26 (1): 65–83. https://doi.org/10.1111/jlca.12530.

Castro, Juan Carlos. 2019. "Río Uruguay. Una síntesis arqueológica." *Revista del Museo de La Plata* 4 (2): 541–84. https://doi.org/10.24215/25456377e088.

Chase-Sardi, Miguel. 1989. "El Tekoha: Su Organizacion Social y Los Efectos Negativos de La Deforestacion Entre Los Mbya-Guarani." *Suplemento Antropológico* 24: 33–41.

Clifford, James, and George E. Marcus, eds. 1986. *Writing Culture: The Poetics and Politics of Ethnography*. Berkeley, CA: University of California Press.

Collier, Benjamin, and Jerry Skees. 2012. "Increasing the Resilience of Financial Intermediaries through Portfolio-Level Insurance against Natural Disasters." *Natural Hazards* 64 (1): 55–72. https://doi.org/10.1007/s11069-012-0227-0.

Collier, Stephen J., and Savannah Cox. 2021. "Governing Urban Resilience: Insurance and the Problematization of Climate Change." *Economy and Society* 50 (2): 275–96. https://doi.org/10.1080/03085147.2021.1904621.

Collier, Stephen J., Rebecca Elliott, and Turo-Kimmo Lehtonen. 2021. "Climate Change and Insurance." *Economy and Society* 50 (2): 158–72. https://doi.org/10.1080/03085147.2021.1903771.

Collins, Jane L. 1986. "The Household and Relations of Production in Southern Peru." *Comparative Studies in Society and History* 28 (4): 651–71.

Colombino, Lia, and Fernando Allen. 2013. *La luz sobre el rostro: Algunos elementos sobre El Kamba Ra'anga*. JASY KAÑY/Luna Escondida. Asunción, Paraguay: FOTOsíntesis S.A.

Connell, Raewyn. 2019. *The Good University: What Universities Actually Do and Why It's Time for Radical Change*. London: Bloomsbury.

Cooper, Melinda. 2010. "Turbulent Worlds Financial Markets and Environmental Crisis." *Theory, Culture & Society* 27 (2–3): 167–90. https://doi.org/10.1177/0263276409358727.

Cooper, Melinda. 2017. *Family Values: Between Neoliberalism and the New Social Conservatism*. Near Futures. New York: Zone Books.

Cosse, Isabella. 2014. "Mafalda: Middle Class, Everyday Life, and Politics in Argentina, 1964–1973." *Hispanic American Historical Review* 94 (1): 35–75. https://doi.org/10.1215/00182168-2390604.

Cunninghame Graham, R.B. 1901. *A Vanished Arcadia: Being Some Account of the Jesuits in Paraguay, 1607 to 1767*. London: W. Heinemann. https://catalog.hathitrust.org/Record/001023746, accessed November 11, 2021.

De Goede, Marieke, and Samuel Randalls. 2009. "Precaution, Preemption: Arts and Technologies of the Actionable Future." *Environment and Planning D: Society and Space* 27 (5): 859–78. https://doi.org/10.1068/d2608.

Elliott, Rebecca. 2021a. *Underwater: Loss, Flood Insurance, and the Moral Economy of Climate Change in the United States*. New York: Columbia University Press.

Elliott, Rebecca. 2021b. "Insurance and the Temporality of Climate Ethics: Accounting for Climate Change in US Flood Insurance." *Economy and Society* 50 (2): 173–95. https://doi.org/10.1080/03085147.2020.1853356.

Ellis, Warren. 2014. *The Planetary Omnibus*. Illustrated edition. New York: DC Comics.

Elyachar, Julia. 2005. *Markets of Dispossession: NGOs, Economic Development, and the State in Cairo*. Durham, NC: Duke University Press.

Emerson, Robert M., Rachel I. Fretz, and Linda L. Shaw. 2011. *Writing Ethnographic Fieldnotes*. Chicago, IL: University of Chicago Press.

Ericson, Richard, Dean Barry, and Aaron Doyle. 2000. "The Moral Hazards of Neo-Liberalism: Lessons from the Private Insurance Industry." *Economy and Society* 29 (4): 532–58. https://doi.org/10.1080/03085140050174778.

Flachs, Andrew. 2019. "Planting and Performing: Anxiety, Aspiration, and 'Scripts' in Telangana Cotton Farming." *American Anthropologist* 121 (1): 48–61. https://doi.org/10.1111/aman.13175.

Folch, Christine. 2010. "Stimulating Consumption: Yerba Mate Myths, Markets, and Meanings from Conquest to Present." *Comparative Studies in Society and History* 52 (1): 6–36. https://doi.org/10.1017/S0010417509990314.

Folch, Christine. 2013. "Surveillance and State Violence in Stroessner's Paraguay: Itaipú Hydroelectric Dam, Archive of Terror." *American Anthropologist* 115 (1): 44–57. https://doi.org/10.1111/j.1548-1433.2012.01534.x.

Folch, Christine. 2019. *Hydropolitics: The Itaipu Dam, Sovereignty, and the Engineering of Modern South America*. Princeton, NJ: Princeton University Press.

Foster, David William. 2013. "Masculinity as Privileged Human Agency in HG Oesterheld's El Eternauta." *TRANSMODERNITY: Journal of Peripheral Cultural Production of the Luso-Hispanic World* 3 (1). https://doi.org/10.5070/T431020837.

Foster, David William. 2016. *El Eternauta, Daytripper, and Beyond: Graphic Narrative in Argentina and Brazil*. Austin, TX: University of Texas Press.

Frutos, Juan Manuel. 1974. "De la reforma agraria al bienestar rural." In *V [5th] Reunión interamericana de ejecutivos de la reforma agraria*, pp. 97–159. Asunción, Paraguay.

Ganson, Barbara Anne. 2005. *The Guaraní Under Spanish Rule in the Río de La Plata*. Stanford, CA: Stanford University Press.

George, Lily, Juan Tauri, and Lindsey Te Ata o Tu MacDonald, eds. 2020. *Indigenous Research Ethics: Claiming Research Sovereignty beyond Deficit and the Colonial Legacy*. Advances in Research Ethics and Integrity. Bingley, UK: Emerald Publishing.

Glowczewski, Barbara, Rosita Henry, and Ton Otto. 2013. "Relations and Products: Dilemmas of Reciprocity in Fieldwork." *The Asia Pacific Journal of Anthropology* 14 (2): 113–25. https://doi.org/10.1080/14442213.2013.768697.

Gray, Ian. 2021. "Hazardous Simulations: Pricing Climate Risk in US Coastal Insurance Markets." *Economy and Society* 50 (2): 196–223. https://doi.org/10.1080/03085147.2020.1853358.

Greene, Daniel. 2021. *The Promise of Access: Technology, Inequality, and the Political Economy of Hope*. Cambridge, MA: MIT Press.

Grove, Kevin. 2021. "Insurantialization and the Moral Economy of Ex Ante Risk Management in the Caribbean." *Economy and Society* 50 (2): 224–47. https://doi.org/10.1080/03085147.2020.1853363.

Günel, Gökçe, Saiba Varma, and Chika Watanabe. 2020. "A Manifesto for Patchwork Ethnography." Fieldsights, Member Voices, June 9. https://culanth.org/fieldsights/a-manifesto-for-patchwork-ethnography, accessed October 17, 2022.

Gupta, Akhil, and James Ferguson, eds. 1997. *Anthropological Locations: Boundaries and Grounds of a Field Science*. Berkeley, CA: University of California Press.

Han, Clara. 2011. "Symptoms of Another Life: Time, Possibility, and Domestic Relations in Chile's Credit Economy." *Cultural Anthropology* 26 (1): 7–32. https://doi.org/10.1111/j.1548-1360.2010.01078.x.

Han, Clara. 2012. *Life in Debt: Times of Care and Violence in Neoliberal Chile.* Berkeley, CA: University of California Press.

Haraway, Donna. 2018. "Making Kin in the Chthulucene: Reproducing Multispecies Justice." In *Making Kin Not Population*, ed. Adele E. Clarke and Donna Haraway, pp. 67–100. Chicago, IL: Prickly Paradigm Press.

Hartigan Jr., John. 2021. "Knowing Animals: Multispecies Ethnography and the Scope of Anthropology." *American Anthropologist* 123 (4): 846–60. https://doi .org/10.1111/aman.13631.

Haywood Ferreira, Rachel H. 2010. "Más Allá, El Eternauta, and the Dawn of the Golden Age of Latin American Science Fiction (1953–59)." *Extrapolation* 51 (2): 281–303. https://doi.org/10.3828/extr.2010.51.2.6.

Heinze, Jerika Loren. 2020. "Gauging the Toll: Auto-Reflexivity, Sexual Violence, and Fieldwork." Fieldsights, Member Voices, September 1. https://culanth.org /fieldsights/gauging-the-toll-auto-reflexivity-sexual-violence-and-fieldwork, accessed July 5, 2022.

Hendrickson, Carol. 2008. "Visual Field Notes: Drawing Insights in the Yucatan." *Visual Anthropology Review* 24 (2): 117–32. https://doi.org/10.1111/j.1548 -7458.2008.00009.x.

Herken Krauer, Juan Carlos. 1984. *Ferrocarriles, conspiraciones y negocios en el Paraguay, 1910–1914*, vol. 4. Serie Historia. Asunción: Arte Nuevo Editores.

Herken Krauer, Juan Carlos. 1989. *La política económica durante la era liberal*, vol. 9. Cuadernos Históricos. Asunción, Paraguay: Archivo del Liberalismo.

Hetherington, Kregg. 2014. "Waiting for the Surveyor: Development Promises and the Temporality of Infrastructure." *The Journal of Latin American and Caribbean Anthropology* 19 (2): 195–211. https://doi.org/10.1111/jlca.12100.

Hetherington, Kregg. 2019. "The Concentration of Killing: Soy, Labor, and the Long Green Revolution." In *How Nature Works: Rethinking Labor on a Troubled Planet*, ed. Sarah Besky and Alex Blanchette, pp. 41–58. Santa Fe, NM: School for Advanced Research Advanced Seminar Press.

Hetherington, Kregg. 2020. "Agribiopolitics: The Health of Plants and Humans in the Age of Monocrops." *Environment and Planning D: Society and Space* 38 (4): 682–98. https://doi.org/10.1177/0263775820912757.

High, Holly. 2011. "Melancholia and Anthropology." *American Ethnologist* 38 (2): 217–33. https://doi.org/10.1111/j.1548-1425.2011.01302.x.

Ingold, Tim. 2005. "The Eye of the Storm: Visual Perception and the Weather." *Visual Studies* 20 (2): 97–104. https://doi.org/10.1080/14725860500243953.

Ingold, Tim. 2010. "Footprints through the Weather-World: Walking, Breathing, Knowing." *Journal of the Royal Anthropological Institute* 16 (S1): S121–S139. https://doi.org/10.1111/j.1467-9655.2010.01613.x.

Jackson, Jean E. 2016. "Changes in Fieldnotes Practice over the Past Thirty Years in US Anthropology." In *eFieldnotes*, ed. Roger Sanjek and Susan W. Tratner, pp. 42–62. Philadelphia, PA: University of Pennsylvania Press.

James, Deborah. 2014. "Deeper into a Hole?" *Current Anthropology* 55 (S9): S17–S29. https://doi.org/10.1086/676123.

Johnson, Leigh. 2013a. "Catastrophe Bonds and Financial Risk: Securing Capital and Rule through Contingency." *Geoforum* 45: 30–40. https://doi.org/10.1016/j.geoforum.2012.04.003.

Johnson, Leigh. 2013b. "Index Insurance and the Articulation of Risk-Bearing Subjects." *Environment and Planning A* 45 (11): 2663–81. https://doi.org/10.1068/a45695.

Johnson, Leigh. 2014. "Geographies of Securitized Catastrophe Risk and the Implications of Climate Change." *Economic Geography* 90 (2): 155–85. https://doi.org/10.1111/ecge.12048.

Johnson, Leigh. 2021. "Rescaling Index Insurance for Climate and Development in Africa." *Economy and Society* 50 (2): 248–74. https://doi.org/10.1080/03085147.2020.1853364.

Kamienkowski, Nicolás M., and Pastor Arenas. 2017. "'Bitter' Manioc (Manihot Esculenta): Its Consumption and the Grater Used by the Indigenous Peoples of the Gran Chaco in Its Preparation." *Journal de la Société des américanistes* 103 (103–2): 205–28. https://doi.org/10.4000/jsa.15230.

Kar, Sohini. 2018. *Financializing Poverty: Labor and Risk in Indian Microfinance.* Palo Alto, CA: Stanford University Press.

Karim, Lamia. 2011. *Microfinance and Its Discontents: Women in Debt in Bangladesh.* Minneapolis, MN: University of Minnesota Press.

King, Edward, and Joanna Page. 2017. *Posthumanism and the Graphic Novel in Latin America.* London, UK: UCL Press.

Kleinpenning, Jan M.G. 1987. *Man and Land in Paraguay.* CEDLA Latin American Studies, vol. 41. Netherlands and USA: FORIS Publications.

Kleinpenning, Jan M.G. 2002. "Strong Reservations about 'New Insights into the Demographics of the Paraguayan War.'" *Latin American Research Review* 37 (3): 137–42.

Kleinpenning, Jan M.G. 2009. *Rural Paraguay 1870–1963: A Geography of Progress, Plunder and Poverty,* vol. 1. Madrid, Spain: Iberoamericana.

Klima, Alan. 2002. *The Funeral Casino: Meditation, Massacre, and Exchange with the Dead in Thailand.* Princeton, NJ: Princeton University Press.

Komporozos-Athanasiou, Aris. 2022. *Speculative Communities: Living with Uncertainty in a Financialized World.* Chicago, IL: University of Chicago Press.

Kraay, Hendrik, and Thomas L. Whigham, eds. 2004. *I Die with My Country: Perspectives on the Paraguayan War, 1864–1870.* Lincoln, NE: University of Nebraska Press.

Krause-Jensen, Jakob. 2013. "Counter-Espionage: Fieldwork among Culture Experts in Bang & Olufsen." In *Organisational Anthropology: Doing Ethnography in and among Complex Organisations,* ed. Christina Garsten and Anette Nyqvist, pp. 43–57. London: Pluto Press.

Kukkonen, Karin. 2010. "Navigating Infinite Earths: Readers, Mental Models, and the Multiverse of Superhero Comics." *Storyworlds: A Journal of Narrative Studies* 2: 39–58. https://doi.org/10.1353/stw.0.0009.

Kusenbach, Margarethe. 2003. "Street Phenomenology: The Go-along as Ethnographic Research Tool." *Ethnography* 4 (3): 455–85. https://doi.org/10.1177/146613810343007.

Lathrap, Donald W. 1970. *The Upper Amazon*. London, UK: Thames & Hudson.

Lavinas, Lena. 2013. "21st Century Welfare." *New Left Review* 84 (6): 5–40.

Lavinas, Lena. 2018. "The Collateralization of Social Policy under Financialized Capitalism." *Development and Change* 49 (2): 502–17. https://doi.org/10.1111/dech.12370.

Lehtonen, Turo-Kimmo. 2017. "Objectifying Climate Change: Weather-Related Catastrophes as Risks and Opportunities for Reinsurance." *Political Theory* 45 (1): 32–51. https://doi.org/10.1177/0090591716680684.

Lehtonen, Turo-Kimmo, and Ine Van Hoyweghen. 2014. "Editorial: Insurance and the Economization of Uncertainty." *Journal of Cultural Economy* 7 (4): 532–40. https://doi.org/10.1080/17530350.2013.875929.

L'Hoeste, Héctor Fernández, and Juan Poblete, eds. 2009. *Redrawing the Nation: National Identity in Latin/o American Comics*. New York: Palgrave Macmillan.

Liendo, Javier García. 2020. "Memory in Pieces: Chola Power's Origin Story and the Quest for Memory in Peru." In *Graphic Indigeneity: Comics in the Americas and Australasia*, ed. Frederick Luis Aldama, pp. 144–67. Jackson, MS: University Press of Mississippi.

LiPuma, Edward. 2017. *The Social Life of Financial Derivatives: Markets, Risk, and Time*. Durham, NC: Duke University Press.

López Mazz, José M., and Rocío M. López Cabral. 2020. "The Presence of Guaraní Groups in the Current Uruguayan Territory." *Journal of Anthropological Archaeology* 59: 101193. https://doi.org/10.1016/j.jaa.2020.101193.

Loponte, Daniel Marcelo, and Mirian Carbonera. 2017. "Distribution, Antiquity and Niche of Pre-Columbian Guaraní Amazonian Horticulturalists in the Misiones Rainforest, Argentina." *Pesquisas, Antropologia* 73: 5–30. São Leopoldo: Instituto Anchietano de Pesquisas. http://www.anchietano.unisinos.br/publicacoes/antropologia/volumes/073/antropologia73.pdf.

Malinowski, Bronislaw. 1984. *Argonauts of the Western Pacific*. Prospect Heights, IL: Waveland Press.

Marcus, George E. 2002. "Beyond Malinowski and After Writing Culture: On the Future of Cultural Anthropology and the Predicament of Ethnography." *The Australian Journal of Anthropology* 13 (2): 191–9. https://doi.org/10.1111/j.1835-9310.2002.tb00199.x.

McGranahan, Carole. 2020. *Writing Anthropology: Essays on Craft and Commitment*. Durham, NC: Duke University Press.

McNaspy, C.J. 1987. "The Archaeology of the Paraguay Reductions (1609–1767)." *World Archaeology* 18 (3): 398–410. https://doi.org/10.1080/00438243.1987.9980014.

Milheira, Rafael Guedes. 2014. "Arqueologia e História Guarani No Sul Da Laguna Dos Patos e Serra Do Sudeste." In *Arqueologia Guarani no Litoral Sul do Brasil*, ed. Rafael Guedes Milheira and Gustavo Peretti Wagner, pp. 125–53. Curitiba, Brazil: Appris.

Moore, Alan. 2009. *Tom Strong Deluxe Edition,* vol. 1. La Jolla, CA: WildStorm.

Morrison, Grant. 2015. *The Multiversity Deluxe Edition.* New York: DC Comics.

Mounk, Yascha. 2020. "No Testing, No Treatment, No Herd Immunity, No Easy Way Out." *The Atlantic*, April 28. https://www.theatlantic.com/ideas/archive /2020/04/stop-waiting-miracle/610795, accessed October 17, 2022.

Murphy, Michelle. 2018. "Against Population, Towards Afterlife." In *Making Kin Not Population*, ed. Adele E. Clarke and Donna Haraway, pp. 101–24. Chicago, IL: Prickly Paradigm Press.

Musharbash, Yasmine, and G. Presterudstuen. 2014. *Monster Anthropology in Australasia and Beyond.* Berlin, Germany: Springer.

Narayan, Kirin. 1999. "Ethnography and Fiction: Where Is the Border?" *Anthropology and Humanism* 24 (2): 134–47. https://doi.org/10.1525/ ahu.1999.24.2.134.

Narayan, Kirin. 2012. *Alive in the Writing.* Chicago, IL: University of Chicago Press.

Nobre, Gabriela Guimarães, Sanne Muis, Ted I.E. Veldkamp, and Philip J. Ward. 2019. "Achieving the Reduction of Disaster Risk by Better Predicting Impacts of El Niño and La Niña." *Progress in Disaster Science* 2: 100022. https://doi.org /10.1016/j.pdisas.2019.100022.

Noelli, Francisco Silva. 1998. "The Tupi: Explaining Origin and Expansions in Terms of Archaeology and of Historical Linguistics." *Antiquity* 72 (277): 648–63. https://doi.org/10.1017/S0003598X00087068.

Noelli, Francisco Silva. 2004. "La distribución geográfica de las evidencias arqueológicas Guaraní." *Revista de Indias* 64 (230): 17–34.

Noelli, Francisco Silva, José Proenza Brochado, and Ângelo Alves Corrêa. 2018. "A linguagem da cerâmica Guaraní: Sobre a persistência das práticas e materialidade (parte 1)." *Revista Brasileira de Linguística Antropológica* 10 (2): 167–200. https://doi.org/10.26512/rbla.v10i2.20935.

Noelli, Francisco Silva, Giovana Cadorin Votre, Marcos César Pereira Santos, Diego Dias Pavei, and Juliano Bitencourt Campos. 2019. "Ñande reko: Fundamentos dos conhecimentos tradicionais ambientais Guaraní." *Revista Brasileira de Linguística Antropológica* 11 (1): 13–45. https://doi.org/10.26512 /rbla.v11i1.23636.

Ocampos, Genoveva. 2016. *El enclave Barthe y el estado paraguayo (1888–1988): Una biografía agraria con sus intrígulis y sus secuelas.* Asunción, Paraguay: Intercontinental Editora.

Oesterheld, Hector German, and Francisco Solano Lopez. 2015. *The Eternonaut.* Seattle, WA: Fantagraphics.

Passaro, Joanne. 1997. "'You Can't Take the Subway to the Field!' Village Epistemologies in the Global Village." In *Anthropological Locations: Grounds of a Field Science*, ed. Akhil Gupta and James Ferguson, pp. 147–62. Berkeley, CA: University of California Press.

Pastore, Carlos. 1972. *La lucha por la tierra en el Paraguay*. Montevideo: Editorial Antequera.

Peterson, Nicole D. 2012. "Developing Climate Adaptation: The Intersection of Climate Research and Development Programmes in Index Insurance." *Development and Change* 43 (2): 557–84. https://doi.org/10.1111/j.1467 -7660.2012.01767.x.

Rabossi, Fernando. 2003. *En las calles de Ciudad del Este una etnografía del comercio de frontera*. Asunción, Paraguay: Centro de Estudios Antropológicos de la Universidad Católica.

Reber, Vera Blinn. 1985. "Commerce and Industry in Nineteenth Century Paraguay: The Example of Yerba Mate." *The Americas* 42 (1): 29–53. https://doi .org/10.2307/1006706.

Reber, Vera Blinn. 2002. "Comment on 'The Paraguayan Rosetta Stone.'" *Latin American Research Review* 37 (3): 129–36.

Richards, Paul. 1993. "Cultivation: Knowledge or Performance?" In *An Anthropological Critique of Development: The Growth of Ignorance*, ed. Mark Hobart, pp. 61–78. New York: Routledge.

Roca, María Victoria. 2019. "Arqueología de las misiones jesuíticas guaraníes en Argentina. Estado de situación." *Folia Histórica del Nordeste* 35: 121–44. http:// dx.doi.org/10.30972/fhn.0353901.

Rohland, Eleonora. 2011. *Sharing the Risk: Fire, Climate, and Disaster: Swiss Re, 1864–1906*. Lancaster, UK: Crucible Books.

Rutherford, Danilyn. 2012. "Kinky Empiricism." *Cultural Anthropology* 27 (3): 465–79. https://doi.org/10.1111/j.1548-1360.2012.01154.x.

Rutherford, Jessica. 2020. "Visualizing an Alternative Mesoamerican Archive: Daniel Parada's Comic Series Zotz." In *Graphic Indigeneity: Comics in the Americas and Australasia*, ed. Frederick Luis Aldama, pp. 168–80. Jackson, MS: University Press of Mississippi.

Santos, Jorge. 2020. "Critical Impulses in Daniel Parada's *Zotz*: A Case Study in Indigenous Comics." In *Graphic Indigeneity: Comics in the Americas and Australasia*, ed. Frederick Luis Aldama, 181–96. Jackson, MS: University Press of Mississippi.

Scheper-Hughes, Nancy. 2000. "Ire in Ireland." *Ethnography* 1 (1): 117–40. https:// doi.org/10.1177/14661380022230660.

Schuster, Caroline E. 2015. *Social Collateral: Women and Microfinance in Paraguay's Smuggling Economy*. Berkeley, CA: University of California Press.

Schuster, Caroline E. 2019. "The Bottlenecks of Free Trade: Paraguay's Mau Cars and Contraband Markets in the Triple Frontier." *The Journal of Latin American and Caribbean Anthropology* 24 (2): 498–517. https://doi.org/10.1111/jlca.12419.

Schuster, Caroline E. 2021a. "'Risky Data' for Inclusive Microinsurance Infrastructures." *Development and Change* 52 (4): 780–804. https://doi.org /10.1111/dech.12663.

Schuster, Caroline E. 2021b. "Weedy Finance: Weather Insurance and Parametric Life on Unstable Grounds." *Cultural Anthropology* 36 (4): 589–617. https://doi .org/10.14506/ca36.4.07.

Schuster, Caroline, and Sohini Kar. 2021. "Subprime Empire: On the In-Betweenness of Finance." *Current Anthropology* 62 (4): 389–411. https://doi.org/10.1086/716066.

Schwittay, Anke F. 2011. "The Financial Inclusion Assemblage: Subjects, Technics, Rationalities." *Critique of Anthropology* 31 (4): 381–401. https://doi.org/10.1177/0308275X11420117.

Seizer, Susan. 1995. "Paradoxes of Visibility in the Field: Rites of Queer Passage in Anthropology." *Public Culture* 8 (1): 73–100. https://doi.org/10.1215/08992363-8-1-73.

Soederberg, Paul. 2016. "Introduction – Risk Management in Global Capitalism." In *Risking Capitalism*, vol. 31, ed. Susanna Soderberg, pp. 1–20. Bingley, UK: Emerald Publishing.

Starn, Orin, ed. 2015. *Writing Culture and the Life of Anthropology*. Durham, NC: Duke University Press.

Stout, Noelle. 2019. *Dispossessed: How Predatory Bureaucracy Foreclosed on the American Middle Class*. Oakland, CA: University of California Press.

Strathern, Marylin, ed. 2000. *Audit Cultures: Anthropological Studies in Accountability, Ethics, and the Academy*. New York: Routledge.

Susnik, Branislava. 2017. *Una visión socio-antropológica del Paraguay del siglo XVIII*. Asunción, Paraguay: Museo Etnográfico "Dr Andrés Barbero."

Taylor, Marcus. 2016. "Risky Ventures: Financial Inclusion, Risk Management and the Uncertain Rise of Index-Based Insurance." In *Risking Capitalism*, vol. 31, ed. Susanna Soderberg, pp. 237–66. Bingley, UK: Emerald Publishing.

Taylor, Zac J., and Jessica L. Weinkle. 2020. "The Riskscapes of Re/Insurance." *Cambridge Journal of Regions, Economy and Society* 13 (2): 405–22. https://doi.org/10.1093/cjres/rsaa015.

Thedvall, Renita. 2013. *Punctuated Entries: Doing Fieldwork in Policy Meetings in the European Union*. London, UK: Pluto Press.

Tripathy, Aneil. 2017. "Translating to Risk: The Legibility of Climate Change and Nature in the Green Bond Market." *Economic Anthropology* 4 (2): 239–50. https://doi.org/10.1002/sea2.12091.

Tucker, Jennifer. 2020. "Outlaw Capital: Accumulation by Transgression on the Paraguay–Brazil Border." *Antipode* 52 (5): 1455–74. https://doi.org/10.1111/anti.12656.

Tuomi, Ilkka. 2019. "Chronotopes of Foresight: Models of Time-Space in Probabilistic, Possibilistic and Constructivist Futures." *Futures & Foresight Science* 1 (2): e11. https://doi.org/10.1002/ffo2.11.

Valentine, David. 2016. "Atmosphere: Context, Detachment, and the View from above Earth." *American Ethnologist* 43 (3). Wiley Online Library: 511–24. https://doi.org/10.1111/amet.12343.

Walker, Robert S., Søren Wichmann, Thomas Mailund, and Curtis J. Atkisson. 2012. "Cultural Phylogenetics of the Tupi Language Family in Lowland South America." *PLoS One* 7 (4): e35025. https://doi.org/10.1371/journal.pone.0035025.

Warren, Harris Gaylord. 1989. "An Interview with Harris Gaylord Warren: From the Borderlands to Paraguay." *The Americas* 45 (4): 443–60. https://doi.org/10.2307/1007307.

Warren, Harris Gaylord, and Katherine F. Warren. 1978. *Paraguay and the Triple Alliance: The Postwar Decade, 1869–1878*, vol. 44. Latin American Monographs. Austin, TX: Institute of Latin American Studies, University of Texas at Austin.

Warren, Harris Gaylord, and Katherine F. Warren. 1985. *Rebirth of the Paraguayan Republic: The First Colorado Era, 1878–1904*. Pitt Latin American Series. Pittsburgh, PA: University of Pittsburgh Press.

Weston, Kath. 2017. *Animate Planet*. Durham, NC: Duke University Press.

Whigham, Thomas L., and Barbara Potthast. 1999. "The Paraguayan Rosetta Stone: New Insights into the Demographics of the Paraguayan War, 1864–1870." *Latin American Research Review* 34 (1): 174–86.

Whigham, Thomas, and Barbara Potthast. 2002. "Refining the Numbers: A Response to Reber and Kleinpenning." *Latin American Research Review* 37 (3): 143–8.

Wilde, Guillermo. 2011. "De las crónicas jesuíticas a las 'etnografías estatales': Realidades y ficciones del orden misional en las fronteras ibéricas." *Nuevo Mundo Mundos Nuevos*. https://doi.org/10.4000/nuevomundo.62238.

Wilde, Guillermo. 2017. "The Missions of Paraguay: Rise, Expansion and Fall." In *A Companion to the Early Modern Catholic Global Missions*, ed. Ronnie Po-Chia Hsa, pp. 73–101. Leiden, Netherlands: Brill.

Wolfman, Marv. 2018. *Crisis on Infinite Earths Companion Deluxe Edition*, vol. 1. Burbank, CA: DC Comics.

World Bank. 2011. "Weather Index Insurance for Agriculture: Guidance for Development Practitioners." Working Paper. Washington, DC: World Bank. https://openknowledge.worldbank.org/handle/10986/26889, accessed November 21, 2021.

Ynsfrán, Edgar L. 1990. *Un giro geopolítico: El milagro de una ciudad [A Geopolitical Turn: The Miracle of a City]*. Asunción, Paraguay: Instituto Paraguayo de Estudios Geopolíticos e Internacionales.

Zaloom, C. 2009. "How to Read the Future: The Yield Curve, Affect, and Financial Prediction." *Public Culture* 21 (2): 245–68. https://doi.org/10.1215/08992363-2008-028.

Zeiderman, Austin. 2013. "Living Dangerously: Biopolitics and Urban Citizenship in Bogotá, Colombia." *American Ethnologist* 40 (1): 71–87. https://doi.org/10.1111/amet.12006.

Zeiderman, Austin. 2016. *Endangered City*. Durham, NC: Duke University Press.

Editors: Sherine Hamdy (University of California, Irvine) and Marc Parenteau (cartoonist)

This groundbreaking series realizes ethnographic research in graphic novel form. The series speaks to a growing interest in comics as a powerful narrative medium and to the desire for a more creative and collaborative anthropology that engages the public with contemporary issues. Books in the series are informed by scholarship and combine text and image in ways that are accessible, open-ended, aesthetically rich, and that foster greater cross-cultural understanding.

Other Books in the Series

Messages from Ukraine, written by Gregg Bucken-Knapp, illustrated by Joonas Sildre (2022)

The King of Bangkok, written by Claudio Sopranzetti, adapted by Chiara Natalucci, illustrated by Sara Fabbri (2021)

Light in Dark Times: The Human Search for Meaning, written by Alisse Waterston, illustrated by Charlotte Corden (2020)

Gringo Love: Stories of Sex Tourism in Brazil, written by Marie-Eve Carrier-Moisan, adapted by William Flynn, illustrated by Débora Santos (2020)

Things That Art: A Graphic Menagerie of Enchanting Curiosity, written and illustrated by Lochlann Jain (2019)

Lissa: A Story about Medical Promise, Friendship, and Revolution, written by Sherine Hamdy and Coleman Nye, illustrated by Sarula Bao and Caroline Brewer, lettering by Marc Parenteau (2017)